What readers have to say

More than a memoir—*The Sp*
logic steps aside and Dr. Jackson is initiated into the magnificent
world of miracle making. This book reveals the infinite potential
of the miracle maker inherent in each and every one of us.
—Pat Landis, M.S., individual & family counseling, Key West, FL

For me this book was a compelling journey where a life of mystical
moments and healing was generously and eloquently shared.
—Joseph Cannatelli, stylist and salon owner, Wilmington, DE
3 Lf tx,

This book will inspire you to believe the unbelievable *is* possible! Our
three-year-old grandson was dying of ARDS (*acute respiratory distress
syndrome*). Immediately after calling Dr. Jackson for distant healing
and prayer, we witnessed one miracle after another. The oxygen level
in his blood steadily rose from 30% to 100%. In 72 hours, the scalded
lining of his lungs began regenerating much more quickly than
expected. The doctor told us it was the most severe case of ARDS he
had seen in 8 years and the fastest recovery. Faith, prayer, and distant
healing helped the doctors save his life and restore his health.
—Ron and Beth Robinson, grateful grandparents, Unionville, PA

The part in the book about his [the author's] parents facing their son's
polio hit me hard. His "quest for coordination" after polio did result
in him developing a perfect jump shot from a technical standpoint. I
coached the game in which he describes himself as being in the
"zone." He sure was—he won the game for us. He has a wonderful,
expressive writing style and I enjoyed reading his words.
—Dan Peterson, retired professional basketball coach, Milan, Italy

Also by Dr. Stephen Royal Jackson

8 Steps to Love
*How to Return to Love When You
Need it the Most—the Moment
Stress & Conflict Begin*

A Matter of Love
*A Fascinating Journey About
Following and Fulfilling
Your Divine Destiny*

Words Become Flesh
*True Stories of How Words
Hidden in Your Heart Become
The Flesh of Your Life*

Love Conquers Stress
*Applying the 8 Steps to Love
to Various Kinds of Stress*

Love, Stress & Sex
*Applying the 8 Steps to Love
to the Stress of Love & Sex*

Slay the Dragon—Not Each Other
*A Guide to Help You Vanquish the Inner
Source of Stress, Anxiety, Anger & Conflict*

Books are available in bookstores through *Ingram Books* in the USA and
Bertram Books in the UK. They can be obtained online at Borders and
Amazon.com.

**For information on books and seminars visit:
www.drsrj.com**

THE SPACE

BETWEEN

STARS

There are two ways to live your life. One is as though nothing is a miracle. The other is as though everything is a miracle.

—Albert Einstein

THE SPACE BETWEEN STARS

A Memoir on the Magical Space
Where Stars & Miracles are Born

Stephen Royal Jackson, Ph.D.

Published by
SET Publishing
Wilmington, Delaware

For information address:
SET Publishing.
2304 Riddle Avenue
Suite 406
Wilmington, Delaware 19806

Cataloging-in-Publication Data is available
from the Library of Congress
LCCN 2008933627
ISBN 978-0-9664809-62

Cover Design by Michael Stack & Jennifer McVeigh
Central cover image of an exploding super nova is
from a photo taken by the Hubble Space Telescope.

Printed in the United States of America

This Is Dedicated To
The One(s) I Love

A Special Thank You To
Rosemary Lane for convincing me that others
could benefit from hearing about my journey,
Jaki Baskow for her immensely generous spirit,
Suzanne Eder for her insight and invaluable input,
Joseph Cannatelli for his constant inspiration,
and Janet for remaining God's gracious gift.

CONTENTS

Narrator's Note

THE IMAGE ON THE COVER COMES FROM A PHOTOGRAPH taken by the Hubble Space Telescope. It is a picture of the explosion of a super nova. Due to its resemblance to the shape of an eye, it was entitled *The Eye of God*. The significance of this image for the theme of this book will become more clear as you proceed through the pages that follow.

You will soon learn that the narrator of this book is different from the writer. I, the narrator, prompted the writer to make the following deviations from the rules of grammar. Personal and possessive pronouns relating to God in the Christian Trinity are capitalized.

Carl Jung and John Mahoney capitalize the word Self in order to set apart its spiritual nature from the body-based personal self (ego). Self is capitalized in sections on Jung and Mahoney. However, I urged the writer to not capitalize the spirit-based sidereal self or true self since a sense of humility is essential to spiritual growth. To capitalize self deifies it. The spiritual self is not God but a spark of the Divine.

You will also find the words "I AM" in large capital letters and "I AM" in small capital letters. The large capital letters are used to refer to God as the Almighty I AM Presence, and the small capital letters are used to refer to the spirit as an individualized expression of God. For example, when identifying with his or her spirit, a person may affirm: "I AM an extension of the Almighty I AM Presence of God."

Heaven is also capitalized. Something seemed awry when Heaven is not capitalized when mentioned in a sentence with planet Earth. Surely, Heaven deserves equal billing with Earth.

Prologue

THIS BOOK IS NOT AN AUTOBIOGRAPHY BUT A MEMOIR narrated by the spirit: the transcendent portion of the writer's soul. The writer contacted his friend Bill McLaughlin, a dedicated English teacher of thirty years. Bill supplied the following commentary on what constitutes a memoir. It is from the book, *Teaching the Universe of Discourse* by James Moffet.

> The narrator tells of what happens essentially to someone else, though he may have been a participator in the action. He identifies himself, states what his relation was to the main character(s) and the events, and expresses reactions to them. Depending on how close he was to the people and events, he had access to information by three possible channels—confidant, eyewitness, membership in a community or chorus. The value of such a narrator is that he can provide and external and at the same time privileged personal view of the protagonist and what happened. The key is often resonance between speaker and spoken-about, first and third persons; what happens in the protagonist resounds in the narrator. Though two different people a vicarious relation binds them. This is the frontier between autobiography and biography, first and third person narrative.

Who resonates better with the protagonist (writer) of this book than his spirit? As the writer's spirit, I have a unique vantage point. Through my elevated awareness, I offer an expansive perspective that also provides a deep and penetrating insight into the inner and outer life of the writer. In this sense, this memoir is truly on "the frontier of autobiography and biography."

I Am Not I

I am not I.
    I am this one
walking beside me whom I do not see,
whom at times I manage to visit,
and whom at other times I forget;
the one who remains silent while I talk,
the one who forgives, sweet, when I hate,
the one who takes a walk when I am indoors,
the one who will remain standing when I die.

—Juan Ramón Jiménez

One

The Spirit Speaks of the Soul

IT WAS AS IF HE WERE SEEING THE STARRY HEAVENS AS A shooting star would if a star had eyes. At first, Stephen sped through space at such a rapid speed that the stars were a blur of streak lines. He suddenly slowed down to a near standstill, and he began moving in slow motion. He was floating in space as noiselessly and effortlessly as a helium-filled balloon being carried aloft by a gentle summer breeze. A framed doorway appeared. An earth-mother stood within it. She was a Native American wearing a beaded deer-skin vest and skirt. Her long ebony-colored hair glistened. Her face was welcoming and happy.

Another framed doorway appeared as he continued his journey through space. In this portal there stood a beautiful young woman with long chestnut-brown hair. She wore a full-length black skirt, high-buttoned black shoes, and a cream-colored high-collared blouse with long sleeves. Her arms were raised above her head while she attempted to pin up her long locks into an ample bun on the top back of her head. Her hair style and apparel appeared to be Victorian. There was a slight resemblance to old sepia-colored photographs of Stephen's maternal grandmother.

Suddenly, he felt himself speed up. He was hurtling through space toward a distant doorway. It was empty and dark as though it was only a door frame suspended in the ever-expanding emptiness of space. No mother-figure was present in this one. He sped through it and came to an abrupt halt. At first, he felt encased in a small body. His tiny arms and hands were grasping for something to hold on to in order to feel some stability. He felt as if the tiny body was floating in a warm liquid. Without warning, he was overcome with fear. Every cell of this little body he was inhabiting was ablaze with fear of the burning, inescapable sensations of gnawing hunger.

A fear of starving to death threatened the existence of every cell as a brush fire gone out of control threatens all in its path. Every cell in this little flesh form was on fire with fear and the searing sensations of hunger. Somehow he sensed this fear dated back to the dawn of human history. Ancient. Primitive. Unrelenting. No relief was forthcoming. Finally, he stopped struggling and faced the fact that there was nowhere to go and nothing to do to escape.

At that very moment of surrender and acceptance, he felt a larger consciousness hovering above and to the right of this little body. As soon as he, as the consciousness encased in the little body, merged with the larger awareness, he felt relief. He felt free of the fear and hunger as he began to observe the overwhelming fear of the pain of starving to death. He was no longer threatened. His perspective shifted from being in the fire of fear and hunger to simply being still and watching the fear and hunger from above. He felt peaceful and calm once he, experiencing himself as the consciousness stuffed into the little form of flesh, merged with the spacious awareness of this transcendent consciousness.

The spaciousness of my awareness was both within and beyond the boundaries of the little body. He stopped identifying with the little body feeling fear and hunger. Minutes passed. Eventually, the gnawing pain of hunger abated, as if absorbed by this larger and calmer consciousness.

Who were these two seemingly separate sets of consciousness? By we, I, the narrator of this book, refer to the one undivided consciousness that later would appear to separate into two. One would appear in a body at 10:12 P.M. on September 3, 1947 and be named Stephen Royal Jackson shortly after emerging from his mother's womb. As for me, the more expansive one who is not limited to the confines of the body, I AM Stephen's spirit. I AM a spark of the Spirit of God, the Almighty I AM, and the soul is an extension of me into the body. I have always been there like a guardian angel watching over him, the embodied soul, and patiently waiting for him to rediscover me. The soul was frantic to *do* something to escape from the fear and hunger. While I was calm, still, and did absolutely nothing but *be* with and watch the fear and the hunger. The soul was identified with *doing*, the spirit with *being*.

* * *

THIS PREBIRTH EXPERIENCE TOOK PLACE WITHIN THE WALLS of a quaint and cozy white-clapboard farmhouse set in the beautiful foothills of the Berkshires. He was attending a workshop held in Southern New England in the early summer of 1995. A small group of individuals participated in a modern version of a shamanic healing session. For nearly three hours, Stephen lay on a rubber mat, breathing deeply, and listening to high-powered music. Shamans used drumming and breathing techniques to achieve altered states of consciousness. While in this state, a person could receive the healing he or she needed physically, mentally, emotionally, and spiritually.

The altered state of consciousness he achieved through the breathing and music helped him relive and heal an early trauma. In addition, with these shamanic techniques, he accessed these prebirth memories.

For Stephen, these memories confirmed that the essential being of each human has three core elements as Saint Paul described: "your whole being—spirit, soul, and body" (1 Thessalonians 5:23). A dozen years after this experience in the womb, he was astonished to hear Christian minister Arthur Burk say of the soul and spirit in the womb: "the soul is inoperative . . . it is the spirit that hears, understands, and remembers." However, to say the soul is inoperative is not to say it does not feel such things as hunger and fear.

Only after donning the soul suit or corporeal costume of the body does the soul stop being an androgynous "it" (a balanced unity of male and female) and experience itself as a separate consciousness embodied as a him or her. Soul begins to identify with the body and forgets about its connection to spirit.

One day, Stephen came across the word *sidereal* (pronounced *sigh-dear-real*). Sidereal means "of or pertaining to the stars." After that he has referred to me, his spirit, as the radiant star of his divine sidereal self. He considers me his spiritual compass, his Polaris (North Star) guiding him through the dark nights of the soul caused by the storms and stress of life.

At the same time that I hover by his body to guide him, I AM also deeply within his body as his innermost heart. To the embodied soul it is a great mystery and paradox how my awareness exists both inside and outside the body. I hear his thoughts and feel what he feels in his body: emotions, desires, sensations, etcetera. My essence is that of a caring, compassionate, and comforting consciousness. I cushion the blows delivered by life. His experience in the womb helped see that he had a choice in times of stress: be still and identify with me, his spirit, or remain stressed and frantic by identifying with his body.

* * *

CURIOUSLY, HIS EXPERIENCE OF ME WAS FOLLOWED BY ONE of the most controversial murder trials in the history of American justice. The night of June 17, 1995, when Stephen was reliving his soul memory of speeding through space, was the night that news footage of O. J. Simpson was broadcast nationwide. He was fleeing from the police in his white Bronco. It was interesting to Stephen how a spiritual experience was paired with a depraved one. The sacred was punctuated by the profane. There was a connection he didn't see at the time. What each event had in common was that both revealed the intense hungers, desires, emotions, and passions that all embodied souls must face. Of course, in saying this, I am setting aside the criminal verdict of Simpson's innocence, and considering the guilt assigned in the Goldman family's civil suit.

With the passage of time, Stephen would revisit the experience in the womb, mulling it over again and again. Gradually, he would deepen his understanding of what happened that night when he was seized by the primal fear and hunger involved in being human.

He felt his mind reeling as he struggled to make sense of what had happened. It seemed to him that what he had experienced had taken place in a realm existing in between inner and outer space. And yet, it somehow seemed to merge them into one space. Subjective. Objective. Real. Symbolic. It was all of these and more. He realized he had been speeding through a place where the starry heavens of both outer and inner space converge. . . .

Stephen wondered if this was *The Twilight Zone,* the TV show from the early 1960s. The show's host Rod Serling had described it as a dimension of sight and sound, of mind and imagination. And it was somewhere that was not limited by the coordinates of time and space.

He then reviewed what happened after passing through the portal of the dark doorway hanging in space, and he realized that he and I had entered his mother's womb and split. He went inside the tiny fetal body; while I hovered alongside. Like a suit of clothes hanging in the closet waiting to be worn, the little body was waiting there in the womb all ready for him to begin wearing.

Clearly, the liquid he felt his little body floating in, his tiny hands groping for something to stabilize him, was the amniotic fluid of his mother's womb. That he was greeted by hunger seemed to be a fitting introduction to life in the body. Stephen thought that perhaps his mother had not eaten recently so that no nourishment was coming to the tiny body. He was transitioning from the formless freedom of the spiritual realm to being in the world of form. What a contrast he was experiencing between total spiritual freedom and total physical dependency.

To Stephen, this hunger was a mirror of the dependency of the body on matter in the form of food. Stephen thought of the Latin word *mater,* and concluded that human beings first depend on matter in the form of *mater* (mother). It is in her womb and, after birth, in her arms, that embodied souls experience the beginning of that this all-too-human love affair with matter, the material world. THESE MYSTERIOUS MOMENTS IN THE WOMB MARKED his most intensely dramatic encounter with me. He came to realize I afforded him a higher and wider view of his life. To deepen his understanding of the nature of our relationship, I often utilize people and circumstances to illustrate what I want to convey.

For example, this very morning, after he wrote the above, I seeded the idea of taking a break and going to the local coffee shop. Once there, I nudged him to notice a mother and child. A small brown-haired boy in the toddler phase was in his mother's arms. Suddenly, he saw a cookie. He squirmed in her arms and, with a sense of urgency, began pointing to the object of his desire. Insistent on grabbing and consuming the cookie, he struggled in her containing embrace. Remaining relaxed, his mother calmly rocked him a bit and quietly coaxed him with no trace of irritation, saying, "Relax."

When Stephen felt fear in those first moments in that tiny fetal body, I held him in the arms of my awareness as a mother holds and comforts her distressed baby. This comforting larger consciousness of the sidereal self is available to all embodied souls; they just have to take steps to stop and still their body and mind. I reveal how to do this in the epilogue.

* * *

STEPHEN HAD AN ANOTHER ENCOUNTER WITH ME hovering next to his much larger, thirty-nine-year-old physical frame. It was following the film *Stand by Me*. The film triggered memories of me being by his side. In the opening scene, Gordy, the main character now an adult (Richard Dreyfus) is seated in his car, reminiscing about the summer before going into seventh grade. Ben E. King is singing the song with the same name as the film. Stephen felt a nostalgia seeping into his thoughts as he listened to the words, "Stand by me . . . oh, stand by me. . . . By the end of the film, he began to have a sense of how I have been the silent presence standing by his side all his life. He felt deeply moved as he realized that as an only child he was never alone.

The movie was an exact match with Stephen's life. It was the summer of 1959. Two boys who were best friends were going into seventh grade. This was the very same year Stephen made the transition to junior high from sixth grade. The music in the film was the transition music leading from Doo-Wop to Soul. Music has a way of taking people right back to the era when they first heard it. Stephen was catapulted back to that summer. He was eleven years old and would be twelve at summer's end when school began.

After the movie, Stephen was sitting in *La Tratoria*, an open-air restaurant set on New York City's Third Avenue. He was filled with gratitude. With tears in his eyes, he thought, *It's all been okay. All of it. The good and the bad.*

Even death seemed perfect in some strange way. "Death is the period at the end of a sentence," he told his date, a Manhattan-based writer. Stephen felt that the end point to earthly existence seemed to somehow give it meaning. "Without some end punctuation," he added, "the sentence is incomplete. In a way, the period gives the sentence an aesthetic quality . . . a kind of stark beauty." Both of his parents had died within the past year.

Various scenes came to mind. One was of having a spaghetti dinner in the middle of summer. It was hot. In the summer of 1959, his family home didn't have air conditioning. Trying to cool off, his father was sitting at the dining-room table wearing a white sleeveless T-shirt. It didn't help much. He still had beads of perspiration on his forehead. Yes, even Stephen's memory of a steamy spaghetti dinner in the heat of summer was just as it should have been. As imperfect as this dinner scene and others were, he wouldn't change a thing. Air conditioning would have somehow ruined the scene instead of salvaging it. His eyes filled with tears of gratitude.

Recalling that summer, he began to feel the presence of a silent, invisible someone hovering by his side but slightly above him. Picturing me as a guardian angel, he imagined my feet to be by his right shoulder with the rest of me hovering six or more feet in the air above him. More tears welled up in his eyes. He suddenly, realized that this observing presence was with him in this hot-summer scene and in other scenes where he was alone as a child. He had desperately wished for a brother. No such luck. But now he realized that he was never alone. There was what felt like an older, wiser consciousness that was somehow part of him and not something other. This wiser part of him had been by his side as far back as he could remember. He saw himself at two years old and felt the older, wiser presence there beside him. Tears of gratitude continued to flow; he now knew he was never alone. Not even in the womb, he now realized.

Moving ahead to the present day, Stephen went to sleep after working on this chapter and awoke in the middle of the night; he was thinking of the word sidereal. He recalled how he discovered this unusual word when writing *A Matter of Love.* Looking up a word in the dictionary, he happened to see sidereal. It appeared to him right after he thought of how each soul coming to Earth has a heavenly origin. He then recalled how he had concluded everyone on Earth has a sidereal self. Sitting up in bed, he had a flash of insight. He saw how the word *sidereal* contained two words: *side* and *real.*

He realized that this tied in with his experience of me being by his side. He began to sense how I have been by his side all of his life, silently observing him and his circumstances. He began to think of me as his *real* true self who exists beyond space and time. In contrast, his sense of self identified with his body and his personal history seemed to be a fiction, an illusion, contaminated and conditioned by life circumstances.

* * *

ONCE WHEN HE WAS PERFORMING ANCIENT THE HEALING practice of Reiki (pronounced *ray key*) on Dee, a woman in late fifties. While working on her knee to relieve her pain, Stephen received a visual of me. He felt the tingling of energy on his scalp. He asked Dee if she saw anything over his head in the dimly lit room. He would turn the lights down to make it easier for people receiving Reiki to relax. Sometimes people receiving Reiki to relieve pain or stress, would see a hazy vortex of white light over his head. One teenager exclaimed, "Dr. J., you have a white tornado over your head." They were talking about a smoky white vortex of energy appearing above his head. But Dee didn't see that. Instead, she said, "I see a silvery silhouette of you standing right next to you, and it is attached to the right side by a silver cord." He was seated and I was not a mirror image. I was standing above him. It was an actual visual of me hovering next to his body.

Over time, Stephen would think of the relation between the two aspects of me (transcendent spirit) and him (embodied soul), as being connected by an umbilical cord of consciousness, the silver cord of light that Dee described. Just as in his womb experience, there were two different vantage points and two different identities, while still remaining connected. One is a body-based identity, and the other spirit-based. The one, bogged down in the body, felt vulnerable to emotions: the little consciousness filled with fear and hunger that he experienced in the womb. I offer a spirit-based identity. I AM a spirit linked to a soul, and, together, we are one being having the experience of being human. I have double vision. I see in both the spiritual and material realms. I remain aware of my heavenly origin before coming to Earth.

Dee's vision of two of him connected by a cord made him think of the two hemispheres of the brain connected by the corpus callosum. Each hemisphere has a different focus, or, in effect, consciousness. The right communicates in images and the left in language. The right focuses on the present moment and the left compares the present with the past and prepares for the future. The left seemed survival oriented and practical and the right creative and artistic. These seemed to be anatomical referents for what he experienced in the womb: a big and a little consciousness connected by a kind of corpus callosum of consciousness.

I guided him to the answer. Yes. There was a correlation. One day a friend excitedly told him about the fantastic experience of a brain scientist/neuroanatomist from Harvard. Dr. Jill Bolte Taylor had a stroke one morning that affected her left hemisphere. Operating almost entirely from her right brain, she felt a sense of expansiveness that extended beyond her body. Everything was energy and she was a being of energy. She felt expansive and too big to fit into her body. She felt she was one with this life-force energy. She felt a bliss and peace she wished others could have.

Virtually cut off from her left brain, she couldn't read the numbers to dial the phone to call for help. Finally after forty-five minutes, she figured out the numbers. When a man answered, she heard the man make unintelligible sounds and when she tried to speak she did the same. Language was foreign to her. Her body-based identity as a brain researcher at Harvard and other particulars were connected to her left brain; but her right brain in charge enabled her to experience her spirit-based sense of herself. This seemed to explain why he experienced me as being on his right side and why Dee had seen the silvery body on the right side, too.

He knew that some spiritual seekers call this silvery body the *etheric double*. But Stephen did not favor esoteric terms. He preferred sticking to what his own experience conveyed to him. His preference was for using the more familiar terms of spirit and soul. Nonetheless, he did feel the word sidereal expressed with precision his experience of me. Sure sidereal seemed strange, but I guided him to it. Besides, the word reverberated in his very being as an echo bounces off the rock walls of a mountain pass.

The two words of *side* and *real* also fit with his experience of my being by his side when he heard Sadé singing *By Your Side*. The song lyrics fit perfectly.

> You think I'd leave your side…You know me better than that. You think, I'd leave you down, when you're down on your knees. I wouldn't do that…If only, you could see into me. Oh, when you're cold, I'll be there, hold you tight, to me. When you're outside …and you can't get in I will show you, you are so much better than you know. When you're lost and you're alone and can't get back again, I'll find you, darling and I'll bring you home. And if you want to cry I am here to dry your eyes and in no time you'll be fine . . . Oh when you're low I'll be . . . by your side . . .

Before he was fully aware of me, he felt the words of the song reflected the love of God, the Divine Beloved, for each and every soul. He was right. However, four months later in October of 1995 (see chapter seven), he had discovered me by his side, I led him to

10

an experience of the Holy Spirit as the Paraclete (2 John 2:1).

Paraclete comes from the Greek *Parakletos* (Comforter), the verb *parakalein* (to comfort), and the prefix *para* (alongside). He would see one difference between accessing me, his spirit, as a comforting presence by his side and accessing the Holy Spirit, the Comforter. The answer lay in the suffix *kalein* (to call). I was always there by his side but the Holy Spirit had to be called: He had to be invited.

* * *

ONE DAY, REFLECTING ON THE TIMES HE IDENTIFIED with me, Stephen got in touch with certain qualities of consciousness. In the womb, he found me to be a fearless observer. Calm. Caring. Clear. He experienced himself as just looking on lovingly with no judgment. At the same time, he felt older and wiser, he also felt youthful and unchanging. When identified with me, he experienced a timeless being beside the body. No doing. Just being.

It seemed as if he were hovering somewhere out of time, looking on all that is with loving eyes. He wondered if he were seeing through the eyes of God with total love and no fear. He felt as if he could see the goodness in all that exists.

Becoming more conscious of me, he began to gain a new sense of himself. He shifted from a body-based sense of self to a spirit-based sense of who he truly was. He now thought of himself as existing both within and beside his body. It was because of these glimpses of me that he began referring to his body as his *soul suit*. or *corporeal costume.*

Before his paternal grandfather died, Stephen demonstrated the idea of the body as clothes that the soul wears. "One day soon, I'm gonna be lying in a box," said Stephen's ninety-two-year-old grandfather; his tone was both resigned and peaceful. Stephen promptly stood up. He took off his brown corduroy sport coat with patches on the elbows and placed it loosely on his shoulders.

Then, letting it drop to the floor, he said, "You won't be in a box. Your body will be lying there like this sport coat. You'll be somewhere else, probably with Grandmom." His grandfather smiled.

The smile and his perfectly brown hair, no gray or white, and no dye, made him appear fifty-two, not ninety-two. Stephen looked at him and felt blessed to have inherited such good genes. Perhaps he could age as gracefully. He thought of how nice it is to have the prospect of a soul suit that will not wear out easily over time.

* * *

SINCE STEPHEN HAS NOT FULLY ACCESSED ALL OF HIS PREBIRTH and post-death soul memories, I will not bring up anything he has not yet encountered. However, I will discuss a concept he has read and heard about: the planning stage before a soul comes to Earth. He had his first glimpse of this stage in the life of a soul when he was in his early twenties. He was reading something said by Edgar Cayce. An interesting analogy was used by Cayce to describe the soul before coming to Earth. Cayce compared the soul to a deep-sea diver.

It is as if before incarnating, the soul is on a ship looking down into a crystal-clear ocean. Each soul's purpose for coming to Earth is clear before entering the body; life looks easy with the expanded view the soul has from aboard the ship. Then the soul dons an old-fashioned diving suit from the era in which Cayce lived.

The suit is bulky and cumbersome; it is topped off with a round metal helmet with a small round glass portal to look through. There is a long rubber air hose attached to the helmet so that the diver can breathe underwater.

Once souls arrive at the bottom of the ocean, they find themselves struggling against the ocean currents. What seemed clear on the deck of the ship is now unclear. Embodied souls forget their life mission decided before birth aboard the ship in the planning stage. The sidereal self of each embodied soul provides clues to help that incarnate soul discover his or her divine destiny.

Stephen loved Cayce's metaphor. The rubber air hose supplying oxygen to the diver, the embodied soul is the umbilical cord of consciousness that can appear as a silver cord of light. The *air* in the hose and the oxygen tank on the ship are an embodied soul's sidereal self keeping the soul connected to the spiritual realm.

He has also come across the notion of a prebirth planning stage in his training in spiritually-based hypnotherapy and in books by Dr. Michael Newton. Stephen was especially impressed by Newton's serendipitous discovery of the life of souls in the spiritual realm before birth and after death. Stephen respected that Newton stumbled upon the life of souls while using regression hypnosis with clients. Newton was acting as a good clinician by attempting to help clients suffering from various kinds of physical, mental, and emotional pain. One day, after using hypnotic pain-management techniques with a man suffering from a persistent pain in his side, the pain did not ease up so Newton decided to regress him by asking the subconscious mind to reveal the source of the pain. Newton was startled to discover the origin went back to his life as a soul before becoming embodied. Since then, Newton reports helping thousands of clients by regressing them to their lives as souls to resolve their problems. He details his clinical findings in his books *Journey of Souls* and *Destiny of Souls*.

From my transcendent perspective, I can say Newton is accurate in his findings. Each soul chooses the parents it is born to as a boy or girl. The parents are chosen so that the soul can have the experiences it needs to fulfill its mission. Hard to swallow? Well, when you see how Stephen's life unfolds, you will see how this makes sense.

Consider the old expression often uttered by disgruntled adolescents to their parents, "I didn't ask to be born!" You did ask. And you did ask to be born to exactly the parents to whom you were born. No matter how dysfunctional they may have been, they are the ones who will help you master what you came here to master all types of challenges. Anxiety. Addiction. Anger. Alcoholism.

Just the other day, Stephen came across recent research on the near-death experiences of children that confirms the element of choice before the soul becomes embodied. For example, one child reported remembering choosing to have a diseased body instead of healthy one. Presumably, the child chose this challenge to advance his spiritual growth more quickly.

Stephen has no memory of whether or not he chose the challenges of polio and glaucoma. However, he is certain of the emotional elements that contributed to him having both conditions.

You will find that I refer to him as Stevie during his childhood years, Steve in his adolescence and young adulthood, and as Stephen from his thirty-third year on. He received his doctorate in clinical and child psychology and became Dr. Stephen Jackson.

On his birthday, he had a session with his Italian psychoanalyst. Hearing it was his birthday, she told him thirty three was significant. "Italians refer to it as *gli anni di Cristo*, the year of Christ since it was the age when Christ was crucified, died, and resurrected," she said. Her warm, soulful brown eyes twinkled as she spoke. "The year of Christ symbolizes a death and rebirth year," she added.

This was true for his thirty-third year because he was now embarking on his work with people as a clinical psychologist.

* * *

ONE MORNING BEFORE DAWN IN THE WINTER of 2007, Stephen awoke from a dream and heard me whisper that I would be the narrator of this book. His job would be to bring my observations about his life as an embodied soul to the printed page. He agreed.

Stephen concluded, *Who else but my spirit, my sidereal self, the transcendent portion of my soul, is better equipped to tell my story? No one is better suited to the task, other than God the Creator and Source of all.* And remember you, an embodied soul, are an extension of me, I AM an extension of the Almighty I AM Presence of God.

May Stephen's story awaken you to the Holy Grail of your innermost heart, your spirit—the radiant star of your own divine sidereal self. Your sidereal self can help you follow the thread of your divine destiny as you learn to listen to the still small voice within you.

Two

Morning Commute

NOVEMBER'S FROST MOON WAS PEEKING THROUGH the dark clouds. Unlike the Harvest Moon of September or the Hunter's Moon of October, this moon has a frosty, pale-white hue as it hangs in the chilly autumn air. Looking out of the window of the morning train, Stephen observed the fading predawn moonlight imparting a soft glow to the fog rising over the river. There was something different about the ride on this morning's 5:40 A.M. commute to Philadelphia. He had a long day ahead of him since he was traveling to see his eye doctor Dr. Lawrence Jindra whose office was in Floral Park, Long Island. He would change trains four times before arriving at the Dr. Jindra's office. The travel time from the Wilmington train station to Floral Park took a little over four hours one-way. This did not include waiting between train changes in Philadelphia, Trenton, Manhattan, and Jamaica Queens, Long Island. But it was worth it to him.

For four years, Stephen had been making the trek by train because Dr. Jindra was well-known for the success he was having in using a new innovative laser surgery for glaucoma. It was now twenty years since Stephen was first diagnosed with the dreaded disease that ultimately steals the sight of those afflicted. His thoughts shifted to last night's mysterious message. . . .

"The computer keeps crashing the job! What's going on!?"

15

Robert exclaimed to Stephen. Robert was feeling exasperated and perplexed. He was preparing for publication the file of Stephen's book *Words Become Flesh*. Finally, after two hours of troubleshooting, Robert solved the mystery. He discovered that there was no value, no label, as in no font, assigned to the empty space between the asterisks used to separate the subsections of each chapter. *And what are asterisks*, Stephen reasoned, *but little stars!* When Robert assigned a value, a font, to the space between the little stars, the file printed.

Both men felt there was a spiritual meaning and message in this mishap. But what was it? Stephen went to sleep wondering what this might mean. What was God, the Divine Beloved, as he had come to call the Creator, telling him? Ever since his Mount Sinai experience in the Mayan Temple of the Moon in Tikal, Guatemala, God was no longer an abstract, distant Deity. He was now a palpably personal and loving, presence, appearing as a radiant light brighter than the sun. No stone tablets came of the event. There were just the stone walls of the pyramid disappearing in the blinding light of God's love. There will be more about this later. *Is my Heavenly Father,* he wondered, *saying that the space between the things we deem important is important? That life crashes when we ignore the space between what is visible to the eye? That the space between the beginning of the journey and the destination is important? Yes,* he concluded, *all of the above are true.*

He recalled a talk he once had with an art professor regarding the importance of the space between what is visible, what we deem important. "The space between and around the objects you are drawing is what is most important. Negative space is what makes your drawing. Let's take this bowl of fruit," the professor had told Stephen, pointing to a painting of a wooden bowl filled with fruit. "It's how an artist handles the space between the pieces of fruit that brings out their depth and richness."

The professor had then said, "Cézanne's use of negative space in those wonderful paintings of bowls of fruit illustrates what I mean." Stephen remembered how he had understood. He saw how the shadows lent a depth and texture to the light on objects. Stephen saw how shadows in the space between Cézanne's apples and pears give them a palpable quality and a rounded richness.

∗ ∗ ∗

THE WELL-LIT, WARM INTERIOR OF THE TRAIN contrasted sharply with the cold, damp darkness outside. On this morning, he took special notice of the numerous empty seats all around him. Eventually, the seats would be filled as the train headed into Philadelphia.

Sensitized to the concept of the space between, he noticed all the empty seats. There was a young man sitting two seats in front of him; there was an empty seat between them. No one was in the seat behind him, either. He allowed his fantasies free reign while he contemplated the space between himself and the world. He peered out of the window. Raindrops were forming beaded clusters on the glass. The space between him and the dark-soupy dawn was filled with the faintest hint of light penetrating the fog over the river.

He thought of his time in Ireland and the mist became the thin froth barely covering the thick, dark brew of a Guiness ale served up by the dawn. The train began to sip its way through the brew along its route. Yes, like the one pint of Guiness he tried (he really disliked the flavor) in an Irish pub in Galway, the bitter-tasting morning began to have an intoxicating effect on him. For he was excited by his heightened awareness of the empty, invisible space between things visible. And he was beginning to realize that the space between what is seen is no empty void; it is teeming with life and countless possibilities.

In the space between Stephen and the slivers of pale sunlight beginning to part the dark clouds draped over the horizon, his associations and fantasies kept rushing in to fill the perceived vacuum left by the space between all that he observed. There was the glass pane, the beads of water on the glass, the darkness laced with the white frothy fog, and the clouds being dissipated by the slowly emerging light. Through the windows across the aisle, he saw the wood and steel of the southbound stretch of train-track.

Turning back toward the river he noticed the shadowy shapes of trees and shrubbery as well as tall weeds. He could make out the islands of river grass and the stalks of dead cattails. His imagination continued to fill the space between him and all around him. The gray of the sky was growing lighter so that the extended gray formed by the river merging with the sky made him think of the skin of a giant elephant.

Now Stephen imagined himself to be Jonah. But, he was in the belly of a big elephant, not a whale. Unlike Jonah, Stephen was on a dawn-to-dusk journey to see his eye doctor on Long Island, not a sea journey taking place in the dark of night. And yet, he probably thought of Jonah because, like Jonah, he was undergoing a dark night of the soul. He was now legally blind and was in danger of becoming totally blind. Lights out. Complete darkness.

Suddenly, he was shocked out of his reflections by a woman's voice saying, "Scientists say there's a thin film of feces all over the planet. That's because there are so many people eating and going to the bathroom." *What!?* The woman who made this comment was seated right behind him. She was talking to the woman seated next to her. Ernest Becker's words from *The Denial of Death* echoed in his mind: "*Man is the god who . . .*" he paused and thought of the word *defecates*, instead of the crude slang term Becker had used. Becker conveyed that no matter how pumped up by the intellect, human beings are humbled by the inevitable fact that they produce their fair share of fecal matter. *What a humbling message,* he chuckled to himself. He had not noticed the women talking when they boarded the train, and he began filling the space between himself and the women with pictures of how he *imagined* they must look.

His W.A.S.P background made it improper and rude to turn around and look at the women; his mother's command, now his own inner dictate kept him in line. "It's not polite to stare." The other woman behind him continued the conversation, "My back-yard is the forest primeval. We have to get it cleared."

"I know what you mean," replied the first woman, "only it's not our yard that's cluttered. It's our home. We have crawl spaces in both our basement and attic. There isn't much space to move in them so we can clear them out. My husband and I have filled the spaces with lots of stuff. We really need to go through them." Whether a crawl space or backyard, they spoke of spaces between. He heard them get up. This was their stop. They moved in front of him to exit the train; he was surprised at the disparity in their size. The names of characters he'd heard his parents speak about when he was a small boy floated into the space of his awareness. Mutt and Jeff. He didn't know anything about them except that one was tall and one was short. He knew not which was which. The woman who had done most of the talking towered over her tiny friend. And to his surprise they were both gray-haired and unremarkable in appearance, even frumpy. In the space between himself and them, he had formed a picture of young, attractive professionals. He envisioned the one talking as a short-haired brunette in a business suit. Sexy. Smart. Instead they were older, gray-haired women in white lab-coats.

Now their comments made sense. They were lab technicians whose daily lives involved looking under a microscope. He thought of how these women made their living: *They investigate the tiny, unseen world of cells, bacteria, and so forth, that is hidden in the space between their eyes and what is visible to the naked eye.*

✳ ✳ ✳

STEPHEN'S BREATH WAS VISIBLE IN THE COLD NIGHT AIR, he felt invigorated. He pulled up his collar and gazed at the night sky. He knew there were eighty-eight constellations. His thoughts had shifted back to the night before. It was a little after 3:00 A.M. when he descended the steps to the sidewalk outside of Robert's office. He spotted a familiar sight for stargazers: the Big Dipper, twinkling in the constellation of the Great Bear.

He was now literally looking at the space between stars. Then he recalled what his college friend Greg told him about the countless points of light dotting the black-velvet blanket of night. As they left the library, Greg pointed to the sky and said, "Those stars we see tonight aren't really there since most of them are many light years away. A light year is the distance that light travels in a year." He reasoned that since the stars in the Big Dipper are eighty-two light years away then the Big Dipper he was seeing in tonight's sky was actually what was in the night sky on November 5, 1923. So the Big Dipper in tonight's sky will not be seen as it is tonight until November 5, 2087. That was a lot to wrap his mind around.

Just how vast the star-studded night sky was seemed too much to contemplate. He had heard scientists say that the Milky Way Galaxy was 100 thousand light years wide and that it contained 100 billion stars. But that was not all. Astronomers estimated there were 100 billion galaxies. Then he remembered the words Winston Churchill used to describe Communism; they could be used to express his feeling about the immensity of the starry heavens: "It is a riddle wrapped up in a mystery inside an enigma." Unfathomable. Incomprehensible. *How small and insignificant we are!* he thought. But then, spiritually, embodied souls are not insignificant; he recalled the words of columnist George Will. Addressing the graduating class of the University of Miami (the year escaped him), Will had this to say:

> If all the stars in the universe were reduced to only the size of the head of a pin, they still would fill the Miami Orange Bowl to overflowing more than three billion times... Astronomically, we are insignificant. But we are the beloved objects of God's care.

Stephen discovered the depth of God's love in his time with the Mayan shamans. There, amid ancient pyramids in the jungles of Guatemala, Stephen realized, *No matter how seemingly insignificant each one of us appears in the vastness of the universe, the Creator of all the galaxies is intimately involved and in love with each one of us.*

The time with the Maya had been magical. He developed a sense of how the Creator of the universe talked to all embodied souls all the time whether they believed in Him or not. The Maya told him, "God talks to us all the time through nature." It was true. In *A Matter of Love*, he called this the daily dialogue with the Divine. The meaningful coincidences of everyday life were part of that dialogue with God the Creator of all the stars and galaxies. Stephen realized that to God every embodied soul is a bright shining star that somehow stands out in the vast universe.

Then he thought of what he once heard Carl Sagan, the famous astronomer, astrophysicist, and astrobiologist say. Sagan claimed that the human body is made of the same stuff as that of which stars are made. Sagan claimed that the iron, calcium, and hydrogen, to name a few of the elements found in any human body, were first found in the stars. *We are such stuff as stars are made of, at least our bodies, our soul suits are,* Stephen thought. His head was reeling with all this about stars and the vastness of the universe, and that somehow each and every embodied soul was significant to the Creator of all the stars and galaxies.

* * *

AFTER PAYING ATTENTION TO THE SPACE BETWEEN HIMSELF and all that he was observing in the physical world, he reflected on the other meanings of the space between. He thought of how he had defined stress. "Stress," he wrote in *8 Steps to Love*, "is the pressure a person feels in response to the perceived gap between (now he would substitute the phrase "space" for the word gap) what a person would love to have happen in any given situation and his or her ability to attain it." This fundamental space is woven into the fabric of the human experience of each embodied soul on Earth. An embodied soul's character could be seen as how he or she handled this space. He thought of the stress of the spaces between that he was facing in his life.

He could feel the vibration of the train lumbering along with all the bumps and the rattling as he contemplated the space between that leads to stress. Right this moment, he was facing the pressure from the gap between where he was now, just leaving Philadelphia for Trenton, and his desire to reach his doctor's office in Floral Park, Long Island on time for his appointment. There was the more troublesome space between his waning eyesight and how he would love to see clearly again. He had the high intraocular pressures that define glaucoma and deliver the damage to the optic nerves. The high intraocular pressures had seriously damaged the optic nerve in both of his eyes.

In the last twenty years, he had done just about whatever could be done to close the gap: medication, two Argon Laser surgeries, Tibetan herbs, acupuncture, and four SLT surgeries. Three years ago, when he first saw Dr. Jindra about having the SLT surgery performed on him, Dr. Jindra was hesitant. He told Stephen that he had a very advanced case of glaucoma and really needed trabeculectomies in both eyes. This was the term for traditional eye surgery (what Stephen preferred to call under-the-knife surgery).

Dr. Jindra told Stephen the bad news: he was already legally blind and on his way to total blindness unless he had surgery soon. Stephen was adamant in his position; he came to Dr. Jindra for the special laser surgery. Dr. Jindra reluctantly agreed to do the SLT surgeries. These laser surgeries did help lower the pressures but it was not low enough given how much damage was already done to his optic nerves. Stephen was eventually going to have to submit to under-the-knife surgery to save his remaining sight. However, in today's upcoming visit, he would be excited to have a recently-arrived-at hypothesis confirmed about the link of stress with his glaucoma.

The heaviness of the harsh reality yielded to some levity; he always maintained a sense of humor. He thought of Mr. Magoo.

He sometimes called himself Dr. Magoo; he was referring to Mr. Magoo the extremely nearsighted, bordering on blind, cartoon character (Jim Backus of *Gilligan's Island* fame did the voice). As a child, Stephen watched the unsuspecting Mr. Magoo walk into walls and step into open manholes on the street, and plummet many feet down the hole. He might end up in the hospital, his leg in traction, and bandaged from head to toe like a mummy. Only his face would be showing.

What made it funny was that he just blithely went through life bumping into things, getting up and moving on. Unstoppable. He was the precursor to the Energizer Bunny. When he first referred to himself as Dr. Magoo, he was only thinking of the ostensible similarity of poor eyesight. However, I prompted him to think of the cartoon character because there was a more important parallel. Mr. Magoo was never fazed by his lack of vision. I felt Stephen needed to be reminded that he had in many ways been unstoppable in his resolve when faced with difficulties. I thought it best to inspire him by appealing to his awareness of the close connection between comedy and tragedy. He was fond of saying, "The faces of tragedy and comedy are twins but for a smile and a frown."

Since the body is the stuff of stars, he said to himself, smiling inside with his tongue in his cheek, *perhaps the answer to the regeneration of his damaged optic nerves may reside in the stars . . . or in the space between them.*

He returned to his reflections on the meaning of the space between stars. *Life is lived,* he concluded, *in the space between what is happening and what we would love to have happen . . . between where we are and where we want to be. . . .* While the train was *en route,* Stephen had ample time to consider the other ways that the space between stars applied to his life. The trance induced by riding the train provided a fertile ground for sprouting new ideas.

* * *

FOR A FEW MOMENTS WHEN HE WAS STARING INTO THE predawn darkness, Stephen briefly thought of the black holes found in the space between stars. But then he was distracted by applying the concept of the space between stars to his physical surroundings. Now, thirty minutes into the first leg of his trip, the streaks of sunlight sliced through the clouds and he began to wonder how the concept of black holes could be applied to inner space. He knew black holes exist in the space between stars. He knew that black holes occur in space when two neutron stars collide and explode or when a neutron star merges with an existing black hole. Hadn't the conflicts between his parents in the first five years of his life, the formative years, been like the collision of the neutron stars: And with these clashes of will, weren't black holes of unhappiness created in the space between them? And hadn't further arguments acted as new neutron stars that merged with the already existing black holes of unhappiness giving birth to new black holes? The images of these dark voids seemed to capture the dark feelings of fear he had had when he witnessed his parents' strife.

What takes place in the space between a small child and his or her parents and what takes place in the space between the parents themselves greatly influences what takes place in the space between surface and depth in the personality of that small child. Painful interactions are internalized. Criticism can become merciless self-criticism. Perfectionistic demands can become inner dictates that lead to depression because they are impossible to fulfill. The personality of an embodied souls is formed in those first years of his or her life on Earth.

One key question arose in his mind: Could black holes, those mysterious holes in the fabric of space provide a clue about the emotional basis of his glaucoma? Being psychologically-minded, Stephen pondered the possible psychogenic origin, or, in other words, the emotional basis of his glaucoma. What was hidden within the space between his failing eyes and wanting his sight restored? Was there an emotional blindness contributing to his glaucoma? He wondered what stars (key factors) contributed to the creation of the black holes that were sucking the light out of his eyes? These black holes of inner space existed in the space between the surface and depth of his personality.

What were the black holes being created in the pressure he felt in the burning desires he experienced in the fiery crucible of his little heart? These were the typical desires of a small child in the space between a child and the shining stars of his or her parents. As stars, parents are two suns who were as vital to a child's survival as the sun is vital to the survival of life on Earth. One black hole was created in the space between his perceived abilities to do well in school and excel in sports as a young child and his desperate desire to live up to his parents' expectations. Another black hole was developed in the space between his helplessness and the fire of his yearning to make up for his parents' unhappiness and pain.

It seemed to Stephen that he had been caught up in the frequent collisions of his parents. *Perhaps his elevated pressures in his eyes were the inner black holes caused by how much I hated and feared it when they fought,* he thought, feeling certain of it. His thoughts were orbiting the theme of the important spaces in his life. . . .

Stephen started to develop a picture of how the black holes in the space between the surface and depth of his personality might be used to explain the emotional basis of his glaucoma. It could be said that inner black holes had led to outer holes in his vision. He was aware of blind spots. Right before he stopped driving, he would not see a car in the lane of oncoming traffic. Then, suddenly, a car would appear by the driver's side front bumper. *What are the black holes in my vision? What am I not seeing? What do I need to see,* he asked himself, his heart and mind in a dizzying frenzy. What about the black holes created in the space between the surface and depth of his personality at an early age? Hadn't his struggle to deal with the pain caused by his father's criticism and perfectionism created some black holes? And hadn't his efforts to cope with the pain caused by his mother's strictness and, at times, coldness created some, too? All these questions and more were as relentless as mosquitoes by a swamp as they assaulted his contemplations. His head was buzzing with the concept of the space between whatever and whomever he deemed important early in his life. These early blueprint years are when an embodied soul's personality is formed.

There had been a lot of unpleasantness he had blocked out of his awareness. Emotional blind spots became black holes swallowing up whatever it was he refused to see: his parents' arguments, his father's harsh criticism, and a coldness in his mother. He hated seeing them not be loving toward each other.

There was an unforgettable dream in which he reexperienced a scene where his parents were arguing in the living room of his childhood home. Stephen recalled feeling terrified. As an adult, he had a dream that caused him to awake in terror. In the drama he had seen his parents arguing. Nothing special. A typical argument. It was one that will take place in numerous households all over the world. But for children it is terrifying and gets repressed. And because the fear remains hidden in a black hole, the child grows up to become an adult who fights in front of his children. No memory of terror remains in the adult who was once a terrified child. Remembering the terror prevents the pattern of fighting from being passed on from one generation to the next.

Now he could see how his life reveals the price people pay by not facing and feeling the hidden hurts and unhappiness of their childhood and adolescence.

In his clinical practice and in his own life, he saw that whatever early hurts and unhappiness a person does not allow himself or herself to feel does not heal. And both genders are doomed to repeat this pattern throughout life, especially in his or her love life. I will not go into the compulsion to repeat here because Stephen has described this tragic feature contributing to human unhappiness in all of his books.

Alice Miller opened his eyes to how buried emotional pain may also express itself in physical symptoms and disease as it did in his glaucoma. In *Words Become Flesh*, he wrote about the following:

> Life is not about the events that befall us but is about the inner conversation we have about what happens around us. However, from my clinical experience, I realize there is a conscious conversation and an unconscious one. It was the unconscious one, composed of repressed emotions, that did the most damage.

> In the recently released book The Body never Lies, Alice Miller uses the lives of famous people—writers, artists, dictators—to demonstrate the devastating effect of repressed emotional pain. In example after example, she reveals how repressed and denied childhood suffering can lead to illness, disease, and premature death.

In Stephen's life, the pain manifested in polio and glaucoma. The glaucoma illustrates the price of emotional blindness resulting from what he was unable to face and feel until late in life.

In many ways, however, Stephen's story is an ordinary one with extraordinary features. No guns were fired. No cigarettes were put out on his flesh. No brutal beatings. There was just ordinary criticism, the kind that will occur in millions of homes tonight. Therefore, in all of his books, he made it one of his missions to equip people with tools to uncover and release buried childhood pain.

He also saw how evil originated in the space between parents and their young child. What parents say and do to their child impacts what happens in the space between the surface and depth of the personality of the child. Parents abused as children repressed their pain in the space between the surface and depth of their personality. Insensitive to what it felt like to be beaten, they often beat their children.

* * *

IT WAS A NATURAL SEGUE FOR HIM TO THE ORIGIN OF EVIL from thinking of the dangerous effects of buried childhood pain. Therefore, in working with people referred by the Department of Probation, Stephen would learn that evil is what happens when an embodied soul hardens his or her heart. The painful interactions between an embodied soul and his or her parents in the earliest years of life are denied and repressed in the space between the surface and depth of an embodied soul's personality. Unable to experience empathy for their own feelings, embodied souls who commit evil have no empathy for the feelings, especially the pain, of others. Stephen described in detail the psychodynamics of evil in *A Matter of Love* in the chapter entitled *Unmasking Evil*.

Beyond what Stephen witnessed with patients, he realized how graphically this was illustrated in Alice Miller's analyses of the biographies of Adolf Hitler and other mass murderers which revealed that repressed childhood pain can lead to evil acts against others. The evil daily abuse, torment, and humiliation inflicted on him by his father is stuffed into a black hole in the space between surface and depth. Hitler then idealized his father and grew up to be a fiendish caricature of him on the world stage.

What was interesting to him right now was that a prophecy was made regarding him coming to understand evil. Three decades earlier in 1975, before deciding to get a doctorate, Stephen consulted a man who many claimed had the gift of prophecy. This man was located in Brooklyn, New York. The bushy-haired man with piercing blue eyes that contrasted with his thick dark locks began the meeting by simply asking Stephen to speak. It didn't matter about what. He only needed to hear Stephen's voice to pick up information about his soul. Just seconds after listening to the mere sound of Stephen's voice, the man said, "You were a crusader fighting in the Holy Land for the Anglican Church and England. You are still a crusader." Despite his doubts about the reality of reincarnation, Stephen could see a metaphorical truth about himself. He was a crusader for the cause of helping others.

Stephen asked, "I'm not sure if I should just go back to school to get a masters degree and be a school psychologist or should I take more time and get a doctorate?"

The man responded, "Let's look at the concept of the crusader. Do you want to ride into battle on your horse holding up a little knife or wielding a large sword?" He then foretold that Stephen would discover the source of good and evil is found within the human mind. The prophecy was indeed fulfilled. Looking back on his clinical experience, he realized that the head cut off from the heart was capable of ghastly evil acts.

After his life-changing spiritual experience in 1995, he discovered that the minds of embodied souls can be influenced by unseen forces. He remembered how startled he was to see into the invisible space between Heaven and Earth to see what he had only heard, read about, or seen in movies: angels and demons. As a trained professional psychologist, this was startling. He could distinguish between hallucinations and visions, and these were visions. Indeed, there was a spirit realm that could affect an embodied soul's thoughts for good or evil.

Nevertheless, the power these negative forces held was because of the vulnerability he felt in the womb: the primal hunger. And this primal hunger is the model for all other hungers and appetites; it leads to the belief that the embodied soul is dependent on something or someone *external* in material reality for happiness, peace of mind and a sense of well-being. This hunger and its derivatives are what Stephen had labeled the dragon of dependency. This was the source of evil acts. He smiled, thinking of comedian Flip Wilson claiming, "The devil made me do it!" *No, Flip, not the devil. The dragon within your mind.*

Stephen had encountered the fundamental choice facing each soul in the womb. Wedged between the realm of matter and the realm of spirit, the soul can choose. Will I identify with my sensory-driven soul suit and be consumed by the hunger for the people, places, and things of the external-material world? Or, will I identify with my eternal spirit and, in effect, consume the hunger in the spaciousness of my awareness? Will I opt for being enslaved by the gods of materialism and consumption? Or, will I choose spiritual freedom and mastery over matter? Do I remember I AM an astronaut *in* this world but I AM not *of* this world? to borrow the words of Jesus.

Just as an astronaut needs his space suit to survive on the moon or Mars so each embodied soul is dependent on his or her soul suit to live on this planet. The problem is that the embodied soul gets hypnotized into believing that he or she needs much *more* than food, water, air, and shelter to survive.

All kinds of things are sought by the embodied soul in the space between him or her and the external world. Junk food, sex with someone with a beautiful soul suit, legal and illegal drugs, alcohol, and control and power over others. The latest styles may be feverishly sought to adorn the corporeal costume. The words from the film *Casablanca* came to mind. He could see Sam at Rick's (Humphrey Bogart) place playing the piano and singing, "It's still the same old story, a fight for love and glory, a case of do or die . . . the fundamental things of life . . . as time goes by." Yes, from murder to harming others in some small way, evil acts are fueled by the embodied soul believing whatever he or she wants, "I must have! And I'll kill to get it!" It is, as the song says, "a case of do or die. . . ."

* * *

OVER THE YEARS, ONE TRUTH STOOD OUT IN BOLD RELIEF: the

power of a love focus over a fear focus in effectively bridging the space between what is and what someone wants. A love focus zeroes in on desired outcomes, and such a focus had been most effective in helping him attain his goals in basketball, psychology, and in his spiritual search. Focusing on what he would love to have happen had enabled him to make shots in basketball, get his doctorate, and grow spiritually into a happier, more loving, and peaceful person.

His train of thought on the space between stars shifted as the train was starting to slow down. The red ribbons of the dawn's early light were replaced by a bright morning sun shining on the skyline of Philadelphia, the City of Brotherly Love. The train he was on and his train of thought had reached a similar destination. *The space between stars,* he decided, *is where stars and miracles are born.* Nothing less than God the Creator, the ultimate power in the universe is in this space. And what is God but the expansive energy of love.

* * *

THE TRAIN WAS JUST PULLING INTO PHILADELPHIA'S 30TH street station and the morning sun was brighter now; he shifted in his seat and stretched. The clouds were gone. Stephen's thoughts drifted back to a much earlier time when he first discovered the power of prayer in the space between loved ones' lips and God's ears. His parents, grandparents, aunts, and uncles whispered their pleas to God when he was stricken with polio. It was uncertain whether he would ever walk again, that is, if he didn't die. . . .

I
The Space Between
Polio & Flow

When you wish upon a star, makes no difference who you are.
When you wish upon a star your dreams come true . . .

—Jiminy Cricket

Unless you become as a child you will not enter the kingdom of Heaven (Matthew 18:3).

—Jesus the Christ

. . . the lucidity that was to constitute his torture at the same time crowns his victory. . . . The struggle itself toward the heights is enough to fill a man's heart. One must imagine Sisyphus happy. (*The Myth of Sisyphus*)

—Albert Camus

Three

Passion for Grace

OCTOBER 1955

"WHERE WOULD I BE IF I HAD NEVER BEEN BORN?" little eight-year-old Stevie asked himself aloud. He was alone in his bedroom one hot August afternoon. With school out, those "lazy, hazy . . . days of summer . . .," that Nat King Cole crooned about, were perfect for daydreaming. Of course, daydreams usually took a backseat to catching frogs and tadpoles in the pond up the street or lazily watching dragonflies hover over the reeds and cattails. Immediately after his question, he had a vision of the star-filled night sky.

The profundity of his vision of the starry heavens was not completely appreciated by him as a child. He was, however, having a dim recollection of how all embodied souls have a heavenly origin. Flashing ahead four decades, Stephen considered how he had been introduced to the Mayan shamans who claimed that the Mayan people were descended from beings from the stars of the Pleiades. They also told him that the ancient Egyptians were descended from star beings who came from the stars found in the constellation of Orion. *Just maybe*, he thought, *there was more to his childhood vision of the stars than he had ever imagined. . . .*

When he was ten years old, he saw the opening scene of the film classic *It's a Wonderful Life*. He felt a tingling flutter up his spine when the stars, representing angels, were talking about the film's hero George Bailey (Jimmy Stewart). After studying with the Mayan shamans, he began to realize that the tingling was a spiritu-

33

al sign or confirmation from me; it signified that he was on the right track. He thought of how the tingling happened at other spiritually significant times. For example, it happened when he was thirteen years old and the bishop touched his forehead to make the sign of the cross during the confirmation ceremony at church.

He then thought of how a star, the Star of Bethlehem, appeared to announce the birth of Jesus. He remembered hearing the exchange from a film on the life of Christ that he had seen as a child. "How will we find this child?" asked the king.

"He shall be found under a star," answered a member of the king's court. The man then added, "What better spokesman can a child have but a star?" Stephen had never forgotten these words, and he wondered, *Maybe every child has a star appear at his or her birth, representing the radiant star of his or her divine sidereal self. It is just not so obvious as it was with the birth of Jesus.*

After envisioning the stars in answer to his question about where he would be if he had never been born, Stevie had the thought, *I very easily might never have been born so I'm lucky to be here.* Right on the heels of this thought, his thinking took a neurotic turn reminiscent of a Woody Allen movie. *Therefore, I should go along with whatever they [his parents] want me to do.*

At that very moment, he chose to conform to his parents' wishes, and, in so doing, Stevie separated from me and any sense of his heavenly origin. He struggled to be what he believed his mother and father *needed* him to be. He desperately desired to fill in the black holes of their unhappiness. Like so many children, some of whom he saw in his private practice, he deeply and desperately loved his parents and wanted them to be happy.

A totally selfless desire? No. For if parents are happy then they are better able to love their children and set them free to be a separate person in their own right. Empowered by that love, children grow into adults who are better able to pursue their hopes and dreams. They find their wings instead of remaining mired in the swamp of their parents' disappointments. Soaring toward the stars of their own dreams replaces the endless Sisyphean effort of trying to fulfill the unfulfilled ambitions of their parents.

This shift from the stars of his own dreams to focus on discerning the desires of his parents would become a lifelong pattern. Later on, in his capacity as a psychologist, he would diagnose this pattern as a hero-saviour complex. Early on, he was crippled by his compassion. His desires that conflicted with those of his parents were set aside. With the inevitability of iron filings being drawn to a magnet, these reflections were drawn back to a pivotal moment in his life. It was a cloudy afternoon in the early autumn of 1954.

* * *

WITHOUT WARNING, EVERY TRACE OF ENERGY DRAINED from Stevie's seven-year-old body. However, he summoned just enough energy to utter the alarming words, "Mommy, I can't move." Lying on his back motionless, he was barely able to speak. His whole body had suddenly gone limp. Strange that he could move the muscles of his throat and around his mouth while the rest of him lay immobilized on the living room floor. He didn't know it yet but like the paralyzing tentacles of a giant squid, polio, also known as infantile paralysis, had an ineluctable hold on his nervous system.

A decade later, after he had become a basketball star in high school, he would read about this very moment on the sports page of the local newspaper. The word "stricken" jumped out at him when he read the line: "He was stricken with polio when he was seven years old."

Stricken was right. It was a perfect description of what he had experienced. Stricken summed up the suddenness with which the dreaded disease descended upon its unsuspecting victims. Images of dangers in nature filled his adult imagination whenever he looked back upon the moment he was stricken. Polio seemed to swoop down on him from out of nowhere with the suddenness of a bird of prey catching a rodent in its talons. While at the same time, the paralyzing effect of polio had spread with the same rapidity as the lethal poison delivered into a victim's blood by the strike of a cobra's fangs. The venomous virus of polio paralyzed his nervous system, making his every breath a struggle. But the giant squid he watched Kirk Douglas battle best captured the monstrous grip polio had on his life. He had seen the film *Twenty thousand Leagues Under the Sea* only a few months before polio paralyzed him on that fateful autumn afternoon.

* * *

LITTLE STEVIE WAS A VICTIM OF THE LAST POLIO EPIDEMIC in his home state. The First State. Delaware. He would eventually hear stories of other victims such as the one about the high-school football star. A stellar running back, high-school senior was running for a touchdown when his body suddenly went limp; he collapsed on the field ten yards short of the end zone. No one was around to tackle him. Polio tackled him instead. Struck down without warning. That's how suddenly it happened when someone was stricken.

Stephen remembered coming home from school that day feeling a little tired. But how could that be! It was Friday, the beginning of the weekend. No school. When his neighbors Jimmy and Georgie knocked at the back door and asked Stevie to come out and play, he declined. He never declined an opportunity to go out and play. He would remain tight with these two playmates until sixth grade.

One Sunday evening, after returning from a fishing trip with his father, he was shocked to hear what they had done. As his mother tucked him in that night, she told him she found the two boys trying to drown his Basset Hound Polly. When she couldn't find Polly, she went up to the local pond. There she found Jimmy and Georgie holding Polly's head underwater and laughing as Polly struggled. Polly survived. After that betrayal, Stevie never played with them again. Polly had been by Stevie's side throughout his elementary school years. He never forgot how she would look at him lovingly with those big sad Basset Hound eyes. She kept him company by lying next to him the whole time he was recovering from polio.

On this afternoon, however, while he was still friends with Jimmy and Georgie, refusing to go out to play meant that something was definitely wrong. He knew it in his gut, but he had no idea how bad it was. He had gone back to the sofa to watch Hopalong Cassidy.

Growing increasingly tired, he lay down on the floor, resting his chin on the back of his hands while he peered up at the TV screen. It then became too difficult to hold his head up. With just a few minutes left in the show, he turned over and watched the rest of the show with his head upside down. When he attempted to get up, he found he couldn't move.

His mother was in the living room with him when he was stricken. Her name was Gertrude. Most referred to her affectionately as Gert or Gerry. He always preferred the name Gerry. She was home from her work at the bank, and she was comfortably ensconced in the large green-cushioned chair. Her feet were resting on the ottoman.

At five-feet-eight inches, she was tall for a woman in those days. She no longer had the shoulder-length blonde hair she did when Stevie was an infant and toddler. Her hair was now considered dirty blonde. Stevie had been born blonde and gradually his hair darkened by the time he started school. Gradually, her hair darkened during the first five years of his life. She also shortened it to look more professional for the work force. Women had a lot to do to be taken seriously in the working world then, especially attractive blue-eyed women like Gerry..

When Stevie communicated his plight to Gerry, she immediately went into action. He saw her demeanor depict the very meaning of her full first name. Gertrude meant "spear maiden." With the swiftness of a warrior , not a worrier, she immediately went from relaxed on a Friday afternoon at the end of her work week to sheer terror. She quickly converted the energy of fear into taking effective action. She lifted her son up in her capable arms, carried him to his bedroom, and promptly called the family doctor, the distinguished Dr. Henry George.

Many years later as an adult, Stephen would attend Richard Wagner's opera *Die Valkyrie*. Seeing this opera helped him better appreciate the archetypal aspects of his mother as she took action in response to his comment that he couldn't move. He saw her strength of will expressed in Wagner's helmeted-warrior maidens, armed with spears and ready for action. For those not familiar with the opera, the powerful sound of the score and voices that resonated with him were popularized in the epic film *Apocalypse Now*. Robert Duvall played an arrogant and ruthless military commander in Vietnam. He boldly and unashamedly tells his men, "I love the smell of Napalm in the morning." In an unforgettable scene involving an aerial attack with helicopters, Duvall's character is wearing an old-fashioned black cavalry hat. He has Wagner's *Ride of the Valkyries* blasting out of the imposing and ominous swarm of helicopters. Like a phalanx of giant deadly wasps accompanied by Wagner's opera, they destroy a village. The straw and bamboo dwellings go up in flames while the villagers futilely seek cover only to be gunned down or burned alive. Referring to the music, he tells his men, "scares the hell out of them."

Fierce. Formidable. These words described the music and his mother. Years before Helen Reddy sang, "I am woman hear me roar in numbers too big to ignore," Gerry could have made these words her war cry as a woman in the work world.

* * *

DOCTORS MADE HOUSE CALLS IN THOSE DAYS AND Dr. Henry George arrived in minutes. After he examined Stevie, he told Gerry the frightening diagnosis. Remaining stoic to cage her fear about her son's deadly diagnosis, Gerry knocked on the door to the master bedroom. Her husband Earl, Stevie's father, was sleeping. Earl was on shift work at the Edgemoor Plant of the DuPont Company; he was sleeping in preparation for the graveyard shift beginning at midnight. It was now nearly 5:00 P.M. Shaken from his slumber by the shocking news, Earl stood in the doorway for a moment, trying to process the fact that his son had polio. Stephen remembered seeing his father's imposing frame fill the doorway; he was a muscular six-feet-three inches, weighing in at two hundred and twenty pounds accented by a slim waist and big chest.

The two of them appeared well-matched physically and emotionally. They shared a fearlessness and strength. Stevie saw no fear in either of their faces as they both processed the news of their only child's deadly diagnosis.

To Stevie, they were both beautiful as a couple and as individuals. He was considered tall, dark, and movie-star handsome. His long, wavy black hair, handsome features, and dark brown eyes contrasted with her blue eyes and brownish-blonde hair.

If Dean Martin and Cary Grant had a baby boy with Clark Gable's presence, he would have grown up to look like Earl. Whereas Gerry's beauty did not resemble any particular movie star, Stevie did see a resemblance to Lana Turner when Gerry was holding him in one of his baby pictures. Her hair was then long and blonde. Gerry's attitude and stance in life was a combination of Bette Davis and Lauren Bacal. They had an iconic quality. Gerry was a phallic female but feminine; she had a confidence and certainty about her. No ifs, ands, or buts was not just a phrase she used to discipline Stevie, it was a motto for her life. She would set her intention and nothing would dissuade her.

In many ways holding an archetypal view of one's parents is true for any child; their parent's have a larger-than-life quality. Small children see their parents as mythological gods and goddesses like those of the Greek myths. But for a kid like Stevie who was part of the first generation to grow up watching television, this was magnified by movie stars and other celebrities making their way into living rooms all across America. These images on the little TV screen and the big movie screen provided a basis for comparison. Children could view their parents and compare them with images on the little and big screen. Modern society's mythology unfolds on TV shows or in theaters on the big screen.

This dynamic duo stood in that doorway for only a few seconds. But for Stevie the moments moved in slow motion as if forever frozen in time. The door frame became the edges of a mental snapshot he would never forget. Their faces did not fully conceal their alarm and concern behind their shared fearlessness and stoicism. Their stoic and fearless facades were something he would grow up watching and wishing he could emulate. But no matter how hard he would try, he couldn't do it.

When Stevie was eight years old, Gerry cautioned him, "Stevie, you're too sensitive." Had he had my awareness at that time, he might have said, "Yes. I'm sensitive to your unhappiness and Daddy's chronic back pain and depression. And I hate myself for being too small and helpless to take away your unhappiness or Daddy's pain and unhappiness!"

Nonetheless, Stevie's early sensitivity forms the foundation of his choice of profession: clinical psychologist. This sensitivity would lead to one of his professors describing him as a "naturally-gifted therapist." No wonder. He was practicing his therapy skills since he was, as the old saying goes, knee-high to a grasshopper.

Watching his parents standing in that doorway, Stevie was not too sensitive. He was too tired to be scared. *What's going on?* he thought with not enough energy left to worry.

Earl was galvanized into action by the news. Within minutes, little Stevie was whisked away and deposited into the backseat of the family car, one of those classic black Oldsmobiles resembling a fat-round beetle. Earl made record time as the fundamental family unit of man, woman, and child rushed to the hospital.

* * *

AS SOON AS HE WAS ADMITTED TO THE HOSPITAL, STEVIE WAS placed in isolation. There he was in a small room all by himself. The windows of his room had iron bars running vertically from top to bottom. To Stevie they looked like the bars of the jail cells he had seen in TV westerns. To Gerry and to his Aunt Dot, it was heartbreaking having to visit him by standing outside of that barred window. For him, he rarely felt alone when family members weren't visiting. Nurses and doctors were often coming in to give pills and needles. It seemed to Stevie that he was always being stuck with needles. That's what stood out in his memories of his time in the hospital. Needles were delivered into his body everywhere. The most dreaded needles were the ones puncturing the hard areas. Those were the areas with no padding. He would never forget the pain of those needles injected into the bony area of the backs of his little hands and in the small of his back near the base of his spine.

Of the soft areas stuck with needles, his buttocks bore the brunt. He would tell his friends how his behind was so sore because the nurses had made it into a pin cushion. By the time he left the hospital, he had had his fill of needles.

Unfortunately for Stevie and so many other children and adults, the famous Salk vaccine did not come out for distribution until the Spring of 1955. It was now nearly December of 1954. In a matter of months, Jonas Salk would be acclaimed as a miracle worker. Somehow Stevie survived his death sentence: the deadly diagnosis of bulbar polio. Years later, he would learn that the bulbar strain of the polio virus was the most deadly.

* * *

SALK'S MAGIC MEDICINE DID NOT PLAY A PART IN Stevie's recovery. Three miracles occurred: he lived, he learned to walk again, and, in less than ten years, he would become coordinated. So what factors could have brought about the birth of the three miracles? What took place in the magical space between dying from polio and surviving? Between being crippled and walking? Between being uncoordinated and flowing with grace and ease on the basketball court?

Was it prayer? Positive thinking? Unwavering faith and certainty? What accounted for the two miracles that were born in the space between death and life and between paralysis and walking? What empowered the medicine delivered directly into his veins by the needles or the medicine he received by mouth? Was it the prayers of his parents, grandparents, aunts, and uncles as well as his friends in his second grade class? And finally, was it Gerry's unwavering intent that her son would not die? From my perspective all of these factors were part of the recipe for his recovery. He would discover that the most important factor of all was that the Creator responds to the absolute certainty of resolute faith.

Two years after the new millennium, he would learn of the power of what kabbalists call certainty consciousness—one of the 72 names or aspects of God. He learned from his Kabbalah teacher Rabbi Ben that it was the absolute certainty of Nachshon, one of the leaders of the twelve tribes of Israel, that led to the parting of the Red Sea. Nachshon demonstrated the faith that Jesus spoke of being able to move mountains. Nachshon entered the sea until the water was up to his nostrils. With the next step, he would have inhaled the briny water were it not for his absolute faith and certainty. Gerry was capable of such certainty. When she was alone with her thoughts, she would quietly whisper to herself: "As God is my witness, no son of mine will die from polio nor will he remain crippled by it."

Gerry's determination helped give birth to the first two miracles: survival and walking. She drove him to physical therapy for three times a week for two years. Once there, Stevie was determined to walk and to get flexibility back into his stiffened spine. He began physical therapy right after leaving the hospital. Among the doctors, there had been serious doubt as to whether he would be able to walk again.

His first steps were taken during physical therapy. He walked between the two wooden rails on either side of the walkway. The wooden rails looked like the parallel bars that he would see in gym class when he was in junior high school.

Stephen remembered that day when he was finally able to put one foot in front of the other without gripping the wooden bars for support. What a day! It was only after a great deal of hard work that he was he able to walk. Physical therapy was taxing. The three times a week for two years (from seven to nine years of age), he dutifully participated in the grueling, hour-long sessions.

These sessions established an early pattern of self-discipline; he became seized by a passion to overcome the crippling effects of polio and become coordinated. It took him five years before he began to get some coordination in his limbs.

When it came to the third miracle, Stevie supplied his own passion and determination. He kept trying to play sports for the five years following those first steps he took toward walking again without support of the parallel bars or crutches. Stevie tried to play whatever sport was in season. He played baseball and football wherever he could whether in playground or backyard pick-up games.

* * *

THE ROLE MODEL OF THE RESCUING HERO PROVIDED solace and inspiration to Stevie throughout his struggle to recover from polio. The rescuing hero's cry was succinctly expressed by the cartoon character Mighty Mouse: "Here I come to save the day! That means that Mighty Mouse is on his way!" How appropriate! These words were emblazoned on his heart. Mighty Mouse mirrored his smallness and helplessness as a child in the face of his own crippling disease. The image of a mouse also expressed his helplessness in the face of his father's chronic pain and depression as well as his mother's unhappiness. Earl tended to deal with suffering by withdrawing and employing the silent treatment. This was hard for Gerry despite her characteristically positive outlook on life.

When Stevie returned home from the hospital, he would watch his favorite TV heroes. He watched them move . . . jump on their horses . . . throw punches . . . . twirl their six guns with great skill . . . and smoothly take the damsel in distress in their arms. They all had one thing in common. Coordination. They were smooth and fluid in their movements. He longed to overcome the lack of coordination that was the legacy of polio.

His favorite hero was Flash Gordon. In fact, the day he arrived home from the hospital, he turned on the television to watch Flash. He arrived home just in time for the daily episode of Flash Gordon. He loved how Flash would always find a way out of the most hopeless situations. Those cliff-hanging episodes mirrored his own life. He didn't realize this at the time. What did he do in response to all those dire circumstances from which Flash escaped? He developed an eternal optimism.

His mother had told him she always had a smile for everyone since she was a child. Interesting. She lived this motto. His father read Norman Vincent Peale and others on the value of positive thinking. But Earl had trouble living it as Gerry did without ever reading about it.

Once at dinner when he was in high school, Gerry made an

observation that the corners of her mouth and Stephen's turned up. While the corners of the mouths of both Stephen's girlfriend and Earl turned down. Optimism versus pessimism. Positive versus negative. It sure seems that opposites do attract.

* * *

WAS POLIO A PHYSICAL EXPRESSION OF A CRIPPLING COMPASSION for his parents' pain, both physical and emotional? Or, was what happened an additional ingredient in the recipe for a rescuer pattern for his relationships throughout his life?

Here he was at the beginning of second grade, and, if he had a crush on a girl, he would dream about her. The scene was always the same. It had remained unchanged since his first crush on Linda, the little blonde in his second grade class who resembled Darla, the cute little star of the TV show *The Little Rascals*. He saw himself in the woods across from his backyard.

There was a huge tree leaning against other trees. It was about to fall, and he wold see his little love interest standing under the tree. She was completely unaware of the danger. At any second, the tree might fall. If she were the one for him, he would be able to save her before the huge trunk of the tree crashed to the forest floor. Of course, he never failed to save the little damsel. Once a girl made it to this little screen test in his dreams, she was the one for him. Their love was a done deal.

Little Linda was the one whom he rescued before that fateful day when he was paralyzed by polio. Before debuitng in his dream, Linda was part of a game at recess. The boys were supposed to capture the girls and place them in the cage formed by the bars of the jungle gym. When little Stevie caught her hand, she spun around and their eyes met. He felt his heart beat a little faster and a flood of warm feelings filled his seven-year-old body. Was it love? It seemed so to him.

The romantic lyrics of Doo-Wop shaped his young imagination. It was the background music of the time along with the ballads of Pat Boone. One day at the beach when he was on vacation with his parents, he thought about Linda. He wouldn't see her until the new school year started in two months. Picturing her pretty face framed with her soft blonde hair, he put his forefinger into the wet sand and traced the words, "I love you, Linda. Then he made his first attempt at imitating Pat Boone singing *Love Letters in the Sand.* "On a day like today, we pass the time away, writing love letters in the sand. . . . A woman lying on a blanket nearby heard him. She sat up and said, "Hey, you sound like Pat Boone." Stevie smiled. He actually thought he sounded like Pat Boone but it sure was nice to have someone else think so. That a stranger said it made it even better. Relatives were not always reliable. They were capable of giving out unwarranted praise to build a kid's confidence.

Romantic lyrics, often filled with a longing for love, were playing on the radio in the mid-fifties. In 1954, the Doo-Wop group *The Willows* sang, "Church bells may ring, angels may sing, I love you darling and I want you for my own. I'll give you anything I own."

This could have been little Stevie's theme song as a budding young romantic. He loved Linda with an undying loyalty for all of second grade. He didn't see her the next year in third grade because she had a different teacher than he did. Each year, he would have a crush on one girl for the entire school year.

More than his elementary school crushes, he loved his parents with a sense of urgency. His father was suffering from relentless back pain from an injury sustained in World War II. Earl had been on a troop transport plane when it was shot down and crashed into the Coral Sea. When the plane crashed and skidded across the hard beds of coral, the impact did damage to Earl's spine. It was a miracle that he survived. No one else did.

The injury led to a condition called spinal arachnoiditis. The pain radiated from his spine as if he were in the grip of a thousand-legged spider squeezing his vertebrae. The condition was crippling. Little Stevie could see his mother's unhappiness and his father's pain. She was unhappy because he would wall her out due to his depression over his constant pain.

Was the physical paralysis about to grip little Stevie a physical expression of his feeling caught in the black holes of his parents' unhappiness? He was sensitive to his father's pain and to his mother's unhappiness. He could also see how Earl was often depressed and unavailable to Gerry emotionally. Stevie felt sandwiched in the space between the twin fears of abandonment and loss buried in his heart: *I'm afraid Daddy is going to die and Mommy is going to leave!* If Stevie could have expressed this directly, he would have cried out, "Daddy don't die! Mommy, don't leave!"

Naturally, he was unable to articulate or even allow any awareness of these overwhelmingly intolerable fears. Instead Stevie was left with a sense of urgency in his love and concern for them. It was a psychotic place to be; it surfaced in the dark of night. He would wake up with heart-pounding, breath-stopping nightmares. In one a skull was trying to sink its teeth into his toes. In another, his little body was blanketed by hundreds of hairy-legged, poisonous spiders.

Once he remembered screaming and his father came in and reassured him there were no spiders. The scary dreams depicted his fear of the outcome of abandonment: left unprotected. On the one side, death (the skull) was nipping at his toes; on the other, his whole body was blanketed by a poisonous, skin-crawling fear (spiders). Surely, this was an emotionally crippling place for Stevie to be.

His early years before polio were beset by these twin fears that his father would die and his mother would leave. The paralysis he felt from these fears had become physically expressed through polio. However, it was not until many years later that he gained greater insight into the emotional and spiritual climate that contributed to the appearance of polio in America.

* * *

THERE WAS A CONNECTION BETWEEN THE BODY-CRIPPLING effects of polio and the emotional crippling caused by overwhelming fear. In 1997, Stephen found confirmation for a fear-based view of polio when he heard Carolyn Myss speak. She pointed out that polio first appeared during the Great Depression of the 1930s. Myss contended that the appearance of polio in America was related to wide-spread and fundamental fear flooding the consciousness of the whole country. Our survival and security were threatened.

America's sense of security crashed with the stock market crash of 1929 and only deepened in the decade of the 1930s. A victim of polio, President F.D.R. ran the country from his wheelchair. As the leader of the country, he mirrored America's sense of being crippled. America was economically crippled as a nation.

It was not until World War II was over that Americans proclaimed, "We're on our feet again!" Myss pointed out that with that shift of consciousness, Jonas Salk was able to discover his life-saving vaccine in 1952, seven years after the war had ended. And, after years of testing, the vaccine was ready for release to the public on April 12, 1955.

Hearing Carolyn Myss on the emotional and spiritual aspects of polio, Stephen felt that familiar spiritual confirmation from me—a surge of energy up his spine.

His body knew the truth of what she was saying about polio. He thought of how he came into the world with insecurity in the air. His mother Gerry discovered she was pregnant with him right after his father Earl lost his business in what was then called Cape Canaveral, Florida. Earl's partner absconded with the funds and left Earl empty handed. Earl had all of his savings in the business. He ended up moving back to Delaware where he ended up having to live with his widowed mother-in-law. Earl was crestfallen. Humiliated. Depressed. Uncertain of his future, the last thing Earl wanted was another mouth to feed. This kind of financial insecurity was the very breeding ground for polio that Myss had described.

✳ ✳ ✳

WITH HIS VERY MASCULINE APPEARANCE AND PRESENCE, Earl seemed fearless to Stevie. At the same time, Earl was more tender and warm than Gerry. He exercised both strength and sensitivity in in response to Stevie's childhood fears. When Stevie awoke from the nightmares of the spiders and the skull, Earl was understanding. He didn't scold him for screaming as some fathers might have done.

When Stevie was ten years old, he was confronted by a scary-looking tough kid from the inner city. Raised in the more genteel suburbs, Stevie had encountered a kid like this before. He and his friend Johnny successfully scaled a chain-link fence topped by barbed wire in order to sneak into a high-school football game. This big burly kid took Johnny's baseball cards and wouldn't give them back. Taking another boy's baseball cards was a serious offense. Trading cards was acceptable; taking them was not.

Scenes of his TV heroes flashed across his mind. Stevie knew he had to stick up for Johnny and rescue his treasured cards. He knew about good guys and bad guys. Good guys protected the underdog. After all, he was a member of the first generation to grow up watching television. He never forgot the day his father brought home their family's first television set. It was in early December 1951. The set was a large wooden cabinet, the size of a chest of drawers, and the tiny television screen was near the top of the large cabinet.

Every night at 5:00 P.M., he watched the same cowboys ride around the same bend, framed by the same backdrop of mountains. The bad guys wore black hats and black mustaches; the good guys wore white hats and were clean shaven. Hopalong Cassidy and the Cisco Kid were exceptions; both wore black hats and black outfits.

Stevie managed to wrestle the bigger kid to the ground and got on top of him, pinning the kid. Stevie then put his knees on the kid's arms rendering the kid helpless. Despite his position of powerlessness, the kid looked up at Stevie with the fires of defiance flashing in his eyes. "Rough tough cream puff. Go ahead and hit me," the kid growled. Stevie was startled by the kid's comment.

With the kid's arms pinned down, Stevie could have easily pummeled him. There was nothing to stop Stevie from repeatedly punching the kid's face except his conscience. His heroes wouldn't do that. John Wayne, Flash Gordon, the Lone Ranger, Hopalong Cassidy, and his other heroes didn't hit a man when he was down. It wasn't fair.

Stevie was unnerved by the kid's bravado. The kid's scary-looking face and the fearlessness in his voice made his defiance even more unsettling. Stevie felt himself squirm inside but hid his fear and bluffed his way into making the kid promise to give back the baseball cards. The bluff worked.

The next day, Earl took Stevie aside. He motioned him toward the glassed-in porch. Earl began, "I hear you were afraid of an ugly kid." *How does he know?* Stevie asked himself. He then did a quick scan of yesterday's encounter. *Johnny must have told his father . . . but I thought I hid my fear well.* Then he remembered. Later that day, Johnny did express how impressed he was with how Stevie had subdued the bully.

Stevie now remembered responding by admitting he was a little scared by the kid's ugly face. The kid's blunt features were accented by his seething hostility. He had been unnerved by the bully's hate-filled eyes and contorted facial expression, his jaw jutting out defiantly along with his wild and unruly head of fiery red hair and tough tone. All this coupled with the fact that he talked tough despite his defeated position. Now, reviewing the kid's looks from an adult perspective, Stephen realized that it wasn't so much that the kid was inherently ugly. It was more that his attitude was ugly.

Earl continued, "Sure an ugly kid can seem tough. But you have to ask yourself, Is he ugly because he has been in a lot of fights? Or, is he just ugly? If he's ugly because he's been in fights then he can't be that tough. And if he's just ugly, his looks have nothing to do with his ability to fight." Stevie just listened. He had heard from his father's friends just how tough a fighter his father had been all of his life.

It was a balmy afternoon in late September, the sunlight coming through the glass gave the room a welcoming warmth. The atmosphere matched Earl's warmth. He would always treasure the memory of how warm and relaxed Earl was as he spoke. His eyes radiated kindness and understanding. Earl never appeared as handsome to his son as he did that day. His tanned face was still bronze from the summer sun. There were no traces of tension in his facial expression or in his tone of voice.

Earl continued, "I was always afraid in any fight I was ever in. I just took that fear and started throwing punches until someone pulled me off the guy." Wow! Stevie was impressed with his father admitting he was always afraid when he fought.

What a blessing this mentoring moment was given the fact that his father had been a boxer in the Army when he was stationed in the South Pacific during World War II. Stevie also knew that his father had grown up with a reputation of being a good fighter ever since he was a little kid. Earl had grown up in a tough section of the inner city. Families from all different ethnic groups were part of this area of the city. It was a microcosm of America: a mini-melting pot. There was a strong sense of territoriality. Turf wars and minor skirmishes were common.

Earl's prowess as a fighter came up in 1985 when Stephen was talking to his Uncle Vinnie, Earl's older brother by three years. Earl had died six months earlier. "I never had to fight when your father was with me. He took care of anyone who tried to start a fight with me," Vinnie told Stephen. Vinnie mentioned this after seeing Sylvester Stallone's Rocky IV. Rocky said something similar to what Earl told his son. Stephen recalled Rocky telling his son that he was afraid and explained that "Frankie Fear is a fighter's friend." He was implying that fear helps a fighter stay focused and effective.

* * *

OVER THE NEXT DECADE OF HIS LIFE, STEVIE STUDIED THE stylish moves of graceful athletes in all sports. A deep yearning for a coordinated body dominated every waking hour of his life. He longed to run with the grace and speed of famous running backs like Crazy Legs Hirsch. Stevie remembered watching his magic moves when he played for the Los Angeles Rams in 1957. He saw Crazy Legs in an Ovaltine commercial following an episode of Captain Midnight.

He also loved the film about the famous Notre Dame football coach, Knute Rockne. Ronald Reagan played the great running back George Gipper. Stevie loved watching the film footage that showed the magical moves of Gipper's broken-field running. Even though the film was Hollywood hokey and sentimental, it gave Stevie hope.

What was it about the fast-footed eluding of tacklers that so excited him? Was it the same as what made him be sure to catch every cliff-hanging episode of Flash Gordon? Yes. It was the same. Similar to how Flash escaped being trapped or killed, the runners avoided the immobilization, the paralysis of being pinned to the field by tacklers. He thought of the way a student pins a butterfly to a square piece of cardboard for a school science project. Flash's death-defying exploits preceded Stevie's interest in specific sports. Flash symbolized the first miracle: eluding death and surviving despite the odds. Of course, he didn't realize any of this, but I did. He only knew he wanted to be coordinated and smooth in his movements. All he knew was that Flash and the runners were smooth. Not until he had been practicing as a psychologist did he appreciate what Flash and the grace of great athletes represented. They were the antidote to the paralysis of polio.

In one episode, Flash fell into a deep mine shaft and the episode ended. How would he get out of this certain death? That was the question. The opening of the next episode answered the question. Stevie loved discovering how Flash escaped. Flash had grabbed a tree root coming out of the wall of the mine shaft and halted his fall. Once again, Flash escaped death.

In another episode, Flash's archenemy Ming the Merciless, had Flash strapped to an operating table in a scientific laboratory. The episode ended with the laser beam of Ming's Death-Ray machine about to slice Flash in half. As usual, in the beginning of the next episode, Stevie was relieved to see Flash break free in the nick of time. Flash was immobilized by Ming just as Stevie had been paralyzed by polio. Flash inspired Stevie with his ability to escape impossible predicaments. Stevie looked forward to his daily dose of inspiration during those first years he was recovering from the effects of polio. Following his training in child psychology, Stephen realized why he was compelled to watch Flash. By identifying with Flash, he was attempting to master the trauma of being paralyzed by polio. Each episode provided a chance to revisit and triumph over the feelings of helplessness and powerlessness of being paralyzed.

51

Stephen thought of the time the topic of childhood heroes came up in graduate school in a class on psychotherapy. Each student was to think of how his or her hero may be reflected in how he or she performed psychotherapy. Flash Gordon embodied the belief that there is always hope. Similarly, he would consider himself the guardian of hope in his role as a therapist. And this hope was not based in any superhuman powers. He was not Superman.

Flash had his own ingenuity and his faithful friends. He realized that similar to Flash, he believed there was always hope for every patient he ever saw in psychotherapy during his training. This core belief never left him even after years of slugging it out in the trenches of clinical practice. Like Flash, he used his creativity and ingenuity to address the difficult problems presented by patients. Flash was pragmatic and so was he in being eclectic in his use of techniques from different therapies. Whatever works and helps was what guided him in his approach to therapy. He then remembered how he related to his classmates an amusing incident from childhood.

One hot July day in 1956, Gerry told Stevie to put on shorts. Stevie refused because his father never wore shorts. Walking through the living room while Stevie was watching an episode of Flash Gordon, Gerry pointed out that Flash was wearing shorts. Indeed, he was, and Stevie noted that Flash looked good in them. As soon as the show ended, Stevie put on shorts. From that day on, shorts were Stevie's first choice on hot summer days.

Flash reappeared in Stephen's life when Stephen was in his late thirties. He met a woman in Manhattan whose mother had dated Buster Crabbe, the actor who played Flash Gordon. She told Stephen how his childhood hero gave her a tea set when she was a little girl. Her response was not as grateful as Stevie's would have been had his hero given him a gift. She was annoyed. Placing her hands on her hips, she said to her mother, "What's wrong with that man!? Doesn't he realize I need more than three place settings?" After learning what Flash meant to Stephen, she gave a gift. She was able to track down on video nineteen chapters of the original episodes of Flash Gordon. Even after all these years, Stephen was surprised to find that watching Flash in action could still bring back the joy he had felt as a child.

After Flash, he found his inspiration by studying the moves of graceful athletes from all sports. One sunny Saturday afternoon in the Fall of 1958, Stevie received a massive dose of inspiration that did more for his recovery from polio than any medicinal injection. He was about to watch an Army-Navy football game on television. The announcer told the story of a West Point player named Pete Dawkins. Through what was described as an aggressive approach to physical therapy, Dawkins was successful in overcoming the effects of polio. Dawkins contracted polio when he was eleven years old. Through a dedicated regimen of exercise, Dawkins became an All-American football player for Army.

Stevie took note that Dawkins disciplined himself to follow a daily exercise routine. It included starting each day with 50 push-ups. This made an impression on Stevie and reinforced his own dedication to daily exercise.

At the time, Stevie didn't know that this would become the personal myth he would aspire to and live out in his own life. Like Dawkins, he would also live the myth of the child who overcomes the effects of polio to become a star athlete. Only the sport he would make his mark in would be basketball. His mother's sport. Gerry was one of that first group of females to play woman's basketball professionally. Before he let his mother take him under her wing, he tried his hand at organized baseball.

* * *

THE FRAGRANCE OF FRESHLY CUT GRASS HERALDED the beginning of baseball season. This emotional link lasted long after baseball lost its hold on him. Little League baseball was the first organized sport that Stevie tried. In his passion for stylish and graceful movements, Stevie studied the batting swing of Dick Stuart of the Pittsburgh Pirates. Stuart would tilt his bat before whipping it around to swat the ball out of the ballpark for one home run after another.

When Stevie copied Stuart's impressive wind up in Little League games, he would inevitably hit straight down the right field line.

His swing was too late to hit it to left or center field as most right-handed batters did. After abandoning Stuart's style, Stevie tried emulating other Major League stars. However, his timing and eye-hand coordination were still affected by the after effects of polio.

"Stevie tries hard, sometimes he tries too hard," Mrs. Darby his fourth grade teacher wrote in the section of his report card reserved for teacher's comments. Her comment referred to academics and to playing sports during recess. He would try hard to hit the ball when up to bat in softball but was rarely successful. This carried over to the next grade.

Then one afternoon in May during recess, Stevie's fifth grade class was playing softball. He was up to bat. As the ball came toward him, he used Stuart's wind up of the bat before swinging hard. He always tried to hit the ball with all his might. This time, he connected bat with ball. The ball soared far into left field. He sprinted to first base and kept going since the left fielder was still running after the ball. There was no fence. Had there been, the ball would have easily cleared the fence and been a home run.

Stevie continued running all the way to third base before the left fielder retrieved the ball. Teammates urged him to stay on third but Stevie was overwhelmed with excitement. He wanted a home run. He didn't make it to home plate in time. He was tagged out in the last second. Recess was over with that play at home plate. Stevie sat there motionless, his eyes filling with tears. His teacher tried to get him to get up and come inside, but he just sat there in the dirt. Deflated. Humiliated. Stevie was inconsolable. His friend Greg stayed by his side while the rest of the class went inside.

One saving grace in his early attempts to become coordinated through baseball was that he had become adept in the outfield. He had a strong arm and could throw a baseball from deep in the outfield to home plate with just one bounce. His crowning achievement came in one Little League game. It was the bottom of the ninth inning. The other team was up to bat. There were two outs and the other team's best hitter was up with the bases loaded. Stevie's team was leading by one run. If Stevie's team could get through the inning with no more runs scored by the other team, then they would win.

Stevie knew it was tricky judging how far a fly ball was going to go in order to move under it and catch it. He stood there in center field waiting and watching. The pitcher on his team did his wind up and delivered a fast ball right down the middle. The pitch was at the knee's of the batter. It was a perfect pitch for a good hitter to use a golf swing to hit a home run. Home-run hitters of that era such as Ted Williams and Mickey Mantle were delighted when a Major League pitcher delivered the ball to the bottom of the strike zone: the height of the batter's knees. The batter would hit the baseball with the same kind of power as that of a professional golfer hitting a golf ball for a long drive.

Sure enough, the batter clobbered the pitch. It was headed to center field. The ball went high into the dimly-lit pre-dusk sky. The sun had set, leaving a few streaks of light in a sky that was getting darker by the second. Stevie struggled to keep from losing sight of the ball as it sailed high; he could just about spot the little sphere as it moved against the backdrop of the darkening sky. The descending darkness made it hard to track the shadowy silhouette of the ball heading his way.

First he started to move in toward the ball, estimating it would drop in front of him. Then he realized it was more likely to go farther than that. Quickly, he began to back up. It was as if he danced a little back and forth cha-cha-cha before getting into position to catch the ball. The whole event happened in mere seconds but to Stevie it all happened in slow motion; he had all kinds of time to think. Should he move in closer? Should he move back? He must get right under it to make the catch and win the game. Then he stopped and firmly planted his feet, being sure to cushion his left-hand glove with his right hand. Bingo. He caught the ball. Game over. He was the hero and his coach patted him on the back. It was a moment he would never forget.

* * *

SIMULTANEOUS WITH BASEBALL, STEVIE TRIED ACROBATICS and

gymnastics. With great admiration, he had observed the muscular gymnasts from the local high school perform their magical moves. These amazing athletes demonstrated impressive control and coordination. What they could do with their v-shaped physiques was something Stevie might have sold me for if he had been given the option. He watched the graceful moves they performed on the rings, the parallel bars, the horse, the high bar, and the floor mats.

These muscled young men exemplified a symmetry in their size and movements. Stevie noticed that they were short in stature and well-proportioned. Washboard abdominal muscles. Deltoids like cannon balls. Steel-plated pectoral muscles. What they could do with their perfected physiques was incredible. One of them did the iron cross on the rings for more than a minute.

Wow! This was yet one more example of how he envied the short guys in his elementary school classes from second to sixth grade. *God help me not grow tall so that I can be short and coordinated,* he would pray. The cool guys in those early grades were in control of their bodies. They were coordinated. Confident. Competent. Later, he would thank God that he didn't get his childhood wish, especially when basketball became his game.

However, thirty years later, he was amused when he had a chance to have his wish granted. He was at a friend's 40th birthday party; her two brothers and her father were all over six-feet-eight. For once in his life, in a setting other than a basketball game, he wasn't the tallest person in the room. Now, even at six-feet-four, he felt like he was the cool short guy. He was in the position of the cool and coordinated short guys of his childhood. The theme of the party was the Rat Pack: Frank Sinatra, Joey Bishop, Peter Lawford, Sammy Davis, and Dean Martin. As he danced that night, he felt compact and smooth as if he were short enough to be a member of the famous Rat Pack.

* * *

Shooting up six inches over the spring and summer from five-feet five inches to five-feet eleven delivered a death blow to his dreams of gymnastics. This door to developing grace and coordination slammed shut. His longer legs made doing handsprings and somersaults in the air much more difficult. This was the summer of 1961 which became the summer of 61 home runs. Roger Maris and Mickey Mantel had vied for the honor of breaking Babe Ruth's longstanding record of 60 home runs. This was also the summer when Stevie became an adolescent, and he became Steve. He moved beyond the whispers of fear and doubt that so many people fill the space between what is and what is desired.

As Stevie, he had learned to fill that space between being paralyzed by polio with belief and hope. Now as a teenager, he possessed a growing certainty. Stevie felt a faith in the invisible hand of God. Deep inside, Stevie knew that what has yet to be seen, becoming coordinated, would come to pass.

He also filled the space between polio and recovery with the three "D's"—dedication, determination, and discipline. He was dedicated to a dream of being graceful and coordinated. The graceful moves of his TV heroes had been replaced by stars in baseball, football, and gymnastics. But these avenues to grace and coordination gave way to the flowing moves of the heroes of the hardwood court. He shifted his focus to studying and trying to replicate the moves of the masters of what he called the ballet in the air. Good-bye gymnastics and baseball. Hello basketball.

Four

Ballet in the Air

FEBRUARY 1965

SIRIUS, THE DOG STAR, IS THE BRIGHTEST STAR IN THE night sky. Since their debut on the Ed Sullivan Show one Sunday night in February of 1964, the singing group known as the Beatles became the brightest star in the star-studded firmament of popular music. The brightest star in the firmament of high school basketball was Lew Alcindor. He later changed his name to Kareem Abdul-Jabbar, and he would go on to become a legendry star in college and professional basketball. At the end of the 1964-65 season, Steve would be named as a High School All-American and be selected along with Lew Alcindor and a handful of players from all over the country to play on the U.S. All-Star Team. Unfortunately, a badly sprained ankle prevented him from participating in the game to be held in Pittsburgh, Pennsylvania.

In his senior year in high school, he was Sirius in his hometown. Following the fourth game of his senior year in high school, he was caught off guard by an article written by Matt Zabitka, a sports writer for the local newspaper. Stephen was averaging 22.2 points per game. The season before, as a junior, he had made First Team All-State. The writer's words made him see how he had made the dreams of becoming coordinated a reality. Those dreams had filled the space between the paralysis of polio and flowing with the grace and ease of an athlete.

"Fantastic, superb, colossal, extraordinary, fabulous. These were some of the accolades heaped on 6-foot-4 Steve Jackson after he had made the spacious Brandywine High School gym his personal shooting gallery last Friday," wrote Matt Zabitka. The article was entitled, *Steve Jackson's Mom Recalls Dark Days*. In effect, the article documented how he had filled the space between being paralyzed with polio and becoming coordinated.

Steve's passion for grace in his moves on the court was noted in the description of him as, "an artful inside and outside shooter." The key word that revealed to him that, indeed, he had achieved his goal was the word "artful." It was more than scoring points to him; it was scoring with style. For him it was all about the aesthetics of athletics. The article continued on to say that the opposing coach described him as having, "too many moves . . . all kinds of shots . . . it's impossible to defense him." No matter what defense a team tried, man-to-man, zone, double teaming him, or, in some cases, triple teaming him, he would still score or assist his teammates in scoring. He was a skillful passer and the article indicated that he led his team in assists on Friday night.

Nevertheless, it was what a college scout said to Zabitka that really validated all the hard work and dedication. "He's one of the best coordinated big players I've seen this year in high school basketball or any year." Although the scout did not identify the college he was representing, the article quoted Lou Zicarelli, Steve's coach, regarding the colleges interested in Steve. A clone in attitude and style of Vince Lombardi, the famous coach of the Green Bay Packers, Zicarelli said, "Steve's reputation has spread across the nation." He indicated that Steve had received attention from colleges all over the country including nationally ranked teams. The article mentioned, "Ohio State, Maryland, Virginia, Duke, Kentucky, North Carolina, Georgia Tech, and North Carolina State." This was only the fourth game of the season and there were more colleges to court him in hopes of enticing him to come to play for their school.

The article went on to say that with each game, "the ranks of the college scouts swell, they come to see the big guy with the tremendous coordination and potent scoring punch." There was that reference to Steve as being coordinated: "Tremendous coordination." Earlier in the article the phrase, "best coordinated" was used. His vision of becoming coordinated had materialized. From watching Flash Gordon's moves to making his own flashy moves on the court, he dreamed of becoming coordinated. He filled the space between paralysis and flow with images of seeing himself flowing with grace and ease.

The article also mentioned that Steve was, "a tenacious defender." Months later when the All-State Team was announced, Steve was referred to as "Mr. Versatility." As a former professional basketball player and a coach, Gerry rarely commented on the points he scored; she expressed more interest in his defense and rebounding. So in 1969, when Steve was named honorable mention All-American, First Team All Middle Atlantic Conference, and First Team All-East (Division 2), the newspaper noted that Steve was not only his team's leading scorer, averaging 19. 7 points per game, he guarded the opposing team's leading scorer, provided the leading scorer was not a center. Gerry had raised him to be a Renaissance man on the court. Her son would be well-rounded and excel in all aspects of her sport.

On the personal side, the article discussed Steve's struggle with polio. It noted, "for some unexplained reason, Steve recuperated enough to walk and felt well enough to tryout for sports." The article also noted that his first efforts to play organized basketball failed, saying, "his coordination wasn't up to par."

Steve was cut from the basketball team in seventh and eighth grade. The article didn't mention how Steve found inspiration in one of the biggest names in basketball at the time: Bob Cousy. Cousy was cut from the junior varsity team at his high school twice. Cousy's coordination was amazing, and he was the first in a long line of basketball stars Steve strove to emulate.

Cousy was called the "Houdini of the hardwood." Steve was mesmerized by Cousy's behind-the-back passes and his behind-the-back dribbling. Bob Cousy's razzle-dazzle style was inspiring to Steve. Cousy played for the legendary Boston Celtics from 1951-1963 but

Steve didn't pay attention to his fluid moves until 1959 when Steve was finally big enough to shoot a basketball. It was in those years when the Boston Celtics won five consecutive NBA titles (1959-1963) that basketball became Steve's focus for developing his coordination. Cousy being cut twice kept Steve from giving up when he was cut from his junior high school team in the seasons of 1959-1960 and 1960-1961.

The article on Steve's mother recalling dark days ended with how his mother was at every game. "She swells with pride at Steve's every move. And she thinks back to that tragic day ten years ago when the doctors warned her that he may never walk again. If he lived." The article had made note of the three miracles: living, walking, and becoming coordinated. His dedication to the dream of becoming coordinated had been realized *and* recognized.

* * *

"TWO SIGNIFICANT EVENTS HAPPENED IN THIS GYM," Stephen said, addressing the next generation of high school basketball players. Within two years, these young men would be attending the high school Stephen attended. He told the aspiring young players seated before him on the gym floor, "One event happened forty years ago yesterday. It was now November 23, 2003, and he was reflecting back to November 22, 1963, the day President John F. Kennedy was assassinated. With a somber tone, he told these future basketball players, "America was never the same after that. We lost our innocence."

Stephen then mentioned the other memorable event involved the time he attained the state of consciousness called the "zone" or "flow." The players knew what he meant. "It's when you can't miss. Every shot seems to go in effortlessly," called out one of the boys.

"The game occurred," he told them, "the day after the Beatles were on the Ed Sullivan Show, the launch pad for what the news media called the British invasion of American music." Stephen described what happened in a scrimmage, an unofficial game, with Coatesville High School, one of Pennsylvania's best high school teams. The eager

61

and hopeful young men were listening attentively as Stephen told them about the game.

The game was not a run-and-gun game but was a slow-down game where both teams could focus on setting up their defense and offense. I remember all my moves flowing. My motions were fluid whether shooting, passing or dribbling. I felt as if my body and mind were in total sync. Every move had an effortless quality. My mind was quiet. No obsessing. No thought. I was in another zone where I was both participating and observing at the same time.

Steve didn't realize it at that time but he was playing in a state of awareness that allowed for a smooth flow of energy. This flow was occurring between me, his spirit as the transcendent observer, and him as the embodied participant. Operating in unison, we moved fluidly through every cell of every muscle he was moving during the game. His inner harmony extended to an outer sense of oneness; he experienced himself as being at one with the ball and the basket.

Stephen told the young men, "I had no idea of how many points I scored." His focus was in the present moment, the province of his right brain. The quantitative calculations of his left brain were switched off. "All I knew," he added, "was that at the sound of the buzzer, we had beaten Coatesville by seven points. In this slow-down game with no fast breaks, we scored 50 points to their 43." Then he smiled as he told them, "One of their players walked over to me, extended his hand to shake mine, saying, 'The All-American, I presume.'"

Stephen then said, "I shook his hand, and said, 'No, that's him over there.' I pointed to our team's 6-foot-8 center." This was the beginning of his junior year and he wouldn't be named All-American until the end of his senior years. Stephen then told the boys, "Right then the score keeper came over to me with the score book in hand and his finger pointing to my name and statistics. I had scored 44 points." To his amazement, he had outscored the other team by one point. He emphasized to the boys, "I did this by being in the zone where I was focused on the moment-to-moment flow of the game. I was giving no thought to my own statistics."

After concluding his talk, Stephen's thoughts went back to Wendy and the Beatles. Wendy was his girlfriend. She had reminded him to watch the Ed Sullivan Show so that he could see and hear the Beatles sing the song, "I Wanna Hold Your Hand." Steve and Wendy had decided that this was their song as a couple.

Looking back, Stephen wondered if love was behind his magical performance in the game against Coatesville. Had love helped to put him into the zone? But during the game he was totally focused on what was happening on the court. Nothing else was on his mind. He had not thought about Wendy.

What did he remember thinking about during the game? Nothing. He had definitely been in an altered state of consciousness. He had been in the peaceful space between thoughts. No stress. No strain. Still, two particular moves remained in his memory.

One was on the baseline just a few feet away from the basket. He spun with his back to the basket while cradling the ball with his right hand without the help of his left hand. And, in one sweeping motion, he gently flipped the ball up toward the hoop. The ball rolled off his fingers and hit nothing but net. Usually, when that close to the basket, he would lay the ball up against the backboard. Finger-roll shots were what Wilt The Stilt Chamberlain did. This shot was more like one of those soft-touch finger-roll shots that he had seen Bob Petit do playing for the St. Louis Hawks. Petit was his mother's favorite offensive player. She admired his graceful moves and soft touch when shooting inside or outside.

The other move was a spin dribble that led to a little lefty hook shot. It was only about three feet from the hoop. It felt so smooth and fluid and it also swished softly through the net for two points. He was left with the beautiful feeling of flowing and the sense that no one could stop this or any other shot he attempted.

Of course, the high he experienced from the love he felt for Wendy the night before had inspired him. If anything, when he was in the zone, he was filled with love in the sense of doing what he loved and loving what he was doing. No future. No past. There was only now.

The eternal now was what he would later learn to call it, borrowing the phrase coined by theologian Paul Tillich.

Yes, the romantic love he felt for Wendy and the love of the game were a similar state of consciousness. Both were characterized by passion, imagination, and beauty. For Steve there was a captivating artistry in basketball. And achieving this artistry took passion and a creative imagination.

In the heat of the moment just as one of his shots was about to be blocked, he would imagine his way to another shot. This was Flash Gordon's influence. He loved the opposition forcing him to create an imaginative way around the obstacle to scoring. If his right-handed shot was about to be blocked, he would switch to his left.

His thoughts shifted back to Wendy and his memories of the Ed Sullivan Show. As always, Ed Sullivan's enthusiastic words opened what would become a legendary show. "Tonight we have a really big shu [show] . . . Please welcome The Beatles." There they were with, of all things, such long hair. John, George, Paul, and Ringo started singing, "Oh yeah, I'll . . . I'll tell you something . . . I think you'll understand . . . I wanna hold your hand . . . I wanna hold your hand. . . ." The hearts of girls in the audience and all over America were excited and throbbing. American's love affair with the Beatles began.

Wendy was a forbidden love; she was a Jewish girl from a rival high school and he was a gentile. Her parents were strict and their young love was out of bounds. It had to be kept secret. She had to sneak upstairs to call him during the commercial break. They were Romeo and Juliet without the feuding family factor. Jewish guys she knew would arrive at her home as if they were dating her. These pseudo suitors would then take her to the parking lot of her high school. Steve would arrive there to pick her up.

Their love lasted from the Beatles until the summer when the Supremes came on the scene. Motown's dream girls took number one on the pop music charts with the lyrics, "Baby, Baby, where did our love go?" These were prophetic words for Wendy and Steve's love. Alas their love went the way of those early loves of adolescence. Their love was not the tumultuous first love filled with angst and heart-break. It was as evanescent as the morning mist. Their love vanished as uneventfully as the flickering flame of a candle vanishes when all that is left is the wick submerged in a puddle of melted wax. Having burned down through the night, the flame's demise comes with a soft puff of breath from young lips, once hot in the dark of night, now cool by dawn's first light.

$$* \quad * \quad *$$

THE NEXT TIME HE ENTERED THE ZONE WAS IN A CLOSE college game. During this game, the Christian idea that embodied souls should love their enemy suddenly made sense to him. It became clear when Steve found himself appreciating his opponent. His loving admiration of his enemy on the court occurred in the first thirty seconds of the game. In this game, Steve was more conscious of being in the zone than he was in high school against Coatesville. Sure he had had other experiences of being in the zone for part of a game. He was aware of the flow of the whole game.

Steve was playing for the University of Delaware, and the opposing team was Bucknell. The teams were evenly matched. The outcome of the game was decided by one point. Delaware won.

To digress a moment, the recruiting race of colleges across the country for Steve to play at their school ended in the South. Steve signed with the Cavaliers of the University of Virginia. He was not aware that the stars figured into his choice. During the planning phase before his descent to Earth, the decision to be born under the sign of Virgo, the Virgin, was loosely linked to his first choice to play for the University of Virginia. A decade later, I led him to get his doctorate in clinical and child psychology at Virginia. However, in the year and a half he spent there as a basketball player, he grew dismayed with what he saw as a lack of solid man-to-man defense.

Steve had been raised on the excellent defenses he had seen in action at the University of Pennsylvania's Palestra. There he had seen the Philadelphia Big Five teams such as Penn, St. Joseph's,

Temple, LaSalle, and Villanova defeat the nation's top contenders for the national title. He saw these teams do this by playing strong defense. Teams from the Southeast, Mid-West, Northeast, and Southwest would blow into town like hot-air balloons and leave defeated and deflated by good defense.

Steve decided to transfer from Virginia to another college. His first consideration was Kentucky, then Villanova, and finally Temple. Steve was very interested in St. Joseph's but changed his mind when their coach Jack Ramsey told Steve he was going to coach the Philadelphia 76ers. Kentucky was first in the nation until little-known Texas Western defeated them in the national finals in 1966. Deemed the biggest upset in the history of college basketball, Texas Western was honored in the 2005 film *Glory Road*.

Delaware was not on Steve's list, but when his first love decided to go there, he abandoned playing basketball in the Atlantic Coast Conference. When he told Gerry that he decided to transfer to Delaware to be close to his girlfriend, Gerry replied, "There goes your basketball career." She was not pleased. To her, giving up the chance to play nationally-ranked teams in almost every game was insane. He knew she was right. Oh, this is yet another example of the price embodied souls pay for love.

In tonight's game against Bucknell, Steve was completely aware of being both a participant and an observer from the opening tip off to the final buzzer. He found himself planning each move. Throughout the entire game, he felt as if part of his consciousness were floating over the whole court like a pervasive mist. It seemed to hover three-feet above the heads of the other players on the court. Strangely, he felt as though he were one step ahead of the other nine players on the court. It was as if he were controlling the whole game while the other players were simply reacting to whatever was happening.

He was aware of a constant stream of silent self-talk that was creating the flow of the game. Of course, the thoughts he had were flashing through his mind in microseconds. Still, he had some sense of words guiding his actions. To present a view of his inner conversation does not do justice to the speed with which everything was unfolding. The merging of the inner and outer game was occurring in one uninterrupted flow that seemed to be in slow motion. In a way, his body moving quickly on the court was a puppet of this observing consciousness. His sense of me as the puppet master was a good way to describe what happens when an embodied soul surrenders control to the transcendent spirit of his or her sidereal self.

The silent self-talk, the inner conversation, blended the present moment with the immediate future. He felt as if he were creating the desired future. At the same time, he spoke with complete certainty as the immediate future moment were a *fait accompli.* No doubts. It was a done deal. Here is a sample of his inner conversation occurring in the present moment in a "now" and "then" format. The running commentary focuses on each succeeding time his team was on offense.

> Now, this time, I'll make a 25- footer on the right side of the court. Now I'll give a head fake and lay the ball up on the other side. Now I'll drive down the right side of the court by the side line, and I'll stop and fake a pass to the baseline. Then, looking out of the corner of my eye, I'll gauge when my teammate will be in a position to score. Then I'll look away and fake a bounce pass to the baseline, and then, without looking at my teammate, I'll whip the ball behind my back and it will land in the hands of my teammate after one bounce, and he'll lay the ball in for two points.

When there was less than a minute left in the game, and his team was down by one point, he said the following to himself, as he ran back down the court to go on defense:

> They [the other team] pass to the right to start their offense, and then they pass the ball back to the left around the top of the key. And when they do, I'll pretend to be tired and I'll drop my left arm down. Then I'll dart out, bat the ball down, and drive the length of the court for a lay-up to put us up by one point.

It happened just as he had planned; he dropped his hand, pretending to be tired. Then he intercepted the pass by batting the ball three feet in front of himself. This gave him a good head start to begin his drive. He then drove the length of the court to score. His team won by one point.

Throughout this game, there was also a welcoming of opposition. He felt a genuine love, admiration, and appreciation of his opponent. The game began with the player Steve was guarding scoring by making what Steve saw as a beautiful move. And he said so. "Nice move," he said to the man he was guarding as they both jogged past half court. A look of surprise showed on the man's face. This set up a pattern of making it okay to express appreciation for a job well done. Throughout the rest of the game, Steve and his opponent freely exchanged praise for each other's moves. By game's end both of them were the leading scorer for their respective team.

Steve realized that the skill of the enemy, the opponent, helped bring out the best in him. He would have to jump a little higher or move a little quicker, or hang in the air a little longer in order to overcome the odds. The opponent was more than the defensive player or players he was up against.

In a broader sense, the opponent was physicality itself with its constraints of time and space. At some level of awareness, he saw through the veil separating the spiritual realm from the physical. The goal of the embodied soul is to achieve transcendence. The goal was to navigate the body beyond the limits of physical life. The goal was to defy gravity and play with the clay of matter by suspending time and transcending space.

What he did understand years later was that transcending time and space did occur when an embodied soul was in this special state of consciousness called the zone or flow. It would be two decades before he would learn of these terms for what he had first experienced for an entire game in 1965 and again in 1969.

In many ways, he was drawn to the beauty and artistry of it all. He was an artist, painting on a large canvas. The canvas was the court, ball, basket, and the clash of his team and the opposing team. At first, in the moments before a game, he might feel some fear. But once a game was underway, he felt love and excitement replace fear.

He also felt gratitude. He was grateful for what the opponent could bring out in him: new abilities and untapped skills. He was excited for the challenge and what could be wrought from the iron-clad defense blocking his way to the hoop.

Much later in life, he would see and appreciate from my spiritual perspective the game quality of life. There was an opponent who provided embodied souls real choices in life. These choices fell somewhere along a continuum in the space between right and wrong, good and evil. The parameters of the playing field or court were time and space. Making wise choices in the heat of the moment was the name of the game. By choosing wisely, the embodied soul could achieve what Stephen would label unconditional-no-matter-what-happens happiness.

* * *

The noise in the gym was so deafening that he couldn't hear himself think. Stephen was remembering what it was like to play high-school basketball from 1962-1965. In those days, a line would form at 4:00 in the afternoon to purchase tickets for an 8:00 P.M. game. When there were no more tickets left to sit in the gym, fans would buy tickets to watch the game in classrooms with closed circuit televisions. Stephen was remembering going up for a jump shot in the corner and feeling buoyed up by the sound reverberating through the gym. It was as if his body were a boat being lifted by a tidal wave of sound. At such times, he was higher in the air than usual when he released his shot and it swished through the net. Every cell of his body seemed to vibrate with the sound of the crowd's excitement.

Stephen was actually remembering a particular moment forever frozen in time. It was a moment that happened more than once. The excitement and enthusiasm of the fans in those days seemed to merge with his muscles thereby lifting his performance higher and higher. He had just lifted the line "higher and higher" from Jackie Wilson's song. Indeed, his love of basketball was taking him higher and higher. . . .

The first time that this particular moment happened was late in the 1962-1963 season. The special moment occurred during a game against an undefeated inner-city team. Best of all, his team beat this tough team and ruined their unblemished record. He was a sophomore starting for the varsity team. Starting varsity as a tenth grader was rare. He was grateful to have developed enough coordination to be in that privileged position; he was finally far out of the long reach of the spectre of polio. By the end of his eleventh grade year, he was first team All-State. That was a rare honor for an eleventh grader. The recognition was wonderful. But it was not what really touched his heart. It was something kinesthetic, a feeling in his body that he felt when his muscles moved smoothly in the air.

"Oh he floats through the air with the greatest of ease, the daring young man on his way to the hoop that he sees . . . his actions are graceful, all the fans he doth please as he finally shoots and scores." Steve put this little verse together borrowing from the lyrics and tune of the circus song about the daring young man on the flying trapeze. This was a description of his heroes and role models who came after Bob Cousy. One of the first to float in the air was Elgin Baylor. Elgin would twist and turn in the air before releasing the ball and scoring. He demonstrated what came to be known as "hang time," the time a player can hang in the air before shooting or passing. Elgin was the precursor of Julius "Dr. J." Irving and Michael "Air" Jordan.

What stood out for him more than winning games or statistics was certain moves he had made: first in high school, then college, and finally in his brief stint in professional basketball. For these moves captured the crowning moments when he attained the grace of the ballet in the air.

* * *

THE BEATLES HAD THEIR MAGICAL MYSTERY TOUR WHILE Steve had the mystery of his magical-mystical moments on the basketball court. These moments took place in two spaces: the space between

70

feet and floor and between ball and basket. The first magical memories occurred in high school. Other memorable moments followed in college and in his brief experience as a professional. But those first magical moments of body-mind coordination stood in stark contrast to his years struggling to gain coordination. In the magic of these memorable moments of twisting and turning in the air, Steve felt fluid and unstoppable. His first memorable moment came in his junior year in a game against P.S. DuPont, an undefeated inner city team. After this game this dynamic team with the colorful nickname the Dynamiters was no longer undefeated.

Steve caught a pass in the foul lane, five feet from the basket, and he went up for a short jump shot. Demonstrating his dexterity, Steve was about to shoot the short jump shot with his left hand—he was right-handed. The hand of the tall and agile center for the opposing team was about to slam Steve's left-handed jump shot into the stands. To avoid having his shot blocked, Steve turned his left hand and moved the ball into the palm of his right hand. Still hanging in the air, he shifted his weight to his right side. And in a pumping motion, he moved the ball to his right hip. Fading back in the air, he shot the ball from his right hip. The ball hit the backboard and swished through the net just as his feet touched the gym floor. He felt as satisfied as he imagined any graceful athlete might: as satisfied as an acrobat doing a series of handsprings and somersaults topped off with a back flip; as satisfied as a diver twisting after he springs from the high dive; as satisfied as a gymnast swinging in perfect symmetry on the rings or high bar. After the game, an opposing player told him that he was standing at half court when he saw Steve make his move in the air. He told Steve that he saw him shift his weight perfectly as he switched from shooting with his left hand to shooting with his right. Such confirmation from an opponent was very gratifying after all those years of working hard to counteract the effects of polio.

In this moment, it was not that Steve jumped high, it was that he displayed his ability to hang or float in the air, defying gravity. He aspired to achieve the hang-time he had seen Elgin Baylor accomplish. Steeve had fairly good jumping ability. But it came only after hours working out with weights doing squats and leg presses. Years later, Stephen would smile at the title of the film *White Men Can't Jump* because he knew from his experience that it contained some truth.

In college, Steve's standing-still vertical jump was 28 inches. His coach told him that this was the same as the average of the Philadelphia 76ers: They had Jumping Johnny Green, a black player whose vertical jump of 36 inches skewed the average a little higher than it might have been otherwise. Green's leaping ability lends credence to the belief that white men can't jump as high as black men can.

Another memorable move also happened in his junior year in a conference championship game against Mount Pleasant, his high school's archrival. There were only three minutes left in a very close game. Steve took two dribbles across the foul line and went up for a jump shot. The center of the opposing team leaped up high and was about to block Steve's shot. Steve would describe the moment by saying, "I was about to have Wilson [the name of the company printed on the ball] imprinted on my forehead."

He ducked his head under the center's outstretched arm, while shifting the ball to his waist. He then swung the ball from his waist flipping an underhanded-scoop shot at the basket. Time seemed to stand still as it always did during these mystical moments. He felt as if he were moving in slow motion. He could see the ball spinning perfectly as it entered the basket. It seemed as if the ball was dead center and, if it had been measured, every part of the ball would have been equidistant from the circular metal rim of the basket.

To top it off, he was fouled and he made the foul shot for a three-point play. He could sense that the other team was demoralized by that shot. He imagined them thinking, "If he can make a shot like that, we don't have a chance. The game is over." But even if the other team's players couldn't formulate such a clear cognition, they lost their momentum as a fighter does when he doubles over after having the wind knocked out of him by a hard punch in the gut.

They seemed dazed and appeared to need a few minutes to recover. By that time the game was over and his team was victorious. Steve always felt it was his performance in that game that gave him the nod for being selected First Team All-State as a junior over Bobby Kendall. Bobby was a senior who was an outstanding player from Mount Pleasant who was an excellent shooter with great hang time on his drives down the lane.

* * *

IN A HIGH-SCHOOL GAME AGAINST A FAST-BREAKING INNER city team, Steve was being triple-teamed in the left corner. He was in his element playing against inner-city players. In the off-season, he left the landscape of his suburban high school for the cityscape where the best ball players practiced their skills. Steve cut his teeth and honed his skills playing playground ball against inner city players. They were hungry. Daring. Uninhibited. Creative. They were all these things that he strove to be.

Using skills learned on the playground, he faked left. The three players were guarding him in a staggered, stair-step shape. They were attempting to stop the triple threat he posed: driving for a lay-up, shooting a jump shot, or making a clear pass to an open teammate.

As Steve faked left, all three players jumped to the left, one after the other in sequence like Snap, Crackle, and Pop of Rice Crispies fame. He then faked right and each defensive player jumped sequentially again. He drove past them on the baseline, leaving his defenders standing there scratching their heads and appearing as baffled as the Three Stooges. Steve was met by a tall defensive player. Steve maneuvered around him by taking to the air about ten feet from the basket.

Gliding like a gazelle soaring over a lion, he floated around the outstretched arms of this tall player blocking his path to the hoop. Steve switched the ball from the left to the right side of his body, pumped the ball from his hip and, in one sweeping motion, banked the shot in from just a few feet from the basket. He was fouled and made the foul shot. Three years later, he used this patented move of his in a college game with the same result: getting fouled and making a three-point play.

In his quest for coordination, Steve did have a few creative moves that he used more than once. One such move was one of those sheer poetry-in-motion moves he copied from his early heroes on the hardwood. He learned the move one day when he watched Elgin drive down the left side of the lane. Elgin motioned as if he were going to shoot a left-handed hook shot. Then, as the defensive player went to block the hook shot, Elgin shifted the ball around his head and into his right hand. Balancing the ball on the palm of his right hand, he pumped it by cocking his elbow. With a flick of the wrist, he banked the shot off the backboard for two points. Elgin was fouled in the process and turned the elegant move into a three-point play.

Steve used this same move twice in his college career with the same result: a three-point play. One time he used it was during a Christmas tournament called The East Carolina Classic. He went up in the air as if he were going to shoot a little lefty hook shot. Then, as he shifted the ball around his head to his right hand, he heard his coach yell, "Don't shoot that shot!" Steve felt a nervous shiver go through his body.

Much to his dismay, Steve was a good boy; he did not want to incur the disapproval of authority figures. This was something he wished he could rid himself of and it was another reason he admired the inner-city ball players. They seemed impervious to needing the approval of authority figures. If anything, they defied authority. During this season, for the first time in his career, he was playing for a coach who could have undermined Steve's confidence. To come into his own, he needed to overcome his dependency on the coach's confidence in him for him to have confidence in himself. The coach was from the Mid-West and he clearly had his favorites for whom he could take credit when they did well. Steve was already a proven player who had left his home state and had now returned.

Steve did not realize it but to assist the growth of his soul, I had guided him into this situation so that he could overcome his need for others to believe in him for him to believe in himself. Now he was forced to find the inner strength of true self-confidence. He rose to the challenge and did so during this season which was his junior year in college. In spite of the shiver of fear from the coach's lack of confidence in Steve's capacity to perform the ballet in the air, Steve made the shot. He steadied himself and banked in the shot just as he had seen Elgin do eight years earlier. Good moves don't have a shelf life.

In fact, he used a variation of this move for his first shot as a professional. In the fall of 1969, he began playing for the Wilmington Blue Bombers, an Eastern League team owned by the Chicago Bulls of the NBA (National Basketball Association).

Steve caught a pass on the left side of the court, five feet back from the foul line. He began his move by dribbling toward the center of the court right by the top of the key. He then did a spin dribble. He spun around reversing his position and began driving down the left side of the lane. He went into the air about eight feet out from the basket. He started to fake a lefty hook shot and the opposing team's center moved into position to block the shot. Steve then rotated the ball behind his head to shoot with his right hand. But then he could see the wingspan of the huge 6 foot-11 center was as wide as the reach of a giant eagle ready to ensnare its prey. Neither shot had a chance of escaping his hands.

Necessity is the mother of invention in basketball as in anything else. He brought the ball back to his left side. Tucking in the ball by his side, he floated past the two outstretched arms of the center, and proceeded to do a two-handed, underhand scoop shot. The ball angled in off the backboard. This was his first two points as a professional. Just as he planned, his airborne acrobatics drew the center into fouling him. He made the foul shot turning his move into a three-point play. Even though his time playing professionally was brief, he was pleased that his first shot in his debut had style.

* * *

WHAT COMPELLED HIM TO ENGAGE IN THESE AIRBORNE acrobatics? Was he compelled to repeat the triumph over the paralysis of polio in order to master the trauma of feeling trapped? Wasn't his excitement over Flash Gordon breaking free of death traps in episode after episode a repeat of bridging the space between hopelessness and hopefulness? But was there something beyond his bout with polio? Was it something related to the fundamental experience of being a soul inhabiting a body and experiencing the whole range of human emotions? Was there a deeper drive shared by all human beings being expressed in the Flash-Gordon cliff-hanging element of his passion for the ballet in the air? Yes, it was this and more. It's something inherent in being an embodied soul captured and captivated by the material realm.

What was the deepest source of his fascination and passion for getting into and out of these defensive traps? What compelled him to see what he could accomplish in the air before gravity reasserted her hold? Could it have something to do with a deeply buried desire or urge to experience spiritual freedom? This is the freedom a soul feels before being in a body buffeted about by the desires, appetites, and hungers that are all part of being human.

Seeing it all through my spiritual eyes, I saw clearly what he was only beginning to glimpse. He was reliving the spiritual freedom he felt as an unencumbered soul floating freely in space without the weight of the body holding him down. During airborne acrobatics, he defied gravity. He was accessing a liberating consciousness. In other words, he was fully in contact with me without realizing it.

In this state of consciousness called flow or the zone, he bridged the space between the material and spiritual realms. The essence of this consciousness was beautifully expressed in those magical moments of hanging in the air or floating forwards during drives or backwards during fade-away jump shots. At a deeper level of awareness, he was mastering the helpless, frightened, and hopeless feeling which he felt when he entered the little baby body in the womb. In his ballet in the air there was certainly the chance for the child he once was to prove to himself that he had escaped from the prison of polio. But more than that there was the compulsion to prove the ascendency of the animating life force of the soul and spirit as well as the power of mind and thought over matter.

I was aware that he was trying to return the timeless and spaceless qualities of the spiritual realm from which he came to Earth. In those moments in the air, he transcended time and space; everything seemed to slow down. He was then seeing the court with the double vision of the jaguar. In those mystical moments, he was seeing through my spiritual eyes and his physical eyes. Deep down in the dark depths of his heart, he was using basketball as a vehicle for satisfying the longing to return to the stars and fly with the angels.

✳ ✳ ✳

NOT ALL OF HIS MEMORABLE MOMENTS IN THE AIR WERE twisting and turning inside shots, some were outside shots. More precisely, they were long jump shots beyond the top of the key, deep in the corner or close to the sidelines. When he was signed to play professional basketball in 1970 by the Carolina Cougars of the ABA (American Basketball Association), it was because he could shoot beyond the three-point line. At that time, the ABA had the three-point shot line and a colorful as well as patriotic red, white, and blue basketball. The NBA didn't have the three-point shot nor did the NCAA (National Collegiate Athletic Association).

Two decades after playing college ball, he ran into players he had played against from Temple, Villanova, and St. Joseph's. It was an impromptu reunion in New York City with players from the same era. The topic arose about the fact that these players did not have the benefit of the three-point line. Many of them, like Steve, scored a lot of their jump shots from behind the newly added three-point line. They all wistfully wondered what their scoring averages would have been if they had that added advantage of the three-point shot.

Steve had some memorable moments in the air involving off-balance jump shots against a top-ranked Rutgers team. The shots drew praise from legendary coach Jim Valvano who was at that time the assistant coach at Rutgers. Actually, the jump shots were not so much off balance. They were not his usual shot that was taken with both feet planted firmly before jumping and releasing the shot.

One jump shot, for example, began as a typical jump shot but quickly started to become a pass play. He was to the right of the top of the key; it was far enough from the basket to be a three-point shot by today's rules. Just as he was about to release the ball, he saw a teammate get open for a lay-up under the left side of the basket.

Holding the ball in the same hand position as he did when he was shooting, Steve started to fire the ball to his teammate. Suddenly, his teammate was no longer open; he was covered by an opposing player. Steve stopped the pass. And, while still hanging in the air, he pulled the ball back into shooting position and released it. The ball sailed through the air, traveling about twenty-five feet before it dropped softly into the basket and curled the net for two points.

* * *

IN HIS PASSION FOR THE AESTHETICS OF ATHLETICS, Steve found mentors. They demonstrated what could be accomplished in the space between . . . between feet and floor, between ball and basket, between the straining muscles of the clashing of the offensive player's body with that of his opponent on defense. Developing graceful moves and a graceful jump shot were helped along by mentors, known personally or from watching live games or televised ones.

In early adolescence, it was on TV that he saw Bob Cousy, Elgin Baylor, Jerry West, Oscar Robertson, Wilt The Stilt Chamberlain, Bill Russell, Bob Petit, and a host of others.

There were also local mentors he encountered on the playground. It was a very special time that was enveloped in an all-pervading ethos of care and concern in the midst of competition. Just as one generation passes on wisdom and knowledge to the next, older players shared what they had learned. They were willing to mentor and guide upcoming players. Steve was an eager student. He closely observed what these older players demonstrated and listened attentively to their instructions.

In the twilight of summer evenings, these local heroes of the hardwood became playground pundits. They offered their counsel on the outdoor-asphalt court. Tutoring sessions took place after the pick-up games were over; these masters of the ballet in the air took fledgling players under their wing. Steve got his wings with the help of these older and wiser players. All his life, he would always feel especially grateful to these gurus of the game of b-ball. He always loved this abbreviation for basketball, but he wondered how baseball hadn't clinched it first. Baseball began with the letter "b" and it was supposed to be America's favorite pastime.

Two of his first mentors provided contrasting perspectives on the art of a strong inside game. Richie McElmoyle was tall and played center; Orville Crabtree was shorter in stature and played guard. Ironically, Orville was nicknamed "Tree." He may have been shorter but his quick hands and razzle-dazzle moves made him tower over others. Both were four years older than Steve, and they were playing college ball. The tutoring took place in the summer of 1963 on the outdoor courts of P.S. DuPont High School. Both Richie and Orville had played together in high school but were now playing for different colleges.

Richie taught Steve drills for developing his left-handed shots close to the hoop. For Richie, it was absolutely imperative to be able to shoot inside shots with both hands. Steve admired Richie's smooth, seemingly seamless moves. He would spin right or left with short hook shots, lefty or righty lay ups, and artful finger-roll and scoop shots. Richie's persistent patience made him an excellent mentor. Steve would use the moves he learned from Richie when the opponent was the same size or shorter than Steve.

Orville, I mean, Tree, taught Steve one particular set of moves which he later used at Virginia. It was Steve's freshman year at UVA and the game was against UNC (the University of North Carolina). UNC had a 7-foot center named Rusty Clark. Tree taught Steve to fake an underhand scoop shot and then to quickly shoot over the defensive player once his arms dropped to block the scoop shot. The reverse was also an option according to Tree's tutelage. He told Steve to fake up toward the basket. And, as soon as the defensive player raised his arms, then Steve could use the underhand scoop shot.

North Carolina's front line was too much for Virginia so the game was not going to be a victory for Virginia. Still, Steve decided to give the game his best shot. He wanted to test Tree's moves to see if they would work against the wingspan of a 7-foot center. They did.

The first time Steve drove the middle of the lane, he faked under and went over and scored with a finger-roll lay-up. The second time he drove down the lane, he faked over and went under with an underhand scoop shot and didn't score but he was fouled. He made the two foul shots.

Staying true to Tree's tradition, he was able to shoot over and under a much taller player. When Tree demonstrated the two moves, he did so with both feet planted firmly under the basket. Steve adapted the moves to being in the air at the end of a drive to the basket. Having made the move his own, he thought he might rename the move from The "Tree Toppler" to Jack's Giant Killer. One of his nicknames was Jack. Both names conveyed the effectiveness of the combined moves, and Steve was excited to have turned them into airborne moves.

* * *

PERHAPS, MORE THAN ANY OTHER ASPECT OF THE BALLET in the air, it was the jump shot that he worked on the most. Steve studied the style of great shooters, and he sought to incorporate the key elements he discerned into his own shot. On occasion, he would look back and remember that there was a time when his jump shot was his life. . . .

Once in the summer of 1965 before he went off to college, Steve broke a date with Paula, a girl from a rival high school with whom he had wanted to go out for quite a while but she was involved with another guy. Finally, she was available and wanted to go out. On that warm August night, the night of what would have been their first date, he was not happy with his jump shot. The games were over and there was plenty of time to go home, shower, and pick up his date. However he called her to cancel because he felt that he needed to work on his shot after the other players left. He was dedicated to perfecting his game.

Once again, to him, the jump shot was a simplified and streamlined version of the ballet in the air. As he had once done with the major world religions, he sought for the essential unity in the diversity of jump shots. In his quest to perfect his jump shot, he searched for the common elements in the variety of styles. University of Florida coach Norm Sloan presented the following formula: elbow, wrist, and fingertips. This mantra condensed three key elements for an effective jump shot. Good shooters tended to keep the elbow of their shooting arm in and under the ball, and they had beautiful follow-throughs. Nevertheless, Steve observed so many styles, and all of them got the job done.

For some reason, he found himself more enamored with the college All-Americans he watched. Maybe it was the excitement and allure of seeing them play in Penn's Palestra, and, on two special occasions, in the Garden (Madison Square Garden) in New York City. Yes, he had seen some professional games live, but he had seen more college games since his high school coach Lou Zicarelli would take his players to inspire and instruct them in the finer points of the game.

The Palestra and the Garden were to Steve what a greenhouse is to a florist; there was beauty everywhere. And, for Steve the beauty of the different jump shots was as varied as the beauty of different flowers. The various shades of red, purple, pink, yellow, blue, and all the subtleties in between, excite the sensibility of a flower lover.

Roses, hyacinths, lilies, and tulips all have their own special style. So did the jump shots of the All-Americans he admired. Flowers came in various colors, shapes, fragrances, and sizes and so did the beauty and artistry of the jump shots of the All-Americans come in all shapes and sizes.

Of all the outstanding All-American players, Steve found himself striving to emulate the jump shots of three particular players over his three years playing high-school basketball. In tenth grade, it was Charles "Cotton" Nash of Kentucky. In eleventh grade, he began to get a glimpse of the Holy Grail of his own authentic shot; he did not use the shot of any other player as a guiding image. That changed after seeing Barry Kramer from NYU (New York University). In the first half of his senior year, he modeled his jump shot and foul shot after Kramer's. Then, in the second half of his senior year, it was Bill Bradley of Princeton. Each one was smooth and graceful.

Just a few weeks before Christmas in 1962, Steve received from his coach one of the best gifts he could imagine: the chance to see Kentucky play in the Palestra. He was in awe as he watched Cotton Nash display his majestic jump shot framed by the sights and sounds of the Palestra. Kentucky defeated Temple 56-52 with Nash nailing nearly half of his team's points. Steve imagined Cotton's long locks of blonde hair combed up and back might be said to resemble a ball of cotton. Was that the origin of his nickname? Or, was it his extremely soft shooting touch? Perhaps both played a part. There was something majestic about his jump shot that Steve wished to adopt for his own shot.

Many of Cotton's shots were taken far from the basket. He seemed to shoot most of them at about a forty-five degree angle, next to or near the sideline. Steve estimated the shots to be in the range of twenty-five feet from the hoop. By today's college rules, these jump shots would be three-point shots. (The three-point shot in college and high school is an arc of 19-feet-9 inches, and in professional basketball it is 23-feet-9 inches.).

When Cotton Nash performed his jump shot, he was as tall and straight as a towering tree. His erect posture made him seem head-and-shoulders over all the other players. Steve memorized Cotton's stylish symmetry as he released his high arcing jump shot over the outstretched hands of Temple defenders. He was being guarded so closely that he was often fouled a split second after the ball left his fingertips. His regal air reminded Steve of how a modern-day golden-hired Greek god might appear.

In contrast to Cotton Nash, Barry Kramer used a single-handed style. It was the finals of the NIT (National Invitation Tournament) in Madison Square Garden. NYU battled Army for third place with Army nosing out NYU 60-59. Steve studied Kramer's style. Hanging in mid-air, Kramer would remove his left hand as a guide, leaving the ball balanced solely on his right hand. Then, true to Norm Sloan's tripartite formula, his elbow was straight under the ball. And when he was ready to release his shot, he would flip his wrist and extend his arm into a flawless follow-through. . . . His extended arm and bent wrist appeared as if his hand reached out and gently placed the ball into the basket. The ball entered the net as softly as a mother hen instinctively lays her eggs in her nest of straw.

Unlike Nash or Kramer, Bill Bradley's shot seemed to have a crouching tiger quality (no pun intended in that he played for the Princeton Tigers of the Ivy League). He appeared to lean in ever so slightly toward the basket before releasing the ball. This was calculated to help him follow up his shot as all shooters should, but many rarely do. Following up one's shot enabled a player to snag the rebound of a missed shot. The player could shoot again or pass off to a teammate for another attempt at scoring a basket.

Steve witnessed his 41-point effort in the 1964 Holiday Festival held in Madison Square Garden. The game was against a highly-favored Michigan team with All-American guard Cazzie Russell and All-American center Bill Buntin. Princeton was defeating Michigan 75-63 when Bradley fouled out. Michigan managed to come back to defeat underdog Princeton 80-78 in Bradley's absence. Following this game, Steve imitated Bradley's foul shot and borrowed elements of his jump shot to integrate into his own shot.

* * *

LONG AFTER HIS BASKETBALL CAREER HAD ENDED, STEPHEN would still occasionally shoot baskets. Usually, he did so alone since it was a kind of body-mind-spirit meditation. Then one day, many years after adolescent and young adult Steve had become Stephen, the professional psychologist, he came across *The Tao of the Jump Shot*, a book by John Fitzsimmons Mahoney.

What Mahoney wrote about the essence of the jump shot dovetailed with his own love affair with the artistry of the jump shot. The cover of the book had a yin and yang symbol on it, suggesting the balance and symmetry of a great jump shot. There is a flow to a great shot, and, as basketball legend Bill Bradley once described, a shot should come out of the "organic flow" of the game. The shot should never be forced.

The perfectly-performed jump shot occurs when a player is in the zone; it flows forth from the state of consciousness where a player feels himself in the flow of the moment. The Tao is the energy flow of the universe. The following passages on the jump shot from Mahoney's book rang true to Stephen.

> The ultimate controller of the shot is not an "I" or conventional self with a name and psychological history, but the Self or Tao that governs the cosmic movement of atoms, cells and stars as well as the simplest human gesture. . . . A well-executed jump shot occurs unimpeded, like clear and flowing water, itself the great symbol of purity. . . . Mental concepts during the shooting act contaminate the pure flow of the shot.

For Stephen, the Self Mahoney refers to as the ultimate shooter is me, his sidereal self. When he acknowledges me as the ultimate shooter, he as the embodied soul, is flowing in harmony with me and my transcendent perspective. Together, we form one flowing unit. Both Heaven and Earth are at work in the unfolding of the jump shot. Being in the flow of the ballet in the air is being at one with the Tao. Stephen found a wonderful descriptions of the experience of flow in Michael Murphy's books, *Golf and the Kingdom* and *The Kingdom of Shivas Irons.*

Set in the misty hills of Scotland, both books reminded him of the magic of the film Brigadoon which was also set in Scotland. The timeless truths and mystical aura of both books mirrored his own mystical experiences in playing basketball as the ballet in the air. Both books featured the spiritual teacher and golf guru, Shivas Irons. Delivering his wisdom, wrapped in his old-world Scottish accent, Shivas coaxed Murphy, "Swing with yer inner body."

It was on a pleasantly warm, golden afternoon in the South of France that Stephen had one of his clearest experiences of shooting with his "inner body," what he preferred to call his energy body. He had this epiphany involving his jump shot while visiting his friend Don. Don had rented a villa on the outskirts of St. Tropez for the summer of 1994. The villa was set high on the end of a peninsula and it offered beautiful views of the blue Mediterranean.

Stephen had just celebrated his forty-seventh birthday. Don had had a basket and backboard installed on a bluff overlooking the bay bordering St. Tropez. Don played high school basketball in a tough and highly competitive league in New York City. Don still had excellent moves despite having recently turned fifty years old. Don and Stephen were playing a game of horse. When one player makes a shot, the other must make the same shot or receive a letter. Whichever player misses a total of five shots, the player loses since the accumulated misses spell horse. Standing on the outdoor basketball court, Stephen could hear the rhythmic sound of the sea. Waves were washing over the rocks down below. The sweet scent of the last roses of summer was in the air. The whole scene was having a hypnotic effect on him. He felt his body relax; all trace of tension dissolved in the sound of the sea. He felt good.

It was Labor Day back home, summer's swan song. Soon the crowded beaches of summer would be empty with autumn's approach. No toil. No effort. There was only the barely audible sound of happy voices of people at play on France's famous Riviera, *Côte d'Azure.*

The lengthening late-afternoon shadows danced arm-in-arm

with the waning yet still bright sun. The sunlight flickered on the rippling waters of the bay; it was as if the sea were a giant mirror that had shattered into thousands of little pieces. The space between each shiny piece of mirror was filled with the shadows of the waves. This dance of light and shadow lent a mystical aura to the scene. Time and space stood still in the chiascuro characterizing the space between the elements of earth, air, sun and sea. No place to go. Nothing to do but shoot hoops within the specific coordinates of time and space containing the outdoor basketball court. The temperature was just right. Not too cool. Not too hot.

Before the game began, Stephen recalled the advice of a coach whose name he couldn't remember, "Always practice your shot as if you were under game conditions. Don't just shoot around." These words made him think of a scene from the film *Butch Cassidy & the Sundance Kid.* Butch (Paul Newman) and Sundance (Robert Redford) have fled to the lush countryside of South America. They've decided to give up a life of crime and apply for jobs as payroll guards. But first they have to pass a shooting test. They are to shoot at cans to demonstrate their shooting skills.

Butch goes first. He does fairly well. But Sundance isn't doing so well as he stands there shooting at the stationary cans. Finally, he asks the supervisor evaluating them for the job, "Can I move?" The supervisor agrees. Once he is allowed to move, as if he is in a gunfight, Sundance mows down every can one after another in rapid-fire succession as if he is shooting a machine gun.

From the beginning of the game of horse until the end, Stephen moved as if he were being guarded in a game. He would ask Don to pass him the ball, and he would begin readying himself to receive the pass. Sometimes, he would imagine he were open (unguarded) and he would catch the ball and go right up for a shot. Other times, he would fake and go up for a shot or dribble as though driving and stop and go up into his jump shot. Shooting had always been about rhythm and flow. This was as true for a gunfighter as Sundance demonstrated as it was for a basketball player. Movement helped to get the meddling mind out of the equation. With the mind quieted, the shooter could achieve a more coordinated mind-body effort.

Literally and figuratively, he was aware of what he described as being, "on his toes," before shooting every shot in this game of horse. Stephen became conscious of his jump shot as a flow of energy beginning with his toes. He felt how his jump shot flowed from his toes and up through his body until the ball was released from his fingertips. He was conscious of being in the flow of the zone, the Tao, even if it were only a game of horse.

There was a heightened sensitivity with each shot. He was reminded of those times in high school when he would shoot baskets in the snow. To increase the sensitivity in his fingertips, he would wear leather gloves. When the gloves came off, he would really feel the ball. Today, however, the sensitivity extended throughout his whole body. He described the extended sensitivity to Don as, "the whole body jump shot." Holistic health was a concept in the air in those days. It meant true health was a matter of body, mind, and spirit.

Here, he thought, *is a holistic jump shot where body, mind, and spirit harmonize in one coherent flow.* Don interrupted the silence surrounding the game of horse. Stephen had lost track of time. His awareness was immersed in the moment-to-moment flow of each shot. Don was keeping track of the game, and broke the trance Stephen was in, saying, "Do you know that you have made 99 shots out of a 100? That's ninety-nine in a row without a miss!" And the truth was Stephen had missed none of his jump shots; he had taken a brief break from shooting jump shots to casually toss up two hook shots. The right-handed hook went into the basket, and the left-handed hook missed. He had shot all of his jump shots with his inner body, or, as he liked to call it, his "energy body."

Sensitizing himself to the flow of energy in his body, he felt it rise from his toes to his fingertips. Stephen now saw how the jump shot happens in the space between Heaven and Earth. The feet push off from the ground, and at the peak of the jump, the player pauses in mid-air before launching the ball to the basket. Focusing on the flow of energy within him had made all the difference in his unerring accuracy on this lovely afternoon with the old world ambience of St. Tropez providing the backdrop. Somehow this setting seemed appropriate since he was accessing an ancient awareness that was not new but was part of old world spiritual wisdom. The only things new were the terms used to label this awareness: zone and flow.

* * *

"IS THAT ALL THERE IS? IS THAT ALL THERE IS? THEN LET'S keep dancing. Let's break out the booze and have a ball, if that's all there is. . . ." Peggy Lee's sultry voice cut through the cool spring breeze wafting into his dorm room. Sitting on the train, Stephen's thoughts went back to the Spring of 1969. The song lyrics were perfectly synchronized with his feelings. He recalled how the song was playing at the moment that he had just received a phone call. It was the call he had hoped would happen.

"You've been picked for First-Team All MAC (Mid-Atlantic Conference), First-Team All East (Division III), and Honorable Mention All-American!" exclaimed the voice on the other end. It was Otto, the team manager. "You're achievement is made all the more sweet because you beat out players from LaSalle for your spot on the first team."

This was the year that LaSalle went undefeated with 23 wins and no losses. LaSalle would have had a good shot at being number one and beating UCLA. UCLA's dynasty extended from the mid-sixties to the early seventies. A large part of UCLA's dominance was due to back-to-back imposing centers: Kareem Abdul Jabbar followed by Bill Walton. LasSalle had a strong center in Ken Durrett but LasSalle never got the chance to defeat UCLA because of a preseason violation of NCAA (National Collegiate Athletic Association) rules.

Rumor had it that the starting five had been given construction jobs for hefty salaries. However, it was discovered that none of the players ever showed up for work, and they still got paid. LaSalle was ineligible to play in the post-season tournament to determine the number one team in the nation. Locally, LaSalle's players dominated the selections made for the first, second, and third teams of the MAC (Mid-Atlantic Conference). Of the honors he received as a basketball player, Steve would count this one his best honor: being the only player not from Philadelphia's Big Five to be named First-Team All-MAC.

Steve sat there stunned. Immobilized. "Is that all there is. . . ." To his surprise, Peggy Lee's words mirrored his mood. Sure he was elated but he also felt empty. Is that all there is? He quickly changed into his gym clothes and ran to the field house to shoot baskets by himself. He knew it would help him think better so he could make sense of his mild anxiety over feeling enveloped in a fog of meaninglessness.

As soon as he shot his first few shots, Steve experienced a calmness spreading within, through, and around his body. It was as if an invisible blanket coupled with a hot cup of chicken noodle soup took away the chills while breaking the fever of his free-floating anxiety. This was the meaning of all the practicing? It was as his philosophy professor Dr. David Norton had said when he quoted Cervantes, "Not the inn but the way." *That's it*, he thought. *It's about the striving . . . the journey . . . not the destination.* He needed to set his sights on a new star to navigate by, a new goal to work toward.

The meaning was to be found in the straining of his muscles and the buckets of perspiration spilled on the gym floor. It was all in the moment-to-moment aliveness penetrating into the mitachondria, the tiny furnaces in the cells of his muscles. What Albert Camus wrote in the *Myth of Sisyphus* said it all.

> . . . the lucidity that was to constitute his torture at the same time crowns his victory . . . The struggle itself toward the heights is enough to fill a man's heart. One must imagine Sisyphus happy.

With every move of his muscles as he shot baskets by himself, Steve was experiencing the visceral and existential truth of Camus' words. Indeed, it is not about arriving at the summit. Sisyphus discovered that his freedom lay in embracing his torture. He is condemned to roll a rock up a hill in hades only to have it roll right back down again. What a beautiful metaphor of the embodied soul feeling trapped in time and space with no freedom from endless effort. The freedom is found in embracing the creative struggle.

Steve was discovering for himself the essential truth that the act of creating, being like God, the Creator, brings joy. Yes. The struggle itself to aspire to fulfill his dreams had been enough to fill his heart! Steve was glad to learn this at twenty-one years old. He realized that the satisfaction of attaining the honors was pale in comparison to the joy of working toward the goals he had set for himself.

At some level of awareness, he sensed that this insight was not entirely complete. Otherwise life is all about constant striving. Is there no peace but that arising from acceptance of the inherent struggle?

Later in life, Stephen would see that it is the peace that comes from recognizing the endless process of desire that brings the joy of spiritual freedom. Fulfill one desire and another desire follows in its place. There really is no place to go and nothing to do that brings ultimate satisfaction. But being in the present moment and identifying with me, his spirit, he realized could bring peace. For I AM the awareness who is aware of the constant rise and fall of desires arising like the dips and swells of an endlessly flowing river. By identifying with me, he could find the peace found in the space between desires. It is the peace of just being. Not doing. An embodied soul simply witnesses what is without taking any action.

* * *

THE TRAIN WAS TRUDGING INTO TRENTON, AND HE WAS staring out of the window lost in thought; he didn't notice how he had fogged up the bottom of the glass pane by his mouth. He was remembering a night that took place over thirty-five years ago. The sun disappeared over the horizon on October 31, 1969. Halloween. He still remembered how that sunset had seemed poetic since the sun had just set on his college basketball career. He thought of how he had literally turned in his newly issued sneakers to the coach before practice began that day. And, before the dust settled, less than twenty four hours later, he signed a contract to play professional basketball. He left the team in spite of the fact that he had another season of eligibility. The season before he had done well even though he had not had the kind of support of the coach he had always had with other coaches.

The year Steve transferred from Virginia back to his home state of Delaware, he became friends with Charlie Parnell. Charlie was a superb player who made All-MAC by beating out players from the Big Five. Charlie accomplished this in his junior year. Steve arrived at the start of Charlie's senior year, and Steve was ineligible to play because transfer players have to wait a year before they can play. It's an NCAA rule. Steve still practiced with the team to keep his skills up, and Charlie befriended Steve during that year.

Over the year, Charlie told Steve how the coach was undermining his confidence. With his confidence sagging, Charlie did not do as well in his senior year as he had done in his junior year.

When Steve was facing his senior year after an outstanding junior year, he feared following in Charlie's footsteps. Steve had maintained his confidence during his junior year in spite of the lack of support from the coach. During the preseason, he saw the coach beginning to do things to sap his confidence, Steve thought it best to leave the team. This way the team had time to adjust to his absence.

Stephen remembered how he felt a little sad yet relieved when night had finally fallen on the college town of Newark, Delaware on October 31, 1969; the street lights had come on as soon as darkness descended. Costumed children, trick-or-treaters, were being escorted by their parents. He promised himself he would not allow himself to regret his decision to end his college basketball career. He would never second guess his decision by always remembering how he felt at the time he decided to leave the team. An embodied soul can only torture himself or herself with regret by forgetting his or her feelings at the time. He was well aware of the old saying, "Hindsight is 20/20." Years later, after he had worked with many adolescents and young adults in therapy, he would wish he had had someone like himself back then with whom to talk. All he needed was a therapist who could have shown him how he needed to slay the dragon of dependency. He needed to take this next step in his psychological and spiritual growth by believing in himself and his ability to perform the ballet in the air even when the coach did not.

"Self-esteem," he would later tell his patients, "is not based on the opinion of others; that's why it's called self-esteem and not 'other esteem.'" His self-esteem as a basketball player is based on an accurate assessment of himself done by himself. He did not know this at the time and he felt hopeless. That's what he would remember. And he would repeat the mantra of compassion he wrote about in his books, "I know in my heart that I would have stayed on the team and played if I could have but I didn't feel I could at the time so I didn't. In short, 'I would have if I could have but I couldn't so I didn't.'"

He remained true to his promise and never allowed himself to be eaten up with regret. It wasn't until thirty-three years had passed that he even looked back and imagined what might have been if he had toughed it out in his senior year as he had in his junior year. He attended a reunion held for his college team in 2002. After that, there was only the occasional wistful wondering of what might have been. . . .

∗ ∗ ∗

HIS THOUGHTS TRAVELED BACK IN TIME TO THE VOW HE made on Easter Sunday 1964. He made it in the presence of his best buddy back then, Kenny Westerside. Kenny followed suit and wrote down a similar vow for baseball. They sealed their vows in an envelope, and put it away, never to be looked at again. On the envelope were the words, "Do not open until the Spring of 1969." Steve's vow read as follows:

I, Stephen Royal Jackson, do solemnly swear that in the year of our Lord nineteen hundred and sixty-nine, I will have attained the honor of All-American, signed a contract to play professionally, and my name will rank with the greats of all time."

Westerside wrote the same vow only his was for baseball. The solemnity of the ceremony resembled the blood-brother ritual that he had engaged in at eight years old with his neighbor, Jimmy who was closer in age to Stevie than Georgie. Jimmy took out his black-handled penknife and opened it. Then each boy made a small cut on the underside of his right wrist. After this, they pressed their cuts together to signify the mixing of their blood to become blood brothers.

Stephen thought about how he had fulfilled his vow by the Spring of 1969. He had attained the first of part of the three parts of his vow. By November of 1969, he would fulfill the second part by signing a contract to play professional basketball. Four years later, he would learn that the third part of his vow was accomplished; his name was in the Basketball Hall of Fame in Springfield, Massachusetts. It was not what he had intended when he made the vow. He had meant to be in there for a distinguished career in college and as a professional. Instead, he was in the hallowed halls for his performance at the University of Delaware in 1969. Still, it was significant that he had written down his vow and it had come true in the space between where he was in 1964 and where he wanted to be in 1969.

Looking back, he was grateful for Peggy Lee and the edgy anxiety and agitation he felt after hearing about his honors. He had been provided an important insight into life and happiness. He understood that something deeper was going on behind the mask of basketball.

In the summer of 2002, he found a beautiful description of the deeper truth underlying his quest for coordination. It was in the opening words of Mahoney's *The Tao of the Jump Shot*. It was thirty-three years after his final season in college.

> Any physical or mental activity that's constructive and creative and aims for perfection helps in our quest for the spiritual foundations of existence.

To put it another way, in the words of the venerable sage from India, Swami Rama, "Only one who remains unaffected by honor or insult can keep the divine flame alive." Yes. Only by slaying the dragon of dependency on the approval of others mirrored in honors and trophies, does the embodied soul soar and savor a little taste of Heaven on Earth. His quest for coordination culminated in the quest for the prefect jump shot. However, his quest was for something deeper. He was searching for me; for as his spirit, I AM the spiritual foundation of the consciousness that is his embodied soul. Basketball was not about statistics. Not about wins and losses. Not about how many points he scored or honors he received. He realized that pursuing excellence in any creative endeavor enables the embodied soul to find his or her sidereal self as a by-product of reaching for the stars. . . .

II

The Space Between
Surface & Depth

Thus shall we think of all this fleeting world, a star at dawn, a bubble in a stream, a flash of lightning in a summer cloud, a flickering lamp, a phantom and a dream. . . . (*A Gradual Awakening*)

—Stephen Levine

You must shine like stars lighting up the sky, as you offer them the message of life" (Philippians 2:16).

—Saint Paul

With man this is impossible, but with God all things are possible (Matthew 19:26).

—Jesus the Christ

Five

Delving into Dreams

SUPER MASSIVE BLACK HOLES ARE AT THE HEART OF LARGE galaxies such as the Milky Way Galaxy, the one in which the Earth resides. The center of the Milky Way galaxy is the "spout" of the teapot-shaped constellation Sagittarius. What appears to be steam rising from the teapot is millions of stars. Behind the stars are dense clouds of gas and dust that hide the heart of the galaxy: a huge black hole that is three-million times as massive as the sun. Could it be that at the heart of the personal galaxy (the personality or personal identity and sense of self) of every embodied soul is a black hole?

Sitting quietly on the train now leaving Trenton for New York City, he continued on his own train of thought; he was reviewing his life through the lens of the space between stars. He began to turn the telescope from outer to inner space by drawing upon his knowledge of depth psychology. He considered how depth psychology delves into the black holes existing in the space between the surface and depth of the personality. His head was reeling with the excitement of spotting the parallels between inner and outer space. It seemed to Stephen that this description of outer space applied to inner space. But how did it apply? The answer involved a consideration of the nature of black holes.

Black holes in outer space exert a strong gravitational pull on whatever comes near them. The gravitational force exerted by black holes is so tremendously powerful that this pull extends out into the space around the black hole and warps that surrounding space. Like the giant, gaping mouth of an invisible monster lurking in the dark depths of space, a black hole swallows whatever comes near it: stars, planets, and spacecraft. Objects disappear and cannot escape from its unseen jaws.

He was now beginning to get a glimpse of what was clear to me. From my transcendent perspective, there are not only parallels between outer and inner space, they are inextricably intertwined and so are indistinguishable. He wondered if this might mean the embodied soul's essential nature is a vast and formless consciousness. In contrast, the body-based personal identity is essentially a mask hiding a void: a gaping black hole. From his experience of hunger in the womb, he knew that this black hole was essentially a wide-open mouth.

Karl Schwarzschild, a mathematician, performed calculations that provided a scientific understanding for black holes. He determined that when mass is compressed into a small enough space, then an extremely strong gravitational influence is exerted on any objects in space surrounding the compressed mass. Einstein replaced the notion that gravity was a force of attraction with the idea that gravity was due to a curvature in space. Einstein was the first to determine that dense objects in space such as stars and planet warp space, causing it to curve.

The warping caused by compression in outer space is similar to the warping caused by repression in inner space of thoughts and emotions. And wasn't hunger and fear of the pain of hunger the first painful experiences he faced shortly after entering the womb? Could fear and hunger and the compression of continuous consumption contribute to the origin of the black holes of inner psychological space?

In his clinical training, he had learned that fear was the basis of all psychopathology. Fear forces the embodied soul to erect mental and emotional defenses: repression, denial, and projection. These defenses are erected early in life to avoid psychological suffering. Fearing parental criticism, disapproval, abandonment, punishment, and rejection, children develop an idealized self-image. If they can live up to this image, then they can avoid these painful experiences.

In *Love Conquers Stress*, Stephen described how this self-image is composed of standards to live up to in order to ward off criticism, punishment, rejections, and disapproval. "I must be perfect. I must never make a mistake. I must be strong and never show fear." The list is long and depends on the values and identities of parents and others a child admires: older siblings, aunts, uncles, grandparents, and so forth.

Beginning to see things from my spiritual perspective, Stephen saw a curious play on the words avoid and void. There is *a void* at the core of the system of defenses set up to *avoid* suffering from all the primary hungers for food and all its derivatives: the hunger for love, approval, money, sex, power, and so forth. How ironic that a black hole exists at the heart of the personal identity (personal galaxy) of every embodied soul. In other words, there is a constantly consuming void at the core of any conventional sense of self based on the body and personal history. What hungers drive an embodied soul and how the embodied soul handles those hungers define his or her personal identity and sense of self. One embodied soul hungers for love and approval while another always needs to be right. Another hungers for power and control. Another hungers for sympathy and love by seeking to suffer. And, at the most basic level, another denies the hunger for food and becomes anorexic.

Stephen would later realize that the core of a black hole is the trapped light of love. Love is my essence and the essence of the soul inhabiting the body. He would come to understand from his clinical experience what William Blake meant when he wrote, "under every grief and pine runs a joy with silken twine." Black holes are stuffed with the dense, dark energy of the negative emotions of fear and anger.

Thwarted hungers fuel the contracted energy of negative emotions, and underlying this contracted energy is the positive energy of love. For if embodied souls didn't love and care then they would not be mad, sad, or glad. Later, he would learn to link dark emotions to the light of love and, in so doing, liberate the light of love in the black holes created by repressed emotions.

Since I AM pure spirit then love is my essence and true identity. Love is also the essence of the embodied soul because we are essentially one undivided consciousness. With his or her vision clouded by being in a body, the embodied soul is not always able to see clearly that his or her true identity is love. The dense darkness of anger and fear can block the light of love. Learning to disentangle from negative emotions by returning to love is a challenge for the embodied soul.

Ultimately, this constructed sense of self is an illusion, a walled-in fortress blocking the light of love. The solidity of the body, the soul suit, the corporeal costume, is also an illusion from my eternal perspective. At death or during other times of expanded awareness, such as those Stephen discovered on the basketball court, a reunion of spirit and soul takes place. Transcendent spirit and embodied soul are momentarily reunited back into one unified consciousness again. By briefly merging with his or her transcendent spirit, an embodied soul is able to soar freely in the spirituel realm.

Love is the cohesive force holding the universe and all the stars and galaxies together. Whereas love is an expansive energy and includes all that is, fear is contracted energy. Fear is the gravitational force of the black holes populating the space between the surface and depth of the personality. Fear swallows the stars of love shining in the vastness of inner space. Not only does fear make the light of love disappear but fear also extinguishes the light given off by the flame of consciousness.

Then he thought of another aspect of the black holes of inner space. The fear at the center of the black holes in the inner space of parents exerts a strong gravitational pull on their child which can warp the child's identity and sense of self. Repressed fear in a parent may be expressed by his or her child. He always loved what Erik Erikson's observation, "The child expresses what the parent represses." He had expressed the fears and insecurities his father had repressed.

He knew there was a way to illuminate the black holes of an embodied soul's personality. He had discovered it over thirty years earlier. The answer was to be found in the strange stories and sometimes bizarre images that visit the embodied soul during sleep. These nightly visitors bring to light the contents trapped in the black holes of inner space.

* * *

FREUD SAID, "DREAMS ARE THE ROYAL ROAD TO THE unconscious." And for Stephen whose middle name is Royal, dreams were Royal's road to his unconscious. This was true even if he tended to interpret his dreams in the tradition of Jung. For Jung, dreams were not disguised as Freud claimed.

Symbols don't disguise as Freud claimed. Sure they may serve an embodied soul's defenses against emotional and mental pain. Yes the symbol may hide a thought or feeling that the conscious mind finds unacceptable. But upon closer inspection, it may beautifully express a dreamer's feelings. The grizzly bear in a child's dream is not a disguise of the fear the child feels for his short-tempered father. It may help keep the dread of the father from becoming fully conscious, but it also beautifully expresses the child's depth of fear for his growling and menacing "grizzly-bear" father. The bear may also express the anger a child fears expressing in response to his father's angry outbursts. Dreams express the invisible inner world of the images behind feelings and thoughts.

To Stephen, dreams were snapshots of an embodied soul's psychodynamics, the *interplay* of the inner play of emotions, portrayed in symbolic language. In Jung's schema, you could say that complexes are black holes swallowing into its darkness the light of consciousness on any given theme. Common complexes are the inferiority complex, the father complex, the mother complex, all of which are complex webs of feelings and thoughts revolving around a central idea like the planets revolve around the sun.

Through his dreams, he discovered a debilitating father complex. At its core, the black hole of his father complex was subsumed by an all-consuming hero-savior complex. This complex turned out to be the large black hole at the heart of his personal galaxy; the complexes of other, smaller black holes cluster around it like unseen satellites. The central organizing principle in his personality, this complex first appeared in a dream he had in 1975, one year before he went off to graduate school at the University of Virginia.

* * *

"I AM CARRYING MY FATHER ON MY BACK AS I STRUGGLE TO run up a fairly steep hill. Nearing the top of the hill, I turn to help my father off my back. But instead of my father, I find a monkey. I feel affection for the monkey. I lovingly lift the monkey off my back and hug him. Upon awakening, I think that my father has been the monkey on my back." Steve was telling Dr. David Hart his dream. "I guess, I'm ready to face and embrace the monkey on my back," Steve chuckled. He was in Jungian analysis with Dr. David Hart. Jungian analysis was an offshoot of psychoanalysis. David Hart went to Zurich and trained directly under the master himself, the renowned Swiss psychiatrist Carl Gustav Jung. This was well after Jung broke with Freud.

Steve had become fascinated with Jung's approach to dreams when studying philosophy in college. He ended up in David Hart's office because he did a masters thesis on Jungian psychology and American Romantic Literature. In order to determine whether his thesis was accurate and in accord with Jung's theory, Steve wanted to talk to a Jungian analyst. He found that the closest analyst was in Swarthmore, Pennsylvania. The analyst was Dr. David Hart. David Hart reviewed and confirmed Steve's thesis before Steve submitted it. In fact, David Hart wrote a glowing preface praising Steve's analysis of the works cited in his thesis. After careful consideration, Steve decided to undergo analysis with the intention of becoming an analyst. A minimum of 100 hours of analysis was required before training could begin.

The outcome of his time with David Hart was not to become an analyst. Instead, in 1975, he decided to return to graduate school to get his doctorate and start his own private practice.

Ascending the long stairway to David Hart's office, Steve always felt enveloped by a sacred stillness. Almost always, he would notice the angled shafts of the late-afternoon sunlight gracing his ascent to his session with David Hart. The light slicing across the length of the stairs seemed to symbolize the inevitable insights he gained in each session. Each insight would send a ray of light into the black holes in his psyche. His standing appointment was always scheduled after the school day was done. He was teaching high school for the three years in which he was in analysis.

The sense of the sacredness was not that it was the stairway to heaven. The ascent was that of the ancient Greeks entering the Temple of Aesculapius. There the seekers would go to sleep, have a dream, and have it interpreted by the keeper of the temple. To each session, Steve would bring his dream journal filled with the dreams he had had since the last session. He would tell the dreams and share his associations as well as his own interpretations. It was as though he were seated in a secret garden, what the ancient Greeks called the *temenos*.

There was a warmth coupled with a comforting scent coming from the carpet in David Hart's waiting room and office. It conjured up scenes of summer vacation with his parents at the beach when he was small. He remembered how wonderful it was to inhale the aroma arising from the grove of pine trees near the cottage where they stayed. He would be walking back from a day at the beach. The grove was just two blocks from the ocean. By late afternoon, the summer sun had baked the bed of golden-brown pine needles to such a degree that the comforting fragrance filled the air by the cottage.

Seemed that it was almost always sunny on the days he had sessions. Short streaks of sunlight slipped through the blinds, creating strips of light and shadow on the carpet in Hart's office; the sun's rays were filled with thin filaments of floating specks of dust. All of this had a hypnotic, sedating effect on Steve and put him into a contemplative mood. After all, he was there to cast light on all that floated into the space of his awareness. The windows were to the far left of Hart's desk and where Steve sat. Typically, his dream journal lay in his lap, open to the page containing the first dream from the previous week that he wanted to discuss.

In the sacred stillness of David Hart's office, Steve would explore the space between the surface and depth of his personality. It was here that he learned how his dreams could help him carry on the dialogue between the conscious and unconscious areas of his mind. He didn't know it but he was fulfilling one of his main missions in coming to Earth: how to fully experience the depth and height of what it means to be human. He was learning how to fully feel his emotions while remaining free to observe them. It is so easy for the embodied soul to become enslaved by emotions and the desires the emotions serve.

He was here to discover and teach others how to fully feel the whole range of human emotions without being hooked and trapped by them. His first challenge in life was to find the physical freedom of moving through life with grace and ease. The challenges of polio and then basketball were his teachers. Now he was embarking on finding mental and emotional freedom in the inner space between surface and depth.

* * *

FOCUSING ON THE IMAGES OF HIS DREAM, STEVE STARTED TO share his thoughts about how his father was a monkey on his back. His father had been critical of him. Steve related to David Hart a scene when he was eight years old. It was summer. School was out, and he was helping Earl first weed, then water the garden in the back-yard. There were stalks of corn, tomatoes, cucumbers, potatoes, lima and string beans. Steve's mouth began to moisten ever so slightly at the mere thought of the medley of fresh veggies from the garden that his mother mixed into her mouth-watering succotash.

He described the scene to David Hart. The sun had set and the evening air was cool. It would be dark soon, so Earl and Stevie stopped working and moved to the driveway by their small white-shingled home. After they put away their tools in the garage, they stood in the driveway. Stevie watched Earl coil the hose around his left hand and elbow before hanging it on the hook attached to the side of the house. With a softness in his face and a warm sincerity in his dark-brown eyes, Earl made a startling admission. Regarding his tendency to be critical of his son, Earl said, "Stevie, it's not you I'm dissatisfied with, it's myself, and I take it out on you."

Even as Stephen sat on the train this very day in 2005, he could still feel the words touch his heart the way it did that summer evening in 1955. When his father would criticize him after that comment, Stevie may have felt a flash of anger, but it would pass quickly. His tendency was to let Earl off the hook because he felt bad for his father's unhappiness with himself and his life.

It broke Stevie's heart to hear how his father was dissatisfied with himself. He wished his father could love himself as much as he did. Stevie admired him. Earl was everything Stevie wanted to be: smart, handsome, strong, muscular, and athletic. He was a hero to his little son.

Earl was still strong despite the debilitating effects of his war injuries—chronic back pain. Stevie would proudly watch his father throw or punt a football far, farther than any of the other fathers in the neighborhood. Sure Earl was critical of his son, or, to use the image from the dream, "on his back." Still, the criticism had spurred on little Stevie and later Big Steve. The criticism was the burr under his saddle that irritated him just enough to achieve. In light of Steve's achievements, "arriving at the top of the hill," the image from the dream, that criticism, once a heavy load to bear, was now a "monkey on his back" for which he was grateful. Steve told David Hart that when his father complained when Steve was in high school, 'You practice more than anyone I know and you still stink," Steve just got mad. He simply practiced even harder with a determined defiance that silently shouted: "I'll show you!"

Steve recalled Earl claimed that his harsh criticism was actually "reverse psychology" designed to motivate him. Sure there was some truth to that. However, years later, Steve would see the conflicting feelings of pride and competition his father harbored about his son's accomplishments both athletic and academic. Focusing on the affection he felt for the monkey in the dream, Steve told David Hart, "If my father were here right now, I'd say, 'Thanks for the criticism, Dad, it made me strive harder.'" As the dream showed, Earl literally rode his son's back all the way to the top. But in the end, Steve made peace with his father's criticism, and the way Earl had lived vicariously through Steve. Earl being carried piggyback also symbolized how Earl had tried to fulfill his unfulfilled ambitions through his son. And Steve accepted that as well.

* * *

AN EARLY MEMORY FLASHED INTO STEVE'S MIND. AGAIN, he was eight years old. Earl was screaming in pain as he struggled to crawl across the floor one night in 1955. This memory was the central one, a shining star, swallowed up in the black hole at the heart of the galaxy of his personal identity: the hero-savior complex. The first emotion he had felt as a little boy was awe.

In relating the memory to David Hart, Steve remembered how stunned he had been that his father was not crying; instead, he was toughing it out and pushing Gerry away when she tried to help him. Steve remembered crying but he was not yet able to access the deeper feelings he felt at the time. The traumatic element was still under the excessively strong gravitational pull of the black hole in which it was hidden. To Stevie, Earl was the wounded war hero who portrayed the masculine ideal of toughness.

Seeing Stevie crying, Gerry left Earl's side to go to her son; his bedroom door was ajar and he could see his father on his hands and knees. He might as well be crawling behind enemy lines with bullets flying over his head and cannon shells exploding. This memory would come up again three more times after he stopped seeing David Hart. It was curious that each insight appeared a decade after the one preceding it: 1985, 1995, and 2005. Each insight illuminated a piece of the core of his complex and its effect on him.

In this instance in 1975, he told David Hart what he recalled his mother saying to him. "She asked me, 'What's wrong?' And I said, "Why isn't he crying?' My mother answered, 'Because men don't cry.'

He then told David Hart how much he hated himself for being weak and crying. "I watched gangster movies to toughen up and learn how not to cry. He studied such films as *The Roaring Twenties* with James Cagney and Humphrey Bogart. One of Cagney's movies, *Public Enemy*, had a scene in which Cagney's character as a boy Stevie's age was being beaten with a belt by his father. Stevie admired how he didn't cry and stayed tough. A few years later, he met a kid who looked like a little James Cagney.

It was a cool summer morning at Boy Scout Camp when Stevie was eleven years old. He was sitting on a dock by a stream that fed into the nearby river. A tough-looking kid from the inner city was sitting next to him. He had blonde hair and was the spitting image of James Cagney. Camp was only for one week. It started on Saturday, and it was now Tuesday. Every day, Stevie received a short letter from his mother. Gerry worked in Maryland not far from where the camp was located so she was able to pop a letter in the mailbox on her way to work. He would receive it that same day. Noticing that Stevie was receiving a letter daily, the Cagney look alike said something that caught Stevie off guard. With a tinge of appreciative longing in his voice, he said, "It must be nice to have parents who care about you."

Attempting to be tough, Stevie struggled to deny his love for his parents, "Nah, I hate 'em." As soon as the words came out of his mouth, he clenched his throat and eyes, trying to fight off the urge to cry. It took a Herculean effort but he managed to choke back the tears. For a second he felt as if his throat were going to explode. He successfully choked off the tears, and the feeling finally passed.

After telling David Hart this during his session, Steve realized that it was not just his own childhood dependency he was struggling to get free of in that moment on the dock. It was feeling responsible for his parents' happiness. He was the brightly shining star in their lives so that when he was away they were faced with each other. Yes, Stevie knew that they loved each other and had a good chemistry. But Earl was difficult to live with, given his chronic pain and depression.

As a child, he was not only expressing his normal dependency, he was expressing what his parents were repressing: their denied dependency on him. In other words, these two tough adults had repressed their unmet dependency needs as children. They now could project these unmet needs for love onto him. They were comfortable with Stevie expressing these needs for them. When Stevie returned home from camp, Earl said, "You were homesick weren't you?' In his heart, Stevie had thought, *No. I'm not. It was good to get away.* But, sensing what his father needed to hear, he said, "Yeah, Dad, it's good to be back home." He was beginning to disentangle his dependency from their need to be needed by him. Not crying was an aspect of the masculine hero he aspired to be. Heroes don't cry. It would be another eleven years when he would see another male ideal, Clark Gable, cry in *Gone With The Wind.* The men's movement to liberate men from the straightjacket of denying their emotions was beginning. Phil Donahue devoted talk shows to the topic of the need for men to cry and express their feelings. The black hole was filled and the hero was set in stone like a statue of male strength. But by then the damage was done. Even now in the three years of seeing David Hart, Steve had never cried in a session. He wouldn't understand why until 1985. It was during a phone session with David Hart following the deaths of Gerry and Earl that Stephen spoke to David Hart about how he had never cried in sessions with him. Stephen described what happened in the following excerpt in *8 Steps to Love.*

I then started with the phrase, 'I never cried in front of you,' and as I did I started to well up with strong feelings in my chest. My eyes started to fill up with tears and I blurted out the words: 'Because I was afraid you would think I wouldn't be able to be a good psychologist since you studied under Jung himself.' I found myself starting to discount the realness of the feelings that were emerging and I wanted to censor them since they seemed so ridiculous. I had been in practice for a while and certainly helping people release their emotional pain through tears was an important part of the healing. Nevertheless, I continued on as I knew that the feelings were true for both my father and for my esteemed mentor.

There, I had cried in front of my mentor. At that same moment, I found myself recalling the book, *Love Story,* which I read while I was on active duty in the Army. I remember how touched I was at the end of the book by a scene with a father and son. The lead male character, Oliver, is leaving the hospital after his young bride and love of his life, Jenny, has just died of cancer. Oliver meets his father in the hallway of the hospital and they stand there just facing each other. The two of them have never felt close and because the father did not approve of his son's marriage, he was even more estranged from his son. I found myself moved by the words in the book describing this scene. 'And then I did something I had never done before in his presence, much less in his arms, I cried.'

It was now 1985, a decade after this session, he was diagnosed with glaucoma. Could tensing against his tears have contributed to his glaucoma? He knew from his dissertation that one measure of emotional stress was vasoconstriction—tension around the blood vessels causing reduced blood flow. Stress had been given a guilty verdict as a factor in heart disease, cancer, and stroke, so why not glaucoma? In today's upcoming visit with Dr. Jindra, he would receive his answer: an answer I already knew from my penetrating perspective.

* * *

IT BROKE GERRY'S HEART HEART TO OVERHEAR HOW HARSHLY Earl criticized her son. Steve didn't know this about his mother until he was in analysis and showed a sculpture he did of a horse-headed man standing with his hands clenched into fists at his side. When Gerry was visiting Steve's house and spotted the sculpture on a shelf in Steve's study, she took one look at the sculpture, smiled, and said, "Oh, your father." She knew nothing of Steve's dream. This then led to a serious discussion of how critical Earl had been.

The clay piece was based on a dream he had. David Hart amplified the dream image of the horse-headed man by referring to Anubis the jackal-headed god of Egyptian Mythology. Anubis was the guardian of the threshold to the underworld. For Jungians, the underworld is psychologically synonymous with the dark depths of the unconscious.

Jungians often amplify dream images by comparing them with archetypal or primordial images found in ancient mythology and fairy tales. Jung found similar motifs from different cultures dating back to the dawn of human history: heroes, dragons, the wise old man, witches, magicians, kings, queens, damsels in distress, death and rebirth, demons, and angels, gods and goddesses. The list is long and varied. All of these archetypal images are inhabitants of the deepest layers in the space between the surface and depth of the personality. They represent the various potential experiences available to the embodied soul's during his or her sojourn on Earth.

According to Jung, these age-old and universal images emerge from what he called the collective unconscious. This was the deepest layer of the mind shared by all humankind. It was where the archetypes came from and the concept of archetypes as timeless truths is what drew Steve to study Jung in the first place.

David Hart did not reduce the dream into such psychological language but preferred to work with the images of the dream. He conveyed an attitude of reverence; what the unconscious had to say was sacred. He advocated simply contemplating the images in the course of one's waking life. Steve felt as if it were God, the Divine, speaking. Synchronicity confirmed the sacredness of dreams when Steve came across a book on a Jungian approach to dreams that referred to dreams as God's forgotten language.

Proceeding with a sense of the sacred in each analytic session, David Hart treated dream images as symbols pointing to an inner, essentially unknowable, mystery. As quickly as a young child crumples a butterfly when grabbing it from the air, the intellect destroys a symbol by attempting to grasp its meaning. David Hart taught Steve that an archetypal symbol was a mystery to mull over. It was important to simply reflect upon them. Steve learned that just contemplating an image from a dream had an almost magical effect on his conscious attitudes. He was fascinated at how images similar to fairy tales and myths from all over the world appeared in his dreams, even though he had no conscious knowledge of them. This seemed to suggest to him that the collective unconscious was as Jung described: indeed, it was a vast repository of ancient wisdom. It was the storehouse of the archetypal or fundamental truths condensed into images common to all embodied souls.

Steve would feel uplifted to a new level after David Hart's amplification of dream images with those from fairy tales or mythology.

What Steve was experiencing was a connection with the spiritual realm of inner space.

The setting of the dream with the Anubis figure was an underground cavern. Steve was swimming in a subterranean pool encircled by a rounded wall of jagged rocks. Suddenly, he was being pursued by a water serpent trying to bite him. It was not a snake since it had a scaly body with webbed feet and a long, thick tail. After escaping from the serpent, he carefully climbed over the rocks to keep from cutting his bare feet. He then spotted a lighted cave within the cavern. It turned out to be an elevator with clay walls. A horse-headed man was operating the elevator. Addressing Steve, the formidable figure said, "I have a son who is a high school teacher." Steve was teaching psychology and philosophy in high school at the time. The dream ends as Steve is about to enter the well-lighted clay elevator. Looking back, Stephen could now see what I knew back then; facing the many facets of his relationship with his father was the key to higher "elevated" consciousness.

Only after he had been a practicing therapist did Stephen realize the horse-headed man was a symbol of a side of himself. He had internalized this aspect of Earl. The figure represented an inner reality: the tough male stance that stood against his softer-feminine side.

$$* \quad * \quad *$$

TOWARD THE END OF HIS THREE YEARS OF ANALYSIS, HE had an archetypal dream that revealed a softening of the inwardly tough stance. He was beginning to develop a tenderness toward his softer, feminine side, what Jung called the archetype of the anima. The animus was the term Jung used for the corresponding male side of a female. The dream depicted an important step in his emotional growth. Using a familiar fairy tale motif, the dream illustrated an inner transformation was taking place.

Steve stood on the top step of a terraced waterfall. The water was gently flowing over a series of broad, flat stone slabs. On the top step, a fish lay on a thin sheet of water. With all but one side being out of the water, the fish was struggling to stay alive; its gills were rapidly opening and closing. It was stuck and needed help. Steve bent down to free the fish. Contrary to common sense, he placed his hands on the stone slab above the fish in an attempt to scoop it up; however the placement of his hands was above the flow of gravity. If he did not move his hands under the fish to lift it up then simply placing his hands where they were would not allow the fish to flow into his hands with the help of gravity.

Something extraordinary happened. Seconds after he placed his hands by the fish, the stranded fish became a human-sized frog. It then slowly began to descend the stone-slab steps of the waterfall until it reached the bottom step where the water emptied into a dark pool. This was where Steve had planned to place the fish if he had been able to scoop him up the little fellow in his hands.

Steve was puzzled by the startling effect of his counter-intuitive effort to help the fish. David Hart amplified the positive effect of Steve acting contrary to common sense, saying, "Jung called the individuation process 'the *opus contra natura*, the work contrary to nature.' Becoming more conscious goes against the natural urge to remain unconscious and comfortable. The witch in fairy tales is a symbol of the urge to keep us unconscious." In his essays on fairy tales, David Hart described being bewitched as a psychological state of remaining unconscious as if under a spell. Being addicted to a substance or to another person could be described as being bewitched. In contrast, the hero is a symbol of the urge to become conscious of the contents of the unconscious.

The next surprising thing in the dream was that the frog gradually began to transform into a beautiful princess with long, flowing blonde hair. Steve was aware of the fairy tale in which a girl kisses a frog who then turns into a handsome prince. Instead of a frog prince, he had dreamt of a frog princess. In either case, a kind gesture led to a transformation of a slimy, cold-blooded creature into a warm-blooded human being.

David Hart amplified the dream by referring to a fairy tale where the hero helps a stranded fish. With its gills gasping, the fish was flopping about on the shore of a lake, desperately trying to get back into the water. Similar to what Steve did in his dream, the hero bent over to pick up the fish and place it back into the lake. Later in the tale, when crossing the lake, the hero drops a pen in the water. The magical writing implement was needed to free the princess from a castle where she was locked away by an evil king. While the hero is despairing over losing the pen, the fish pops up out of the water with the pen in its mouth. The fish saves the day. Now the hero is able to complete his quest and free the princess. When Steve inquired about the pen, David Hart said, "The pen symbolized giving the anima, represented by the imprisoned princess, a chance to express her feelings."

A few months later, Steve discovered that there was a Russian fairy tale entitled *The Frog Princess*. Freudians had reduced the tale of the frog prince to that of nothing but a pubescent girl learning to overcome her aversion to her emergent sexuality. The slimy frog of her menstruation and the feeling that boys are icky is replaced by a humanizing of her sexual instincts.

Surely Steve's dream had something to do with his corporeality and sexuality. In Jungian terms, he was integrating his anima. Changing from a fish to a frog to a fairy tale princess represented the development of a more intimate relationship to his emotional life. He was moving from cold-blooded fish, living in the dark depths of the unconscious, to an amphibian, inhabiting both land (conscious) and water (unconscious). And finally, his ability to express his feelings was becoming more human and under his control instead of remaining instinctual and reactive. This was symbolized by the head of the frog disappearing and being replaced by the head of a blonde-haired princess.

This process also illustrated an important inner truth that would keep coming up in the course of his analysis; what first appears as unappealing or unacceptable to the conscious mind is transformed when it is embraced. That which is first rejected by the conscious mind is found to be quite valuable. For example, repressed feelings of fear and anger, though unpleasant, can be harnessed and transformed by simply being conscious of them. A valuable liberation of trapped emotional energy is released. The energy of either emotion is available for conscious use. And also available for conscious use is the mental energy used to repress and deny unacceptable feelings.

Steve would also learn from David Hart how fairy tales illustrate the wisdom of Jung's assertion that life required both a heroic, take-charge attitude, and a religious or spiritual attitude of surrender to a power greater than the ego. By surrendering to the greater wisdom of the Self, the ego or conscious mind could overcome any obstacle life presented. For Jung the Self with a capital "S" was the spark of the divine who spoke through dreams. The little self of the conscious mind, the ego, needed to learn to look to dreams and synchronicities (Jung's term for meaningful coincidences) for guidance. Jung was really talking about the embodied soul needing to learn to reconnect with his or her spirit: the radiant star of his or her divine sidereal self. Steve's time in analysis with David Hart was preparing him for reconnecting with me and following my guidance toward fulfilling his divine destiny.

* * *

THE FROG-PRINCESS DREAM REVEALED HOW HE WAS STARTING to get in touch with his softer side hidden behind the tough male stance. He was internalizing the compassionate listening presence of David Hart. Steve could see why Jung described the individuation process as the *opus contra natura*. Learning to listen and not to do or to solve is to go against the natural urge to act. The goal is to learn to listen to whatever thoughts, feelings, fantasies, and dreams were emerging into awareness from the space between surface and depth.

The hardened clay of the horse-headed man was an apt portrayal of his own rigid defenses against the deeply hidden hurts of his early childhood. He would find that true inner strength was not to be found in the hard-as-stone figure of the horse-headed man, the Anubis symbol, but in the quiet presence of David Hart appearing in a dream. Sometimes it might be represented by a colleague. Either way, the listening and witnessing presence gave Stephen the courage to face the fears emerging from the most vulnerable and helpless years in an embodied soul's life on Earth: early childhood.

* * *

A YEAR LATER, ONE MONTH AFTER HIS ANALYSIS HAD ENDED, Steve had a very telling dream on the night following the first day of graduate school at the University of Virginia. During the last part of the class, students were asked to share their thoughts on what they would like to research for their dissertation. Part of his decision to return to get his doctorate was that he finally had a topic he wanted to research. His understanding was that a dissertation involved an original piece of research. When the grandmotherly professor asked him what he wanted to research, he answered, "Dream analysis." To which the professor responded with a stern emphasis in her tone, "You can't do research on that topic!" He was stunned. *My God*, he thought, *I've waited to return to graduate school only after I have finally come up with an area to research!*

Steve may have been scared, but he felt flushed with anger, imagining his face was red. He told his friends what happened, stressing, "I've been in analysis, and I'm not going to get neurotic about this!" That night he had a dream that his father Earl was standing tall and bare-chested by a stream filled with logs that were the length and width of telephone poles. Earl appeared to be the height and weight he was when Steve was in high school: 6-foot-3 and two hundred and twenty pounds. At that time, Earl had a big chest and a small waist bookended by bulging biceps and broad shoulders with cannon ball deltoids. He looked powerful as he lifted up what appeared to be at least six logs and then threw them over his head to clear the log jam.

Steve's first thought was that his father was a "powerful influence" in his life. Then he recalled that his position in the dream was looking up as if from a trench below the slight incline the stream was on. Positioning his body by bending slightly and looking up, he imagined speaking to the dream image of his father. Before he knew what was happening, Steve found himself blurting out as if from the eight-year-old boy in him, "Daddy, will you love me even if I can't beat up every kid on the block as you could? Even if I can't hit a home run every time I step up to the plate? Even if I'm not an All-American and don't get a Ph.D.?" He sobbed deeply as he blurted out the words.

Later in his training, he would learn that the powerful image of his father in the dream was the all-powerful oedipal father. This is the archaic image fashioned by little boys roughly between the ages of four to eight. In this stage of development, a little boy experiences his father as the biggest, strongest man in the world. But this image is not just one of admiration; it is one fraught with fear. Therefore, the archaic image gets repressed but lives on unchanged in the dark depths of the space between surface and depth.

The dream had nothing to do with his current father. In fact, Steve told Earl about the dream, and Earl expressed how proud he was of his son since Steve had graduated college. Steve knew his father loved him. That was not the issue; the issue was what Steve felt he needed to be to be loved by himself. Sure his father's early criticism contributed to Steve's desire to achieve in sports and school. But the image he desperately needed to please was the father he had fashioned in his mind.

Similar to the stars of the silver screen, the early images of the people embodied souls love as children never age. They are forever preserved in their roles as embodiments of idealized standards of perfection. Both the child and later the adult aspire to be like them. These archaic images are compressed into the black holes of the dark depths of inner space where they exert a strong gravitational pull on an embodied soul's emotions, thoughts, and actions. Being hidden, their influence is unrelenting and extends throughout the entire life of an embodied soul until uncovered. Once brought into the light of day, these fantasied artifacts can be examined and, in effect, reshaped and modified. The embodied soul can then re-sculpt the images into realistic standards on which to base their self-esteem.

In Steve's case, this archaic image of his father from early childhood was a condensed portrayal of the conditions Steve felt he needed to fulfill in order to be loved. These unrealistic standards were the unconscious basis for his self-worth: what the famous psychologist Carl Rogers called the "conditions of worth." The searchlight of consciousness revealed the source of his feeling so threatened by the professor saying he could not write about dreams for a dissertation. Here was the source of his anxiety hidden under the blaze of his angry protests, "I won't get neurotic over this!" he had kept repeating to his friends and to himself.

This image of Earl clearing the log jam was not only the heroic ideal he wanted to live up to; it was another component of his hero-savior complex. The early heroes he watched on television and his later sports heroes had helped him in his quest for coordination.

The professor's dismissal of dreams as a viable topic for a dissertation cut him to the quick as his father's criticism had. The critical comment threatened his goal of getting his doctorate. This was the intellectual component of the idealized self-image which Steve had fashioned within himself just as he had sculpted the horse-headed man. Both were his creations. For the inner and the outer creation, he used the raw material of his concrete experiences with his critical father. And to both, he brought the same kind of definitive and dogged determination. Both were created in the subjectivity governing the space between father and son just as any impression any child has of his or her father or mother is something completely independent of the actual parent. This was clear to me and would become clearer to him once he began to look at his life less though the eyes of his soul suit and more through my spiritual eyes.

∗ ∗ ∗

A DREAM STEVE HAD A FEW YEARS EARLIER REVEALED another facet he had internalized from his interactions with his father. Earl was hard on his son even if it was born of his dissatisfaction with himself. Criticism is criticism. It can break the heart and wound the the soul of the child. The dream opens with a scene on the bottom floor of a tall modern office building. It is late at night and no one is around. Steve suddenly senses danger. He starts running for the elevator. Looking behind him, he sees the bearded giant pursuing him. The giant is dressed in Medieval garb. He is wearing a large black belt with a large buckle, a white shirt with puffy sleeves and no collar and laces by the neck instead of buttons. His pants are black with laces and are tucked into a pair of big black boots. Suddenly, the scene changes. Steve is no longer an adult; he is now a child about four years old. The building changes, too. He was now on top of an old watchtower that seemed to be set in a Swiss village from an earlier century. Trouble in the form of marauders or invading armies can be easily spotted for miles around from the tall tower. A huge bell would be rung to warn the villagers and those inhabiting cottages in the surrounding countryside. The giant appears. There is also a little girl, and strangely he feels she is somehow part of him: a little soulmate. She takes Stevie by the hand and leads him away from the giant to the other side of the rooftop patio. Without any hesitation, he follows. Together, they step up onto a low ledge. They then leap off the little ledge and grab the thick rope that rings a huge bell. The sound of the bell awakens the entire village and the people living on the outskirts of the village. Looking down, Stevie sees the darkness is dotted with light. The village and surrounding countryside are all aglow since a large group of people carrying candles are gathering en masse around the base of the tall tower.

The scene shifts. The two children are standing at the base of the tower next to the giant. He is lying on his back defeated. A black-robed holy man with white hair and a long white beard appears next to the giant. For some reason the holy man is called a priest-rabbi. This holy man who combines the Jewish and Christian traditions, reaches into the mouth of the giant and quickly snatches the bottom row of his teeth. The wise old man stands there next to the children with the bottom row of teeth hanging in his hand like a horseshoe. When Steve wakes up from the dream, he thinks, *Without his bottom teeth, the giant has no bite.*

Discussing this dream with David Hart, Steve saw only the archetypal aspect. An elevation of consciousness and the joining together of the male and female, boy and girl, had somehow led to the toppling of the giant. It seemed that the awakening of the village was connected to the giant ending up at the base of the tower. Then the archetype of the wise old man took away the bite of the giant. David Hart had encouraged Steve to hold the images of the dream in his awareness. Steve simply felt good by staying with the Hansel and Gretel feeling of the dream. Just as they defeated the witch, Stevie and the little girl defeated the giant with the help of the holy man.

A decade later, the dream took on new meaning after Stephen had accrued experience working with children. Revisiting the dream, he thought of how little children see adults as giants. In fairy tales, the criticism of parents is beautifully portrayed as a giant who wants to gobble up children. Biting sarcasm and criticism coming from a beloved parent really does "eat up" a child's self- worth.

He considered how the little girl in his dream represents the vulnerable feelings and sensitivities he struggled to deny as a little boy. Here is the origin of the disparaging claims called out by boys to any boy showing his feelings by shedding tears on the playground, "You're such a girl! You're a sissy!"

Behind the eyes of the little boy he once was, fighting back tears, little Stevie wanted to cry out for his daddy's love as he did in the log-jam dream. The giant became an element within him as an adolescent and as an adult. Now as an adult he was as hard on himself as his father had been on him when he was little. And, Stephen realized how he could be critical of the women he loved from high school on. He needed to remember how his father's criticism hurt and didn't help.

Working with children in therapy, he now saw the little girl in his dream as the key figure in the dream. She begins the process that saves the day. Now it was clear to him that she symbolized the need to *feel* how he had been hurt. And the priest-rabbi, symbolizing the wisdom of the Judeo-Christian ethic, pointed to the need to replace criticism with loving kindness, tenderness, and patience.

He now thought of how he had honored the dream by making

119

a sculpture of the main characters: the two children, the wise old man, and the defeated giant. Not knowing exactly why at the time, he gave this sculpture to David Hart. He didn't give him any of his other clay pieces. Now, looking back, he could see how appropriate it was that he chose this one. David Hart had epitomized patience in witnessing the outpouring of feelings, thoughts, and dreams arising in the space between the surface and depth of his personality. For over the three years David Hart sat and listened without criticism. David Hart received the unconscious projection of the archetype of the wise old man, also a symbol of the Self, thereby imbuing him as the analyst with the spiritual wisdom and authority of the Self.

One of the goals of analysis involves withdrawing the image of the Self from the analyst and finding the Self within. Eventually, Stephen would realize how he had projected me onto David Hart. Now looking back, he knew it was I, his spirit, his sidereal self, who was being represented in the dream as the priest-rabbi.

* * *

WITHIN THE DREAM OF CLEARING THE LOG JAM, LAY THE roots of the fear underlying his decision to end his college basketball career. He was terrified of not living up to the standards of the internalized image of the all-powerful father of his oedipal period. He feared failing on the one hand, and, insofar as he had projected this image onto the authority figure of his coach, he had externalized the fear of incurring the disapproval of the coach. It didn't matter that projecting the image of his father onto the coach was like projecting Godzilla onto Jiminy Cricket. The coach was physically much shorter and smaller than his father. All later male authority figures for the embodied soul carry the projected image of the early father. Subconsciously, they are all the Great and powerful Wizard of Oz. This holds even if these men may be the stooped-over little man behind the curtain operating the levers that create the wizard's scary image.

In the role of the Anubis figure in the subterranean cavern

dream, Earl operated an illuminated elevator. He set an example for his son that elevated his son's aspirations and put Steve on the path to seeking wisdom. Earl was always reading and quoting from books on the world's great philosophers: Plato, Aristotle, and others. He had books on and by Freud. He studied hypnosis. By trade, Earl was an accountant. But his passion was psychology and philosophy.

Earl even read self-help books before there was such a category. Two in particular stood out: *Psycho-Cybernetics* by Maxwell Maltz, and *Your Key to Happiness* by Harold Sherman. Besides spurring his son on with his criticism, Earl inspired Steve to seek the truth and to investigate the vastness of inner space and the powers of the mind. His father's influence as well as the emotional wounding he received at the hands of his father led Steve to study psychology, philosophy, and led him to David Hart's door.

The dream of little eight-year-old Stevie looking up in awe at his father clearing the log jam revealed another set of feelings buried in the black hole of his hero-savior complex. Under all of young adult Steve's ambition to achieve athletically and academically was a sensitive little boy who wanted his daddy's love. But even more than that was the pressure to fulfill his daddy's unfulfilled athletic and academic ambitions. Little Stevie longed to help his daddy be happy. Certainly, little eight-year-old Stevie felt the ever-present pressure of his daddy's need to live vicariously through his son's achievements. What had he said to Stevie? "It's not you I'm dissatisfied with, it's myself." So as a child, adolescent, and young adult, Steve felt the need to grant his father's wish by proxy. Deep down, he wanted to give to his father the love and support to encourage him. Stevie sensed how his father had not received this support from his family growing up. "No one came to my games. No one showed any interest when I played sports," he'd told Stevie more than once.

There was an additional aspect to the anxiety twenty-eight-year-old Steve felt in the log jam dream. Steve really did not have a clear set of standards by which to determine if he had achieved more than his father. First, the goal was not to outdo his father. The goal was to help fulfill the unfulfilled ambitions of his father. Within the dream, these ambitions were represented by the athletic honor of All-American and the academic honor of Ph.D.

In competing with his father, Steve competed with what he would refer to in *Words Become Flesh* as the "I could have been a contender complex." In the film *On the Waterfront*, Marlon Brando sits in the back of a cab with his brother (Rod Steiger). Brando soulfully expresses his regrets over having to throw a prize fight with the top contender and give up his chance to be the Heavyweight Champion of the World. "I could have been a contender. I could have been somebody. . . ."

It's interesting to note that according to men who served with him in the South Pacific during World War II, Earl could have done well as a professional fighter if his back hadn't been injured.

The problem is how do you compete with the ghost of what might have been. It's easier to compete with a specific set of standards such as Dad hit 30 home runs in little league and his son hits 31 so the son wins. Steve didn't have such concrete markers to measure where he stood in relation to Earl. Then again, when a son's unconscious goal is to fulfill his father's unfulfilled ambitions, then beating Dad becomes a nebulous goal as well.

Steve had a dream during his analysis with David Hart that depicted this lack of clarity in his competition with his father. Steve and Earl were in a swimming pool awaiting the appearance of an unnamed champion swimmer. The swimming competition is to take place in an Olympic-sized pool by Boston's bay. Before the champion arrives, the bay begins to encroach on the pool. The boundary lines of the pool disappear. And, as the bay empties into the ocean, there are no markers to use to determine the winner of the competition.

It had been difficult for Stephen to accept himself because he did not have an actual standard by which to measure himself, and the reason he didn't needled him with guilt. Earl did not have the opportunities his son had when he was growing up. And then, he was cut down by the war; Earl never realized his potential athletically or academically. Stephen was always competing with what Earl *might* have been or *could* have been. Stephen struggled to measure up to a ghost . . . a phantom . . . a dream. . . .

* * *

WHAT WAS THE ROUTE THAT LED STEVE TO START DELVING into dreams in the first place? Earl had books on and by Freud but none on or by Jung. How and where did Steve discover Jung?

One beautiful spring day in 1970, the final semester of his senior year in college, Steve had an intellectual epiphany. He was struck by the lightning of an *ah hah!* moment, while listening to the opening lecture of a course entitled *American Philosophy*. Dr. David Norton said the following words that lit a fire in Steve's heart and mind: "The ground of philosophy is human experience. The method is reflection on that experience. And the aim is to improve the quality of life."

Yes! Steve's thoughts echoed a resounding affirmation. These words reverberated off the cavern walls of his heart and mind. *That's what I have been doing since my junior year in high school, and it's what I love to do!* he thought. He was on fire with excitement.

Professor Norton's words reflected the self-knowledge school of philosophy. It originated with Socrates' famous dictum: "Know thyself." Steve learned that philosophy meant love of wisdom. The root words *phileo* (love) and *Sophia* (goddess of wisdom). A statue of her was said to be in King Solomon's temple. And, on the ceiling of the Sistine Chapel, she is the female figure in Michelangelo's painting. God's left arm is around her as He reaches out with His right arm to touch Adam's finger. Now he knew that even in his quest for coordination, he was seeking something else. Something deeper. He was seeking Sophia. Wisdom.

In the spring semester of his junior year in college, Steve had discovered the socratic method in *Ancient Philosophy* and *Ancient History*. Both were taught by the distinguished Dr. Eve Clift. She had had many conversations with Albert Einstein when she was at Johns Hopkins. This white-haired woman embodied wisdom. Her lecture on the socratic method of questioning was eye-opening for Steve. Simply writing out questions in a free and spontaneous way did uncover answers hidden within the space between surface and depth. He found that it helped him sort through the swamp of his emotions on any given topic or concern.

Spurred on by Norton's words that philosophy aimed to improve the quality of life, Steve went to graduate school for a masters degree in philosophy. Within one semester, he discovered that the self-knowledge school was not the focus of most of his courses. The primary focus was on language analysis with emphasis on Wittgenstein. The curriculum ignored the topics David Norton lectured on and wrote about. Norton focused on human existence and such topics as the philosophy of love and death.

Meanwhile, unbeknownst to Steve, academic psychology was looking to the philosophers who wrote about the conditions and parameters of human existence: Sartre, Heidegger, Kierkegaard, Nietzche, Schopenhauer, and others. Some were not philosophers per se but novelists and poets interested in exploring the heights and depths of the human experience: Camus, Kafka, and Rilke.

In the spring semester of 1967, Steve began the semester with the intention of majoring in psychology. He signed up for a course entitled *Learning and Motivation*. He was excited about the course. He imagined that he would receive answers to key questions: What motivates people? What are the deeper, hidden motivations underlying the mask of motivations on the surface of what people say and do?

The semester began with each student being assigned a white rat. Students were to go to the laboratory where the rats were caged. Once there, students performed experiments intended to illustrate the principles of learning and motivation. B.F. Skinner, Hull, and Watson were the notables studied by the class. No Freud. No Jung. The course was about rats, pigeons, and reflexes.

Later on, after Steve had been Stephen, the practicing clinical psychologist, he would see a tremendous value to that course with the white rats. Behavioral Psychology with its emphasis on conditioning did help explain a lot about human beings. He would see how the concept of conditioning could be used to help people relieve their stress, anxiety, and depression. But back in that first class on learning and motivation, he was disheartened and decided to major in history.

What better way to understand human behavior than to study the past, he thought back then when he changed his major from psychology to history. He would minor in psychology. The choice was to major in it and be bored for three years, or take core courses and then apply to a graduate program in clinical psychology. Then he did something with regard to psychology that he had done with basketball. He wrote down a vow, sealed it, and put it away never to see it again. It was not as dramatic as the one he did for basketball. He simply wrote that he would major in history and get a broad view of mankind's past. He would take psychology courses relevant to applying to clinical psychology programs. He would complete a clinical program and become a clinical psychologist in private practice where he would help many people.

In the meantime, it was four years later and he was now pursuing a masters degree in philosophy. It was a dream that made him realize that the graduate program in philosophy was not for him. In the dream, he was taking a psychology course with David Norton and not philosophy. Books for the course included Abraham Maslow's *Toward a Psychology of Being*, and Carl Jung's *The Archetypes of the Collective Unconscious*.

After reflecting on his dream, he realized that he was really interested in psychology. In reality, Norton's undergraduate courses in philosophy had introduced Steve to the works of Maslow and Jung. Steve dropped out of the philosophy program and began to read Jung. He also began to keep a dream journal. He taught himself Jung's approach to deciphering dreams.

His dreams had revealed that pursuing a degree in philosophy was not in his best interest. Philosophy was not going to satisfy his interest in improving the quality of people's lives. Still, he did not yet trust academic psychology. A creative academic option appeared on the academic horizon.

* * *

"DREAMS COMPENSATE FOR THE ONE-SIDEDNESS OF THE conscious attitude," Steve said, presenting Jung's theory in a nutshell to Dr.

Gordenstein at the University of Delaware. Professor Gordenstein was the head of the innovative interdisciplinary field called *American Studies*. A student could shape a course of study in line with his or her interests. Steve continued his pursuit of wisdom in courses such as *American Intellectual History, Psychoanalysis and Twentieth Century American Literature*, and *Philosophical Ideas in Contemporary American Literature*. Intellectual history excited Steve since it investigated the history of ideas and their impact on the quality of human life. Here was a way for Steve to study the history of the ideas of great thinkers.

Steve continued speaking to Dr. Gordenstein, "And, according to Jung, the art and literature of an age act as a dream does by unconsciously attempting to compensate for the one-sidedness of an age's world view." Steve was proposing to do his masters thesis on how nineteenth century American Romantic Literature contained images and themes that were unconsciously striving to make up for the one-sidedness of the world view of the age. Thus, his masters thesis on Jungian dream psychology and nineteenth century American Romantic literature was born. He drew from the writings of Cooper, Poe, Hawthorne, and Melville.

In his thesis, Steve pointed out, to the dismay of great thinkers such as Thoreau and Emerson, the rational world view led to the exploitation of nature. Man was to dominate and not work with nature. Reason was to rule. Emotion was to be repressed. Head over heart was the order of the day. In pursuing a rational ideal of perfection, embodied souls had to deny their feet of clay, or, in other words, the imperfections and limitations imposed on them by their soul suits.

Stories by Nathaniel Hawthorne act as a dream does by bringing up the hidden dark side of the social persona embodied souls present to others. Hawthorne presented images of the dark shadow cast by those professing to live in the light. In *Young Goodman Brown*, Hawthorne portrayed the dark side of stalwart members of the community (church officials and political figures, etcetera). By day they were model citizens, but by night became Satan worshippers. They could be seen chanting strange incantations while cir-

126

cling a fire deep in the dark forest at night.

In *The Birthmark*, Hawthorne described a mad doctor obsessed with making his beautiful wife perfect. The crazed doctor tries to remove a birthmark which he views as an imperfect blight on her beauty. He discovers that cutting into her flesh culminates in the mark receding with each deeper incision. Finally, the doctor sees that the mark resembles a tiny crimson hand that is clutching her very heart. To remove it would clearly kill her. His assistant, depicted as a crude and simple man of inferior intelligence, expresses unexpected wisdom; he tries to dissuade the doctor from removing the mark. The assistant is an example of what Jung called the shadow archetype. The shadow embodies impulses, attitudes, feelings, and thoughts that are incompatible with a shining self-image. However, the shadow enriches the personality of an embodied soul if it is accepted and not denied. What the shadow offers can be quite helpful if heeded as it would have been for the doctor had he heeded the advice of his assistant.

Another dream-like depiction of the dangers of the outlook of the age he found was in *Moby-Dick*. Herman Melville portrays the narcissistic rage of an egomaniac who is out of control. Captain Ahab is obsessed with revenge against the white whale who took a piece of Ahab's leg, forcing him to replace the lost part of his limb with a peg-leg. Melville describes how every time Ahab walked on deck, the thud of his wooden leg was a reminder of his loss.

Ahab saw the whale as a "mask" for something hidden behind nature. In this sense, Moby-Dick was a symbol of Jung's concept of the Self. Steve saw Jung's concept of the Self as similar to what that great American thinker and inventor Benjamin Franklin called the"divinity in our humanity."

Years later, Stephen would know that through the image of the white whale, Melville was glimpsing the radiant star of his divine sidereal self, his spirit, the transcendent portion of his embodied soul. But the world view of the age depicted in Ahab did not allow for seeing and living in accord with the Self symbolized by Moby Dick.

To Ahab, the whale represented some malevolent force behind

nature. His twisted heart flooded with resentment, Ahab wanted to strike through that mask. Ahab's attitude is that of an inflated egoistic attitude taken on by an embodied soul. This attitude must die before a symbolic rebirth of a religious or spiritual attitude. This is an attitude with which an embodied soul is now able to see God in nature. Spirit is in matter as the ancient alchemists believed.

In his thesis, Steve described how Starbuck, Ahab's first mate on the ship, attempted to reason with Ahab. Starbuck tried to convince Ahab to abandon his pursuit of the white whale. Starbuck reminded Ahab of the mission which was to bring back as much whale oil as they could safely carry back to port.

* * *

STEPHEN WAS STARTLED FROM HIS REVERIE FOR A MOMENT. The sunlight suddenly vanished. He was sitting in darkness . . . the vibration of a muffled rumbling diverted his attention. The New Jersey Transit train had entered one of the tunnels leading into the next stop. "New York's Penn Station. Gather up your belonging before leaving the train," the conductor announced, his voice echoing through the air.

Overhead lights came on, and he returned to his reflections. More than thirty years since he had written his thesis, he found it interesting that the reason for whaling was to bring light. The boiled-down blubber of the magnificent beasts of the sea was to be used to light the lamps of homes, businesses, and streets in towns all over New England. Harpooning this creature from the depths, subjecting its remains to fire, and harvesting the remains—a precious oil for light—seemed an exercise in alchemy. By having to penetrate the black holes of inner space, the embodied soul can release the light captured there. Hidden in the void at the center of the galaxy of each embodied soul's personal identity lies the light of God. In the darkness at the core of each embodied soul's constructed identity shines the radiant star of his or her divine sidereal self.

He then recalled how, during this period, he was an Ahab burning with his own inner fire. Only his fervor was for understanding. He, too, wanted to strike through the mask, and gain an understanding of himself and the mystery of life. He recalled the words of a song from a film he saw in the early 1970s starring Michael Caine: "What's it all about Alfie? Is it just for the moment we live?" Certainly, life wasn't about a hedonistic pursuit of pleasure as the aging womanizer Alfie discovered. *What was life all about?* Stephen thought, remembering how twenty-eight-year-old Steve had sensed eternal truths resonating in Melville's tale about a search for a white whale. Life was lived in the moment. Now. Not past. Not future. And right now, he was reflecting back and reviewing his journey as an embodied soul. He turned his attention back to the climactic end of the tale about a whale.

Quequeg, the primitive man covered by tatoos, makes the coffin that saves Ishmael, the narrator of *Moby-Dick*. After the ship sinks, the wooden coffin becomes a life buoy that surfaces from the sea to save Ishmael until he is rescued by the ship named Rachel searching for her "lost children." The ship's name alludes to Jeremiah's poignant prophecy regarding the wailing mothers of Bethlehem lamenting the loss of their sons: "Rachel weeping for her children and refusing to be comforted because they are no more" (Matthew. 2:18).

Indeed, the repressive effect of the rational world view of the nineteenth century seemed hellbent on raping and plundering nature and her wealth of treasures. This outlook left the embodied souls of that time rudderless, ship wrecked, as though abandoned and adrift at sea. At that time, Steve sought the source of this alienation from nature.

In *American Intellectual History*, Steve learned that the roots of the world view of the nineteenth century could be traced back three hundred years. The Puritans led by John Winthrop founded the Massachusetts Bay Colony which led to the founding of Boston. In 1629, Winthrop gave his famous *City on a Hill* sermon in which he described the Puritans pact with God. They were to establish an exemplary Christian community which was to be a "beacon" for other communities to follow.

The flames of Steve's philosophical fervor were being fanned by his exposure to how ideas had impacted American history. He was fascinated at how differing ideas about humankind's relationship with nature could lead to bloodshed and senseless slaughter. At first, the Pequot Indians and the Puritans got along well together. In fact, the Pequot helped the Puritans survive in the harsh new world. They provided the Puritans with natural herbal remedies garnered from nature to restore their foreign friends to health.

Eventually, the two groups clashed over contrasting views of nature. The Pequot saw the presence of Great Spirit, God, in nature and so they respected and even saw the sacredness in nature. They sought to live in harmony with nature.

The Puritans were greatly offended by such a view. Man was to exercise dominion over nature. Dominion became dominance without the Native American regard and respect for the environment. By the nineteenth century, this adversarial relationship with nature, along with the industrial revolution, led to the exploitation and rape of nature, decried by Emerson and Thoreau. As for the Pequot and the Puritans, a harmonious partnership ended badly. The Puritans either slaughtered their previous partners or captured and traded them as slaves in the West Indies in exchange for sugar and rum.

How tragic it was to Stephen that the Puritans saw the Pequot position on nature as challenging their Christian belief that man was to have dominion over nature. As all Native Americans, the Pequot knew that dominion did not mean seeing nature as the enemy. But to the Puritans living in harmony meant the Pequot were worshipping the creation and not the Creator. To the contrary, Stephen would later learn from the Mayan Indians in Central America that God the Creator constantly communicates to man through nature. Creator and His creation were connected.

Stephen was excited when he came across a recording by Arthur Burk, a Christian minister. Burk told of how God revealed to him the part that the Native Americans were to play in His plan for revealing Himself in the New World of America.

To the English and the Europeans colonizing the New world,

God gave the task of bringing to America the knowledge of Christ Jesus, the Second Person of the Trinity. To the African slaves, God gave the task of bringing forth an awareness of the Holy Spirit, the Third Person of the Trinity. But it was to the Native Americans, that God gave the task of revealing Himself, the First Person of the Trinity God the Father. He was known as Great Spirit to the Native Americans.

The Native Americans had a deep awareness of God the Father working though nature, His creation. To illustrate their respect for the power and authority for the role of father, Burk pointed out that, to the Native Americans, the president was the Great White Father. As you will see in chapter seven, Stephen developed a deeper connection to God in the cathedral of nature than he had in going to church. And, as you will see, during his time with the Maya, he unexpectedly encountered the Holy Trinity in a most immediate and amazing way.

* * *

THIS MORNING, STEPHEN COULD SEE HOW DELVING INTO history is like delving into a dream. He was seeing though my spiritual eyes. Both are symbolic of the spiritual meaning of the soul's sojourn on Earth. Now, sitting on the Long Island Railroad train, he looked at the flickering reflections of passing scenery, and he thought of Boston's Beacon Hill. Somehow the two sides of this famous mound of earth seemed symbolic.

As if he were delving into a dream, he allowed his imagination free reign as he began to amplify the image of Beacon Hill by drawing on the mound's history. He first thought of Mount Rushmore with those heads of American presidents, their faces etched in stone. He imagined how the South and North sides of Beacon Hill might be seen as the cranium, the skull, housing the Puritan psyche. The light (conscious) and dark (unconscious) sides of the collective American mind of those in positions of wealth and political power.

Since the time of the Puritans, the sunny south side has been occupied by the privileged aristocracy. These descendants of the

Puritans became known as Boston Brahmins. This was the name given to Boston's elite in 1860 by Oliver Wendell Holmes Senior who was himself one of them. The label was borrowed from the Brahmins of India, the priestly upper echelon of India's caste system. As with the term Puritan, there is the connotation of spiritual purity with the term Brahmin. God's elite.

In contrast, the largest African-American community in Boston occupied the colder, less sunny north side. Negro slaves were originally brought over by the British, and they were released after the British withdrew following the American Revolutionary War. Most former slaves settled on the North side of Beacon Hill.

The warm, sunny side where the wealthy lived was the *beacon*, the shining persona presented for all the world to see. And, as with any embodied soul striving to project a shining self-image to the world, a shadow side of that image is cast. In this case, the poor blacks, many of whom had worked as servants of the rich on the South side.

The history of Beacon Hill provided an intrapsychic snapshot of the contradictions seeking unification in the collective American psyche of the founding fathers. Thinking of this, Stephen again envisioned the mound of Beacon Hill as a kind of Mount Rushmore; only it was just one face showing. It was the face of the prototypical American who first came and founded this country. And the back of the head represented the repressed material that was incompatible with the pious image being professed.

The repressive tendency of the conscious mind was reflected in the Puritans in their slaughter of the Pequot and in their later participation in the Salem Witch Trials in 1690. And yet, the Boston Brahmins, the heirs of the Puritans, joined with members of the black community to run the underground railroad to free slaves fleeing from the South.

Slavery first arrived in America in 1619 and it was abolished in Massachusetts in 1783. And, in 1850, with the Fugitive Slave Law making it illegal to aid and harbor slaves escaping from their owners,, the two sides of Beacon Hill joined hands. They defied the Fugitive Slave Law by operating the underground railroad. Boston's wealthy white—WASP (White-Anglo-Saxon-Protestant)—

elite and Boston's black community living in poverty, were united in the fight for freedom. The opposites were unified: high and low, rich and poor, black and white.

Now, as he looked back, Stephen thought that the origin of the opulence of the Boston Brahmins involved an interesting irony. The Puritans and their descendants made the bulk of their money in the shipping industry. And what did they import? They brought to Boston Harbor boat loads of rum, sugar, teas, silks, and spice— not everything nice. Addictive substances. Such luxuries sink hooks into the flesh.

Alcohol and sugar ultimately enslave their partakers. By being habit-forming, they lead to repeat business. How ironic that those who held themselves to be pure made their wealth by pandering to the base motives to which many an embodied soul falls prey. Teetotaler or rummy, the result is similar. A daily trip to the pub, or all those teaspoons of sugar in all those cups of tea or coffee. It adds up.

Continuous consumption occurs daily. The partakers vary: the rich attending a late-afternoon high tea in a fancy parlor with sugary pastries; high-society socialites imbibing rum cocktails at a stylish *soirèe* attended by the so-called very important; or a working-class man sweetening his tea or coffee at home before going to work.

Freedom fighters against slavery funded their fight with profits from substances that enslave and steal freedom. Or, to put it another way, staunch defenders of independence dealt in substances that created an unhealthy dependence. Given my vantage point, I suppose it's just another American, land of freedom, irony, or, perhaps, a simply human irony.

* * *

OVER THE NEXT DECADE, STEPHEN WOULD RECEIVE his doctorate in clinical and child psychology by doing his clinical internship at a psychiatric hospital in New England. He would stay there and start a private practice, and he was not aware of the thread of destiny weaving through his choice to live in the land of Hawthorne and Melville. However, when he drove from Virginia to Connecticut to begin his internship, he had an unexpected surprise. He was pulling away from the toll booth on the Cross Bronx Expressway when he looked up and saw the sign for New England.

He was suddenly overwhelmed with emotion and tears came into his eyes. A thought flashed through his mind: *I'm returning home.* But he had never lived there, at least not in this lifetime. Even with no evidence to support it, the inexplicably mysterious feeling of New England being home remained. It was more than a memory of some distant past life; it foreshadowed the fact that his spiritual homecoming would take place in New England.

He would make New England his home from the summer of 1979 until the winter of 1997. It was interesting to him that the years he lived there involved a simple reversal of the seven and the nine. In *Words Become Flesh*, he wrote about his time in New England and how, reminiscent of Hawthorne, he encountered his first case of Satanic ritual abuse there. The good by day *did* do evil by night.

> It was in a small New England town that people sought me out for therapy to relieve their suffering and, in a sense, their persecution. New England is the land where the Puritans sought relief from their religious persecution. It is also where Hawthorne and Melville delved into the dark depths of the human heart. After my time there, I discovered what darkness and suffering are hidden behind the facade of those black-shuttered, white-clapboard homes.

Whatever else may have been the allure of New England, he saw something deeply symbolic about this land of sharp contrasts: barren rocky coasts with crashing waves and soft meadows with wild flowers caressed by gentle breezes.

Again, he thought of the symbolic, dream-like quality of the story of Beacon Hill. The embodied soul's quest for freedom seemed somehow mirrored in the Northern and Southern slopes working together for freedom. It seemed that the embodied soul's struggle to reconcile the divisive duality expressed in the longings of spirit and flesh were evident everywhere in this land of inner and outer contrasts. . . .

Six

Glimpsing the Grail

OCTOBER 1985

THERE ARE ONLY 5000 STARS VISIBLE TO THE NAKED EYE, provided you are far from city lights on a moonless night. Likewise, when the focus of the embodied soul shifts from the obsession with the bright lights and objects of the outer world of matter to gazing within, then the starry heavens of inner space come into view. Each morning embodied souls emerge from sleep and the world of dreams. And, with the light of the morning sun, the memories of their dreams quickly vanish. The light of day captures the soul's attention.

So it is with embodied souls remembering that, indeed, they are the stuff of spirit and come from a different dimension. Emerging from the darkness of the womb into the light of the everyday world, embodied souls forget their origin in the starry heavens where inner and outer space converge. Astronomers speak of the brightness seen by the eyes looking up from Earth at the night sky as opposed to real brightness. For example, in tonight's sky, the full moon lines up with Venus, Saturn, and Regulus, the brightest star in Leo the Lion. Standing on Earth without the knowledge afforded by telescopes and the science of astronomy, the moon appears brightest since it is closest to Earth. Next in brightness comes Venus then Saturn, and finally Regulus. But in truth, Saturn is many times brighter than Venus, and Regulus, the least bright in the grouping, is actually a hundred times brighter than the sun from which the moon, Venus, and Saturn all derive their light. They are not stars. Only stars like the sun generate their own light. Planets and moons are simply mirrors that reflect the true light emanating from another source.

Is that true of us as embodied souls? Stephen wondered. *Do we simply reflect the light* OF *God, the Creator of Heaven and Earth? Or, are we little stars, suns, who generate our own light, and, in so doing, are made in the image of God?* I knew the answer even though he was unsure. Each soul is a mini-creator and not simply a mirror reflecting God's light. In a sense, just as each star generates its own light as it burns helium, each soul generates its own light. And that light is an extension of the light of God's love. The space between stars suggests that each star is solitary as it radiates light in the darkness of the night sky like diamonds set by a jeweler against a black velvet cloth. But in that apparent separateness there is an invisible connection with the Creator. But before he thought of me as a star, he imagined me as the Grail: the sacred cup sought by the knights of King Arthur.

Whether Christian, Jewish, Buddhist, Muslim, Hindu, etcetera, or even atheist, each embodied soul is consciously or unconsciously on a quest. The goal of the quest is beautifully expressed in the the psychological and spiritual mystery symbolized by the Holy Grail. The knight kneeling before the radiance of the Grail at the end of the quest portrays a mysterious reunion. The embodied soul (the knight) reunites with the transcendent spirit. To put it another way, the body-based sense of self or identity is replaced by the spirit-based sense of self or identity.

* * *

AT THIS POINT, STEPHEN TRADED IN THE IMAGE OF THE embodied soul as a deep-sea diver that Edgar Cayce had espoused for the space-age analogy of an astronaut. An astronaut wears a space suit to survive on the moon or other planets with an atmosphere unlike home on Earth. Similarly, a soul dons its soul suit, a physical body, so it can live in the atmosphere of Earth which is unlike the soul's spiritual home.

In addition, Stephen also began to reconsider the original archeological metaphor of the inner space of the mind employed by Freud and Jung. The mind had layers. The surface was the conscious mind with the deeper layers being levels of the unconscious. Using their topographical map of the mind, the following could be said about this next phase of Stephen's life. At thirty-three years old, he donned his miner's helmet with its searchlight of consciousness lighting the way, and he began his descent into the dark depths of the mind and heart.

Now as the train was nearing the stop for his doctor's office on Long Island, he watched the flickering images of trees and homes near the train tracks appear and disappear in rapid succession. All the while, his imagination was still captivated by the concept of the space between stars.

Looking back to 1985 through the lens of this new metaphor, he saw his work as a clinical psychologist as that of an astronaut exploring the depths of inner space. He had used the searchlight of consciousness to illuminate the black holes in his own dark depths and those of his patients. The earthbound hero of ancient and Medieval myths, legends, fables, and fairy tales was being blended into the image of the space-age explorer. As he thought about it, Flash Gordon and James T. Kirk of the starship *Enterprise* were simply space-age knights. And like King Arthur's knights, they, too, were in search of the Grail. Both the ancient and modern knight exemplified the age-old archetype of the hero. Like the knights of old, the space-age knight demonstrated the same heroism and courage necessary for facing and overcoming the fears that accompany psychological and spiritual growth.

From his own analysis with David Hart, Stephen knew that such growth culminated in finding and expressing the Grail of an embodied soul's true self. And, as mentioned before, the true self is just another name for me: the sidereal self. I have access to all the painful feelings that the embodied soul stuffs into a black hole. And, I AM the awareness who is able to embrace the seemingly irreconcilable feelings of love and anger left over from childhood.

The image of the Grail as a cup symbolizes a container that can hold all the feelings facing the soul inhabiting a human body. Souls come here to experience all that is involved in being human: love, hate, fear, anger, envy, jealousy, greed, despair, joy, bliss, ecstasy, and the list goes on. I guided Stephen to write in *8 Steps to Love*, the goal is to learn to "live from love instead of from fear and anger." This is accomplished by learning to transform the contracted energy of all negative emotions back into the peaceful power and expansive energy of love. In this phase of his life, Stephen was not yet aware of this.

In *A Matter of Love*, written after the new millennium, Stephen came to think of the Grail as the Holy Grail of his heart, that is to say, his innermost heart. Here is where all emotions are contained into both unconditional love and unconditional-no-matter-what-happens happiness. But in his journey at this point, he was only beginning to get a glimpse of how love is the ultimate power in the universe.

For Stephen, the search for the Grail of his true self was intensified by the deaths of his parents less than a year apart: the Fall of 1984 for his mother Gerry and the Summer of 1985 for his father Earl. Gerry's death was totally unexpected; Earl's was a whole other matter. Then, the day before Thanksgiving 1985, he discovered he had an advanced case of glaucoma. . . .

∗ ∗ ∗

IT WAS A SUNNY AUTUMN AFTERNOON, THE PHONE RANG and rang, indicating that the answering service was trying to reach him. What was so urgent? Usually, there was only one ring and the answering service picked up. Stephen noted that there were still ten minutes left in the session with Jeff, a depressed adolescent who also had a strong mother that reminded Stephen of Gerry. Stephen interrupted the session to take the call. "Dr. Jackson your mother has had a massive stroke and is in the hospital. . . ." The words had a numbing effect. She had just visited Stephen in Connecticut and was now at her brother Hank's house in Delaware. She stepped out of the shower, and, after drying herself off, slipped into her robe and suddenly slumped to the floor. An aneurysm in her brain had burst. A few hours later, she was pronounced brain dead.

Stephen was stunned. If anyone was likely to die he thought it would be Earl, given his health problems. Gerry had been the caregiver, suffering in silence. Strong to the end.

When he arrived in Delaware, Stephen cried for the first time as soon as he saw and hugged his Aunt Barbara, his mother's older sister. Her features resembled Gerry's and this facilitated the flow of his tears. Until then, it still didn't seem quite real. Then he saw his father. Earl was insistent about pulling the plug on the machine keeping her breathing. "Stevie, what am I going to do?" Earl cried, the tears streaming down his cheeks. "She's not there, Stevie. She wouldn't want to be kept alive by any artificial measures. Both of us wrote this in our living wills." Earl was right: her soul had already exited her body. It was Friday night. By early Sunday morning her kidneys stopped, and her body shut down; her soul had rejoined her spirit, her sidereal self, and was hovering nearby, observing her loved ones.

Weeks later, when going through her will, Stephen felt her presence when her sense of humor came through in the words, "Well, if you are reading this, it means that I am no longer on this Earth. You better be careful to do as I ask, or I might come back to haunt you." Stephen smiled with tears in his eyes when he read these words aloud for his father to hear. Earl also smiled. He was remembering Gerry's wonderful sense of humor.

Seeing his mother on her deathbed and hearing her forced, labored breathing would not be the last time he would see her. A dozen years later, five months before the sun set on the twentieth century, she appeared to him in the middle of a steamy August night in 1999. He awakened to see her as if through a portal, looking young and beautiful. From somewhere, he was told that she was appearing as she did when she was twenty-nine years old. She was in a white robe like a toga. Her hair and the robe were fluttering; she seemed to be flying through the starry heavens.

When he looked into her radiant blue eyes, he felt an intense electrifying energy shoot into him. It was as if he were looking into the eyes of a spiritual master. Instead of a tender reunion with his mother, he felt he was receiving an important spiritual message. That night, he had thought of her when he was giving a talk to a Church group on how to master stress. Gerry had an unwavering way of setting her intentions where there was no room for doubt about attaining her goals. He was being given a message to set his intentions as firmly as she had. Rather than silently saying, *Oh, hi Mom, I've missed you* . . . he felt, *Yes, Master!* was more in order.

Six months later, there was a startling request. It was a request made in what was an extremely intimate moment between father and son. Such raw honesty and love was expressed in the space between a father and a son. The request arose while Earl was riding with Stephen to get sandwiches to take back to Vinnie's house. Earl was now residing with his brother Vinnie. Not making eye contact but looking straight ahead through the windshield, Earl began, "There's something I want to tell you but I don't want you to be all torn up about it . . ."

Anticipating his father's solemn message, Stephen interjected, "What are you telling me? You want to kill yourself?"

"Look," Earl continued, "I've lived my life. Every morning when I wake up I'm in pain." Earl was referring to his chronic physical pain but, at the same time, he was in pain over losing Gerry, his life partner. He went on to say, "Look at me, I can't find another woman looking like this." Earl was dismayed by how frail he was. He was terribly thin since the stroke he had a year earlier following the gastrectomy that removed his whole stomach. He was not able to eat much since the pouch the surgeon had made to substitute for a stomach held very little. There was no way to put weight on and get back to the size he had been for most of his adult life.

"I love you and I'd really miss you, and I can understand what you're feeling," Stephen said, his eyes filling up as he tightened against being torn up in deference to Earl's request. He then added, "Will you let me know if you really get serious about this?"

Earl nodded. In retrospect, Stephen saw the nod not so much as an assent to Stephen's question; it was more of a half-hearted acknowledgement of the fact that Stephen had spoken.

A few weeks later, Stephen told his friend Ken, also a psychologist, about this exchange with his father. Ken summed up what Earl was saying, "In effect, your father was saying to you, 'Son, I'm tired and in pain, and if you don't need a father any longer, then I'd like to leave this world.'"

A month later, Stephen had a dream. In the dream, Earl was about to walk into a lake that reminded Stephen of the lake where King Arthur was handed the sword Excalibur by the Lady of the Lake. When he is up to his waist, Earl turns and asks Stephen to write his departing note. Stephen replies, saying, "I'm not going to write your note because people will think I killed you. You have to write your own note." Earl understands and writes his own note. Earl then wades into the lake until the water comes up to his shoulders. He then dips down, his head disappearing under the still waters of the lake.

The scene shifts. Gerry appears. (In reality, she has been gone for eight months.) She is standing on the chiseled steps of a gray stone cathedral. Looking down at Stephen, she announces, "Your father burst into tears at the moment of his death."

Alarmed, Stephen responds, "You're on the other side. Why didn't you greet him so that he didn't have to cross over alone and scared?"

Gerry ignores Stephens comment. Stoically, she declares, "Years ago your grandfather gave me and your father an egg and you two eggs." By her feet lay a clay bowl with four white eggs, the size of a hen's eggs. The scene faded and the dream ended.

Stephen spoke to David Hart about the dream. David Hart made note of Stephen's need to protect his father from pain, in this instance, the emotional pain of death. David Hart said, "We all have to face our fate alone, and we can't do it for someone else."

After the session with David Hart, he decided to use a combination of the Jungian process of dreaming the dream onward with active imagination and the Gestalt Therapy technique of playing the part of other characters in the dream. Actively imagining himself back into the dream, he speaks to his mother, saying, "You're on the other side. Why didn't you greet him and ease his pain about crossing over?"

Playing the part of Gerry, he answers, "I had to cross over alone. Nobody was here to help me." (As an aside, this was a dream with a message for Stephen and not a depiction of how it actually is when souls cross over. Deceased loved ones and others are there to greet the soul now released from the body.) Instantly, Stephen saw how his pattern of trying to rescue his father was being highlighted. He had tried to save Earl from pain since he was a child. Even in graduate school, he brought Earl tapes to help him relax and take the edge off Earl's chronic physical pain. Learning to let go of the need to take away his father's and mother's pain and that of others was something he would have to keep learning over and over again.

Thirteen years later, in 8 Steps to Love, he would call this process of breaking the rescuer pattern slaying the dragon of dependency. And this dragon is the mistaken belief that embodied souls are dependent on something external to themselves to feel good and be at peace. He would see in the lives of his patients what he came to see in his own life. People need to realize in relation to their loved ones: "My pain over your pain is still my pain and is my responsibility to take care of within myself. I DO NOT need you to be happy before I can be happy. I am responsible for my own happiness and you are responsible for your happiness."

* * *

THREE MONTHS AFTER THE DREAM ABOUT HIS FATHER, ON July, 29, 1985, Stephen was finishing his last session before going to lunch. The man he was seeing was the same age as his father. Stephen saw the man to the door and picked up the mail left in the waiting room. At the very moment that he opened the envelope containing information about his upcoming twentieth-high-school reunion, he felt his knees buckle slightly, and the following words entered his mind: "It's good you left Delaware, moved to Connecticut, and set up your practice." The voice in his head was his own but the wording seemed to be something his father might say. He happened to look up at the clock. It was ten minutes after one.

When he came back from lunch, he saw his wife walking down the sidewalk from his office building. She looked somber as she spoke and reached out to hug him, saying, "At ten after one, your father shot himself."

Suddenly, he knew his father's soul had come to him and spoken those words he heard at 1:10 P.M. Stephen then thought of how his father had been a staunch believer in a person's right to die. Since the early 1970s, Earl had been studying the ethics of that right. Looking back, Stephen realized Earl was probably drawn to the topic because of the chronic, inescapable back pain he experienced throughout his whole adult life.

These thoughts of how Earl had exercised what he believed to be his right were replaced by the nagging thought, *Why now?* Earl was going to be coming to Connecticut to spend a week with Stephen and Kathy. Later, Stephen would realize that Earl was probably intent on ending his life, and he did not want to do so in his son's home and put Stephen in the position of finding him dead. Instead, Earl arranged it so that his brother Vinnie would be the one to find him.

The note left by Earl read, "Stevie, please understand. It's what I want. I've lived my life, and now I'm going out for a long swim." Earl loved to swim and in his note he requested that his remains be cremated and sent to his long-time friend Chip in the Florida Keys. He wanted Chip to take his ashes out in his boat and scatter them in the ocean.

There was an eerie synchronicity from the previous night. Debbie, the patient he was to see right after lunch had threatened to kill herself the night before. Up until that day and until he left his practice twelve years later, that was the only serious suicide threat made by a patient. She was short in stature but she had the black hair, brown eyes, and skin tone of Earl. And something about her brown eyes and features bore a slight resemblance to Earl's.

Reflecting on Earl's note, Stephen teared up as he recalled what would become one of his most cherished memories. It was the last time he had seen his father. It was in late June, a month before Earl took his own life. Stephen and Earl were sitting in the living room at Vinnie's home. No one else was present. Earl was sorting through important papers and he would occasionally look up to speak to Stephen about financial considerations and taxes since Gerry's death. In retrospect, Stephen saw what he was doing as trying to get his affairs in order before he died.

Stephen was reading *How Analysis Cures* by the famous psychoanalyst Dr. Heinz Kohut. Earl's voice softened after speaking about his financial account with Merrill Lynch. Earl took note of the book on Stephen's lap, and, with a sparkle in his eyes, he said, "You love your field, and you love keeping abreast of it." Stephen noticed the warmth in his father's face as he spoke. He was deeply moved by such a simple and direct statement because it signified that his father truly saw who he was and what was important to him.

What a moment for Stephen! Earl had said in just a few words, *I see you Son, and I understand what you love and value.* Earl was also looking on with admiration and longing for something he had never had: the chance to pursue a profession he loved. He loved psychology and philosophy but never got the chance to teach both as his son had done nor to practice psychology as Stephen was currently dong.

∗ ∗ ∗

A YEAR AFTER HIS MOTHER'S DEATH, AND JUST TWO MONTHS after his father's, he was struck by a sentence written by Jungian psychologist Robert Johnson. Johnson suggested something to the effect that a man gets a glimpse of the Grail of his true self in adolescence just as the Knight Parsifal did at the very beginning of his quest for the Grail. He was described as a foolish young man with a pure heart filled with compassion. And then again, just as Parsifal did when he was older, a man gets another chance at attaining the

Grail in mid-life. Now his dream from two nights ago made more sense.

The dream began with Stephen standing on the top of a mountain. He heard a voice say, "Look up and you'll see God." The words "fear and trembling" from an essay by the Danish theologian and philosopher Søren Kierkegaard came to mind. The words expressed the fear and excitement he felt coursing through his body as he leaned back to look up. Later, he would see these words in the Bible, "work out your salvation with fear and trembling for it is God who works in you to will and act according to His good purpose" (Philippians 2:12-13). He would learn that a good modern translation of the word salvation was freedom: freedom from addiction, fear, guilt, and anger.

When he forced himself to move through his fear and trembling and craned his head back so that his eyes finally looked skyward, he was stunned. There were no bolts of lightning nor was there a hoary-headed and bearded man like Michelangelo's painting of God and Adam on the ceiling of the Sistine Chapel. Instead, he saw the face of a sixteen-year-old version of himself. The youthful eyes were full of life as they peered out of the white, billowy clouds with an expectant enthusiasm.

The right arm of Stephen's adolescent self reached down. And as it did, the arm elongated, stretching like rubber. Stephen extended his hand and his arm also elongated until his fingers touched his sixteen-year-old self. It was as if an electrical circuit was closed and a tremendous surge of energy was released. Stephen was filled with the feelings of awe associated with profound religious experiences; he thought of Moses encountering the Burning Bush. But there was no lightning. No thunderclap.

Nonetheless, it was as if there were an immediate liberation of light and sound. Fifteen years later, he would learn that mystics of various traditions—Jewish, Christian, Islamic, Hindu—had the following in common. In the mystic's experience of God, the Divine, there is often a powerful combination of light and sound.

He would have been at a loss for understanding the link the dream made between God and his sixteen-year-old self if it weren't for the synchronicity of what Robert Johnson wrote about the reappearance of the Grail in mid-life as a second adolescence. Having focused on the needs of others at home and work, the man in mid-life may appear adolescent and selfish, even foolish, as he buys himself a red sports car. Such behavior is often referred to in a pejorative way as "adolescent." But that was Johnson's point. In order to get another chance at the Grail, a man must be willing to feel foolish. Johnson did not mean a man should act out and do foolish adolescent things. The man needs to get in touch with the adolescent within himself.

Stephen decided to call David Hart for a phone session. He mentioned the new aliveness he felt following the dream of contacting his sixteen-year-old self. David Hart removed the stigma regarding adolescence by pointing out that adolescence is the time when the first spiritual struggles and questions emerge. Who am I? What do I really want to do with my life? Why am I here? Such questions reemerge in mid-life, and they were for Stephen.

* * *

SUDDENLY, THE WORD GRAIL SEPARATED INTO G-RAIL at the very moment the train pulled into Floral Park, Long Island. Walking from the station to his Dr. Jindra's office, he thought of the letter "G" as standing for God. Glimpsing the Grail is getting back on the track of one's true Self, or, in my terms, an embodied soul getting in touch with his or her mission for coming to Earth. He thought of how therapy was often seen as a process of resuming one's psychological and spiritual growth at the point where it was derailed. The God-rail was the track heading toward becoming the person one was meant to be. Getting back on the God-rail involved becoming the person who utilizes and expresses his or her unique God-given gifts and talents.

The dream of looking up to see God seemed to signify that, at 38 years of age, Stephen was getting another chance at the Grail. Literally, in the dream, he was getting back in touch with his authentic, true self when he was sixteen years old.

146

For Stephen, the age of sixteen was significant. That was when he was emerging out of the shadows cast by his parents and by his heroes on the hardwood. He was finding himself: what he liked and what he disliked. He discovered and defined his own style. He had found his own style in all aspects: clothes, hair, the way he walked and talked. Longer hair replaced the flat-top.

In basketball, which was his life at that time, his first glimpse of the Grail appeared in his style of shooting. At first, both his foul shot and jump shot were his own. Neither were copied from any older players whose shooting styles he admired. But then, in his senior year in high school, just after he turned seventeen, he lost sight of the Grail. He began experimenting with his jump shot and foul shot. It was as if he were trying on so many different styles of clothes. Instead of shooting from the internal locus of control centered in his true Self, he focused outside of himself on conforming to an external image of the shooting style of the players he admired. He strove to move his muscles in accord with an external picture instead of allowing his body to align with the inner guidance of his true self as he had done at sixteen.

In his quest to be the best he could be, he sought to emulate the excellence he saw in other players but in so doing abandoned his own authentic style. Fortunately for him, he was good enough to pull it off without impairing his performance. He had chameleon-like ability to copy the style of the champions of the game.

Shortly after his fathers' death, Stephen was shooting baskets with his long-time friend Greer who had been the sixth man on his high school team. They had been friends since sixth grade. Greer had gone with him to see Barry Kramer play in Madison Square Garden in 1964. Both of them were enamored with Kramer's slick style.

Remembering this, Stephen said, "You probably don't know this, but I stopped shooting my own jump shot and foul shot, and started copying the shots of players I admired. Here, I'll show you. I'll take a shot and see if you can guess what famous player from the past I'm imitating." He then demonstrated one player's jump shot after another by introducing each shot with, "Now whose shot do you think this one is?" He started with All-Americans from the early 1960s: Barry Kramer, then Bill Bradley.

Then, Stephen did his impression of professional players from back then. First was Jerry West, then Oscar Robertson, followed by Rick Barry. Greer guessed each one easily, chuckling at the remarkable resemblance of each shot to the player being copied.

After he finished his basketball impressions, Stephen showed Greer the Grail of his own true jump shot and foul shot. He told Greer that when he went back to shooting his own foul shot in college, he was ranked fifteenth in the nation with an 87-percent shooting average at the foul line. Not only did it feel better to act in accord with his true self, but it yielded better results.

$$* * *$$

OTHER DREAMS AND SYNCHRONICITIES FOLLOWED. SYMBOLS and signs, the former from dreams, the latter from daily life, were working together to help Stephen be successful in his mid-life chance at attaining the Grail of his true Self. He was being led to the discovery of who he was apart from how others and life conditions had defined him.

On the day marking the one-year anniversary of his mother's death, Stephen was watching an episode of the television show *Spenser for Hire*, starring Robert Urich. The words of wisdom Spenser shared with a young man named Jimmy were a perfect fit for Stephen. "You're not just someone Kathy [his wife's name] loves, and you're not just your father's son. You're something independent of all of that. Don't give up who you are for anybody ever!" Spenser also referenced something Winston Churchill said to inspire Jimmy. It was something about the measure of a man being how he reacts in a crisis.

That night Stephen had readily agreed with his wife that they should celebrate Christmas at her parents' home near the Connecticut shore as had been a family tradition. He assented to his wife's request in spite of the fact that earlier that morning before going to his office, he had expressed his wish. He wanted to spend Christmas in the new home. Even though set on a mountain in Connecticut, the new house reminded Stephen of his parents' home on Florida's West Coast. Like his parents' home, this one had a swimming pool. The day he put a bid on the house, he felt a warm glow in his heart, especially when he noticed how the sunlight reflecting off the pool was dancing on the ceiling of the foyer. At that moment, fond memories of visiting his parents in sunny Florida flooded his thoughts. Having Christmas in the new home would be like spending it with his recently deceased parents.

That evening, when his wife told him she had changed her mind, and asked if he would mind celebrating Christmas at her parents' home, he replied, "Sure. Why not?" Christmas was three months away. It was now the beginning of October. He had responded with his "good boy," pleasing and accommodating pattern; he shrugged off his desire and went along with her wish.

Unbeknownst to him, something else was rumbling within him in the space between surface and depth. He awoke from two dreams feeling unsettled and unable to get back to sleep. In the first dream, Stephen was at the new house lounging in the hot tub and listening to Bobby Darin singing, "Splish, Splash, I was taking a bath . . . rub a dub just relaxing in the tub, thinking everything was all right." The song was coming from an old-fashioned vinyl forty-five record. Bobby Darin's voice came to an abrupt halt; the sound of the record being scratched startled Stephen. Now contrary to the song, everything was not all right, and his enjoyment was interrupted. He turned to see his wife's cat Chiquita jump on the record. Standing there, she looked defiant. Stephen stood up immediately and confronted Chiquita. He wanted to grab her and pull her off the record, but he hesitated. Growling and hissing with her teeth bared, she was hunched up, positioning herself to bite and scratch him if he tried. He thought of it as a Mexican stand-off. For a second in the dream, he was puzzled why he thought of the word Mexican. Then he remembered. His wife told him how she had found Chiquita in Mexico and brought her home. The dream ended and a new one began.

In this next dream, Stephen saw Bobby, a boy he knew in high school. Bobby was seated in a dentist chair. Referring to the boy in the chair, a voice in the background said, "At the moment of his death, his eyes became clear." He had been drained of his life fluid by a Venus Fly Trap. Stephen had a quick visual of a flower with teeth. The fluid was clear, and not red as blood would be. Bobby was a handsome football player. All the girl's loved him; his good looks resembled Wally, the teen heartthrob on the TV show *Leave it to Beaver*. He never had to go after what he wanted. Things came to him with little or no effort on his part. He never had to risk rejection or defeat.

This dream shifted to a scene from a high school basketball game featuring Vic, a crowd-pleasing player from a rival school. Vic was engaged in a razzle-dazzle move as he floated through the air ready to make a fancy pass. In the midst of Vic's move, Stephen hears from sone unknown figure in the shadows that his wife had married Vic before she married him. He was instantly jealous.

Immediately upon awakening, Stephen knew what his wife having been married to Vic before him symbolized. Vic was the crowd-pleasing part of Stephen. In a symbolic sense, he believed his wife had married the eager-to-please and heroic self-image that Stephen had fashioned in early childhood to please his parents. When identified with this self-image, he sought to satisfy the needs of loved ones above his other needs, beyond his primary need to please. His anger in the dream meant that he believed that his wife did not love him as the person he was; instead, he felt that she loved him for how he pleased her by giving into her wishes. His hidden motto was that of the genie in a bottle, "Your wish is my command." However, he was more generous than the genie; he granted many more than the standard three wishes.

The anger he felt in the dream over Kathy's marriage to Vic tied in with Bobby dying because a Venus Fly Trap had drained him of his life fluid. Death was the price paid for love. And what did death symbolize? It meant deadening himself to his own desires apart from the overriding desire to please. Stephen realized his anger at his wife for marrying Vic in the dream was misplaced. If she married Stephen because he pleased her, whose fault was that? Deep down, he did not feel he was worthy of love as a person in

150

his own right. He felt loved for what he could do or provide, not for who he really was inside.

The death of Bobby also meant that the Bobby part of his personality needed to die so that a new identity could be born. The pleaser needed to die so that Stephen could find and begin to express the Grail of his true Self.

Feeling agitated by the dreams, Stephen got out of bed, careful not to disturb Kathy. He went into the small sitting room off the master bedroom, and began to meditate on the dream images of the hissing cat and the Venus Fly Trap. He found himself focusing on the round row of the plant's teeth, and the bared teeth and flared claws of his wife's kitty. Seated on the floor and surrounded by darkness, he heard the clock downstairs chime four times. It was 4:00 A.M.

A question suddenly soared into his awareness with the power of a determined bird of prey. *When am I going to find my teeth and claws!?* He saw his wife in his mind's eye, and he imagined addressing her: *I killed myself trying to please my parents. Now they're dead! I'm not going to turn you into them or your parents into them! I'm going to start doing what I want to do.* A raging river of aliveness surged through every cell of his body. He knew he must make his wishes known to his wife in the morning. In some way, he felt his life depended on it. This didn't mean that he couldn't choose to go along with her desire to have Christmas at her parents' home. But it did mean that he needed to express and no longer repress or suppress his own desires. There would be no more knee-jerk reflexive responding to his wife's wishes. Conflict did not have to involve yelling and arguing or the silent treatment he had witnessed in childhood with his parents and sought desperately to avoid as an adult.

Stephen then wondered about the significance of Bobby's eyes becoming clear at the moment of his death, when all the life fluid left his body. The implication was that Bobby's vision had been unclear. And what about the mystery of the fluid draining that somehow caused Bobby's eyes to clear? Was the Bobby part of his personality the part who was blind to any needs apart from the need to please? Or, was there a problem with Stephen's eyes? He had recently noticed he was not seeing sports on television quite as clearly as he had before. Movies were fine. But in watching football or basketball games, he couldn't follow the action as well as he had before. In typical male fashion, he considered buying a big screen television before getting his eyes checked. Soon the mystery would be solved.

* * *

AN AMAZING THING HAPPENED THE NIGHT FOLLOWING his awakening to the discovery of his own *teeth* and *claws*. Stephen received a late-night phone call from Ken Westerside, his high-school buddy whom he hadn't seen nor heard from for two decades. They had made their Easter Sunday pact in 1964, and both had left their home state to go to college. Ken went to Arkansas, and he, to Virginia. When Stephen answered the phone call, the voice on the other end cried out, "Dr. Jackson, I wanna kill myself!" An unmistakable chuckle followed. Instantly, Stephen recognized the voice from the past. It was Ken pretending to be suicidal. Later, Stephen would see that the joke of suicide turned out to have some symbolic value.

Ken couldn't explain it, but he felt compelled to call. Somehow Stephen's intense emotional breakthrough traveled the hundreds of miles from Connecticut to Delaware, cutting through the dark of night like a supernatural flash of lightning. Stephen knew he had touched that place in his heart that he did when he was sixteen years old and glimpsed the Grail for the first time. An intense aliveness flowed through their adolescent bodies. Now a renewed aliveness was knocking on the door to their hearts. Back then, both of them were confident and fully in touch with who they were and what they wanted out of life.

It was now twenty years since he had seen Westerside. Now, following the death of Stephen's parents, Westerside was calling after midnight. He was pretending to be a patient contemplating suicide. The fake cry for help was something more deeply symbolic than either of them knew. They were both on the verge of a spiritual and psychological rebirth. Each was a reminder to the other of the first time both had glimpsed the Grail of their true Selves.

Stephen would now find out whether Ken had fulfilled his Easter-Sunday-1964 vow. Had writing down his vow worked magic for Ken as well? It had. Writing down his vow had helped. Ken was named All-American for college baseball, signed a contract to play professional baseball, and his name was in the Baseball Hall of Fame in Cooperstown, New York. Like Stephen, his name was now next to baseball's greatest players of all time but not for his play as a professional as he had intended. Just as it had been for Stephen, it was for Ken being named All-American in college. Still, they both had bridged the space between where they were in 1964 and where they wanted to be in five years. The magic of their love for their respective sports had filled that space and both had fulfilled their vows, even if it wasn't exactly as they had intended.

They made arrangements to meet back in their hometown of Wilmington, Delaware. Stephen had been planning to visit his Uncle Vinnie. There was something comforting about visiting his father's brother since Earl was gone. Jung had written of how a man's psychological growth gets a jolt of energy with the recognition that his life is all up to him now that Dad, the "Big Guy," is gone.

The moment they saw and embraced each other after all those years, Stephen caught a glimpse of the television out of the corner of his eye. One of the *Star Trek* movies was on. Ken and Stephen shook hands and embraced with their free arms at the very moment Captain Kirk (William Shatner) and Mr. Spock (Leonard Nimoy) were embracing. There was some similarity between Spock and Ken as there was between Stephen and Kirk. One parallel was that Ken had black hair like Spock, and Stephen, brown like Kirk. Similar to Ken and Stephen, Spock and Kirk were being reunited at that very moment. In the movie, Spock had been thought dead. The theme of both reunions was that of a symbolic death and rebirth.

Stephen wondered what the synchronicity spoke to in Ken's life. It turned out that Ken had a sixteen-year-old son with whom he was having trouble relating. Reuniting with Stephen made him remember when he was that age. Moreover, Stephen had a lot of experience working with adolescent boys in his training and practice as a psychologist. Ken's call was an outer confirmation of an inner shift in Stephen that needed to be nurtured as a seed sown in a garden needs water and fertilizer.

Returning to his Uncle's after seeing Ken, Stephen noticed a sign that read *Pearle Vision Center*. He remembered the dream of Bobby's eyes becoming clear at the moment of his death. Stephen decided to have his vision checked to see if he needed glasses. The optician told him he needed to see an optometrist first, and gave him the name of one. The optometrist was located on the same road as Stephen's childhood home. This seemed significant after the optometrist performed a few routine tests. Then came the shock. "You have a serious case of glaucoma. You're pressures are extremely high. You need to see an ophthalmologist right away. Your eye pressures need to be lowered." He then explained, "Glaucoma is due to a build up of fluid in the eye which raises intraocular pressure. The elevated pressure damages the optic nerve, and, if left untreated, causes blindness. For traditional medicine, there is no cure for glaucoma and all that can be done is to slow down the progression of the disease. The drains in the meshwork of the eyes are not doing their job. Eye drops and/or surgery can lower the pressure by making it easier for the fluid to drain before new fluid enters the eyes." Stephen appreciated the brutal honesty and went straight to the recommended ophthalmologist.

What an amazing synchronicity! The dream had a physical and a psychological meaning. The fluid draining out of Bobby's eyes made his vision become clear. Fortunately, Stephen listened to the still small inner voice nudging him to go to *Pearle Vision Center*. Listening to my message, he might be able to prevent going blind. Still, the dream revealed that he had an emotional blindness when it came to his other needs apart from his need to please or rescue.

* * *

NOW, WALKING NEXT TO THE TRAIN TRACKS, HE THOUGHT OF how another two decades had passed by. For all these years, he had been on two quests regarding his glaucoma. He was on a quest for a cure in the sense of finding a way to regenerate the damaged optic nerves. This quest depended on fulfilling the quest to control his eye pressure by keeping them low to prevent any more damage to the optic nerves. He had come to Dr. Jindra precisely because the laser he used seemed to offer a way to, in effect, wake up the dormant drain cells so they would keep the fluid flowing. That way, pressures would remain low without the use of eye-drop medications with their negative side effects. His thoughts were on whether decreased blood flow was a factor, and, if so, then he would consider herbs and other ways to increase that flow.

The visit began with a vision test for visual acuity, checking his eye pressures and an eye examination by Dr. Jindra. After the exam was finished, Dr. Jindra told Stephen that there was another test related to glaucoma that he recommended. It was called the Intraocular Blood Flow Analysis. Stephen took the test. Sure enough, he had restricted blood flow within the capillaries of his his eyes. Voilà! His recently-arrived-at hypothesis regarding tension playing a part in the physical mechanism of glaucoma was confirmed. Walking back to the station to catch the train, he resolved to take steps to increase the blood flow in his eyes; he would use herbs and do certain exercises.

When he returned four months later, he took the blood-flow test again. He succeeded: blood flow had increased significantly. This was the good news; the bad news was that he still needed under-the-knife-surgery despite the four special laser surgeries he had since 2002. Stephen sat back on the train as he started the first leg of the trip home from Dr. Jindra's office.

The Long Island train sped along. He found himself under the hypnotic spell of the constantly appearing and disappearing images of the passing sights, an amalgam of steel, asphalt, cement, brick, foliage, and people. He thought of how people lived their lives in the space within and between the stores and apartment buildings, houses, and streets of the neighborhoods. In the flash of a moment, he caught a brief glimpse of children playing by parked cars. At first, his thoughts were also whizzing by in a blur. Looking away, his thoughts slowed down and he focused on old memories.

* * *

FINDING THE GRAIL OF HIS TRUE SELF, A MAN MUST LOOK through the haze of memory to see who he is apart from his father. Discovering who he is in space and time as a unique individual in his own right, a man takes a step toward encountering his ultimately true and real Self, the radiant star of his divine sidereal self. Although, he had brief encounters with me during this psychology phase of his life, Stephen would not be fully aware of me until the next phase of his life: the spiritual phase.

Stephen then recalled that day in 1985 when he was having lunch with Bob, a colleague. Bob shared how he was outstanding as a pianist when he was a teenager. But he was afraid to play on the stage of the auditorium at school because he didn't want his peers to resent him. He told Stephen, "I admire how you weren't afraid to be the best you could be."

Shaking his head and laughing, Stephen responded to Bob, "No, it wasn't that I was not afraid to be the best I could. I thought I *had* to be the best just to be liked. It didn't occur to me that others might resent me. I was so blind to my abilities, I couldn't fathom someone envying me." For years, Stephen had looked at himself through the lens of his father's criticism.

Then, looking puzzled, Bob asked him, "How can someone who has so much going for him not know it!?" Stephen was nonplussed. He didn't know how to respond.

How? I'll tell you how. He was emotionally blind to any sense of his own worth. Feelings of inferiority drove him to be the best. Until he had made his first athletic honor as an eleventh grader in high school, he had not experienced the conflict between striving to be the best and being liked. At first, the two were linked together, forging one chain of desire. He had so lived in the shadow of his father that he could not *see* how being the best might lead to others being resentful and envious.

Then Stephen remembered that at the time that he had received his basketball honors in college, he had a dream that his father died. It felt so very real. The king must die for the prince to become king. This is an age-old archetypal stage in a man's growth.

Memories of his father floated into the spaciousness of his awareness. The first scene took place while Stephen was visiting his parents Gerry and Earl at their home in Key Largo, Florida for Christmas 1977. It was the second year of graduate school in clinical and child psychology. Stephen and Earl were in the swimming pool. Earl was recovering from a stroke he suffered during the surgery to remove bleeding ulcers in the lining of his stomach. He had lost nearly sixty pounds from his large frame. He was a shadow of the man he was but he was in good spirits and his sense of humor was as buoyant as ever instead of sinking in what could have easily been a sea of despair. Father and son were pretending to spar while standing in the shallow end of the pool. Earl was laughing. Stephen stopped and became serious. Addressing Earl, Stephen said, "You know Dad, I have come to some realizations in defining who I am in relation to you. I realize that there are some things that you can do that I will never surpass."

"Oh, no," Earl quickly added, "You have degrees and I don't. You are a college graduate with a masters degree and now on your way to getting a doctorate and you achieved all those honors in basketball—"

"No! Dad," Stephen interrupted. "Listen to what I am saying. Sure I have degrees, and I've attained some honors. But think about it. I realize that you were a better overall athlete than I was. Why just last year before your surgery and your move to Florida, we played croquet. You zipped through the wickets and returned to clobber my ball into the neighbor's corn field." The house Earl and Gerry moved from was set amid farmland in Maryland. Stephen gave other examples of Earl's ability in other sports such as baseball, football, and golf.

Earl listened intently, and responded, "I see what you mean."

Stephen went on and said, "I also realize you are better at math than I am and always will be, even though I have **improved**. But when it comes to basketball even if both of us were in **our** prime, I would always outdo you because I have your upper body and Mom's legs." Earl chuckled and agreed.

Stephen then added, "And when it comes to looks, I used to feel you had the edge, but I've come to appreciate my looks after years of feeling I could never measure up to you. I now feel that, despite our differences, we're evenly matched when compared to each other in our respective primes."

Stephen felt so good as he laid out to his father the facts he had come to terms with in defining himself as a man. It was a good exercise in self-acceptance. After his experience in the pool, he saw the importance of men facing and accepting the space between their strengths and those of their fathers. He would suggest such an exchange for the men in his practice whose sagging self-esteem needed bolstering. He always loved that line from one of Clint Eastwood's film appearances as police detective Dirty Harry Callahan. At the end of the film, Harry looks on as the police car carrying the corrupt police chief (Hal Holbrook) explodes into flames. Speaking through clenched teeth, hard-boiled Harry mutters under his breath, "A man's got to know his limitations."

* * *

THE NEXT MEMORY WAS ONE THAT CAPTURED the spiritual seeker and warrior essence of his father as well as Gerry's fighting spirit. Growing up in a tough section of town, Earl learned to defend himself with his fists. Most cities in the 1920s and 1930s had a section like the famous Hell's Kitchen in New York City. Earl encountered a brutish tough guy from Hell's Kitchen when he was in Virginia, serving in President F.D.R.'s Civilian Conservation Corp (C.C.C.). The scene was in the cafeteria of the camp. The tough guy was taking food from the plates of the men around him. No one dared protest. When he went to take food from Earl, he suddenly found the prongs of a fork pinning his hand to the table. That ended his pilfering from the plates of others.

As the train rumbled on Stephen's thoughts went back to when Steve was a freshman at the University of Virginia. It was a week after Christmas of 1965, Steve was home for semester break from the University of Virginia. It was his freshman year. Earl had just finished reading an article in *Guideposts* magazine about a medical doctor from the University of Virginia who was pronounced dead for ten minutes and came back to life. Earl related how the doctor had an incredible experience of his soul leaving his body and encountering a being of brilliant light whom he identified as Christ Jesus. The article described the journey Christ took him on that allowed him to explore different dimensions in the space between Heaven and Earth. The whole experience took place while his body lay lifeless on his hospital bed. The man was Dr. George G. Ritchie, Jr. Steve would later meet him and Dr. Ritchie would become an influential man in Steve's life.

Ritchie's experience inspired Dr. Raymond Moody to interview numerous patients who had died and come back to life. Such experiences became known as the near-death experience. He presented his findings in his book *Life After Life*, released twelve years later. Interestingly, it came out a few months after Earl had a near-death experience during surgery. Earl found himself speeding through a tunnel toward a brilliant light. But before he could reach the light, Earl was jarred back to the operating table by the shock from the electric charge delivered by the clamps used to restart his heart. The details of his encounter with Dr. Ritchie and how the near-death experience can help embodied souls deal more effectively with stress and conflict can be found in *8 Steps to Love*.

Stephen's discussion with Earl about Ritchie's story was interrupted. It was time to shovel the driveway. The snow had stopped, and the sun had come out. Due to his back pain, Earl had to leave shoveling to Steve and Gerry. A few minutes after staring to shovel, the neighbors appeared on their back steps: the mother, the father, their thirty-year-old son. There had been a history of quiet feuding. It seemed the neighbors never got over Earl complaining about the boys playing baseball in their front yard and putting the glassed-in porch at risk. A passively aggressive feud began. For example, the mother would leave egg shells and coffee grounds on the property line just a few feet from the clothesline where Gerry hung the wash. And it continued even though Earl helped clear the back of their property to make a field in which the boys next door could play baseball and football.

On this afternoon, the mother called out to Gerry and Steve, "You're throwing snow on our property!" Yes, some of the snow was spilling over onto their land; however, their driveway was on the other side of their property. The small amount of snow coming their way was doing no harm.

"Go to hell!" Gerry replied in a matter-of-fact tone. The father and the thirty-year-old son stormed off the steps and headed toward Steve and Gerry. Steve started peeling off his hooded sweatshirt in preparation for the ensuing fight.

At that moment, Earl awoke from the comfort of his easy chair where he had been napping. He was awakened by the commotion outside. He had no shirt or shoes on since he rose quickly from his nap to see what was happening. The back door opened and Earl emerged onto the cement landing at the top of the back steps. It was late afternoon and the sun was still shining brightly but it was cold. Earl was unaffected by the cold. Standing on the top of the back steps with his chest out and stomach in, looking a little like a hairy-chested Charles Atlas, he raised his right hand, pointed his index finger in the direction of the neighbors and bellowed, "I've got the ol' man!" implying Steve had the son and Gerry, the mother. Everyone stopped in their tracks. The neighbors retreated and went back inside their house. Earl had spoken with the authority of a field general directing his troops. One primordial family unit of man, woman, and child pitted against another.

* * *

THE COURAGE EARL DEVELOPED GROWING UP IN THE inner city during the Roaring Twenties and the Great Depression was displayed at the Battle of Dutch New Guinea in World War II. He dove into treacherous seas to save drowning men. For his bravery, he received the Soldier's Medal for Valor. What left a lasting mark on Stephen was that Earl's heroic efforts occurred three years to the day that Stephen was born.

Stephen didn't know the hidden significance of this synchronicity until I revealed it one night in a dream. In the dream, he realized he was one of the men Earl rescued. In reliving the rescue scene, he could taste the salt water filling his nose and mouth as he sunk below the waves. He blacked out just as Earl grabbed him and pulled him to the surface. Lying on the beach with Earl pressing on his chest, he remembered expelling the water and beginning to breathe. Reliving that moment, he reexperienced how deeply indebted he felt to Earl for risking his own life to save him. Unfortunately, the man died seven months later in another battle. Being raised in the Episcopal Church, he had not believed in reincarnation. But this was so real and offered another explanation of his childhood feelings of wanting to rescue his father from his chronic pain that was the bitter legacy of the war. It would be in the next phase of his life that he would discover that the early church fathers did believe in reincarnation; he would also find out that a Church council in the sixth century had ordered all references to reincarnation to be removed from the Bible. I'll say more about that later.

Nevertheless, I knew that the soul of this soldier returned and was born as Stephen. This source of his sense of responsibility for his father was something Stephen needed to *see* after he first processed his childhood feelings. The past indebtedness and the present life feeling from early childhood melded together into what felt like a red-hot wedge of iron buried in his heart. The indebted soldier Stephen had been now struggled to help the man who had saved him from a watery death.

* * *

JUST FOUR MONTHS FOLLOWING EARL'S DEATH, STEPHEN and his Uncle Vinnie went to the movies to see Sylvester Stallone battle a towering Russian in *Rocky IV*. After the movie, Stephen's Uncle

Vinnie told him, "I never had to fight when your father was with me. If anyone gave me trouble, your father took care of it." Even though Vinnie was two years older than Earl, he was three inches shorter. Both lifted weights as adolescents and weighed in at about the same poundage. Vinnie could take care of himself but didn't have to do so when accompanied by Earl. Needless to say, they were close and that's why Earl went to live with Vinnie after Gerry died.

From his training and experience in working with men in therapy, Stephen gained a deeper understanding of Earl being so quick to defend and protect his older brother. Sure, on the surface, he loved his brother and consequently protected him if someone started a fight with Vinnie. There were signs that Earl harbored a repressed rivalrous rage at Vinnie. Earl's sister Dorothy (Aunt Dot) told Stephen about the early sibling rivalry that took place in the space between brothers. "When they were little, Vinnie teased and picked on your father unmercifully. They were just two years apart. Vinnie had a sharp tongue that could cut you to the quick," she said. Stephen realized Vinnie's aggression toward Earl was because he had been dethroned as the first child. And after Earl, three sisters followed.

When Stephen was little Stevie, Earl read books on increasing your vocabulary with titles such as *Ten Weeks to Words of Power*. Earl would share with his son some of the words he was learning. One such word he shared had an emotional charge for Earl. The word was *invidious* which meant offensively unfair. To illustrate the word, Earl told his little son that his mother would compare him unfavorably to Vinnie when they were little boys. Earl felt it was unfair because Vinnie was older. Earl would tell Stevie how his mother would say, "Why can't you be like Vinnie?"

Considering his father's early emotional history, Stephen could see how his father had projected his anger at his brother onto others. Then, playing out his inner conflict between loving and hating Vinnie,, Earl could step in and protect Vinnie. He was, in effect, unconsciously protecting his brother Vinnie from his own rivalrous and retaliatory rage at how Vinnie had picked on him and at how he was unfairly compared to Vinnie when they were growing up. As Stephen was to see over and over again clinically with other men, Earl externalized his inner conflict in order to resolve it, so that his love would win out over his buried feelings of anger.

Stephen would eventually *see* that a similar emotional dynamic contributed to his glaucoma. This was one of the first times where Freud's unveiling of how most embodied souls harbor conflicts between love and hate toward loved ones. He would also see how his glaucoma fit Freud's definition of a symptom as a "compromise solution" between a wish and a fear.

* * *

WHAT DID HE NEED TO *SEE* TO HEAL HIS EYES? The answer lay hidden in a black hole at the core of his hero-savior complex. The black hole was created by repression of the feelings and desires related to the traumatic childhood memory of Earl screaming in pain while crawling across the floor. It first came up in the session in 1975 that was described in the last chapter. It had surfaced again, but, unlike ten years ago, the memory was accompanied with intense emotion. It was a few weeks after the phone consultation when he was able to cry in front of David Hart for the first time.

It was now 1985 and Stephen was once again describing the scene in a session with David Hart. The session occurred just a few months after Earl died. Stephen was tearfully recalling the scene of that night in 1955 when he was eight years old. Again, he recounted how Earl was screaming because the pain in his back was excruciating and unrelenting. Earl was crawling across the floor to get to the bathroom. Little Stevie knew his father had pain but he had never heard him scream before. Usually, Earl was stoic about it. Pain killers prescribed by the physician were not working. Stevie was watching from his bedroom. He was kneeling on his bed praying to God to take away his Daddy's pain. Gerry was trying to help Earl but Earl was waving her away, refusing her efforts to assist him.

As he was retelling the scene to David Hart, Stephen suddenly had a breakthrough that led to an important insight into guilt. Reliving the moment he saw his father crawling, he blurted out to Earl, "I want to take away your pain because I love you so much! I hate myself for being so small and helpless! I hate myself for not being able to do anything to help you!" It was as if a light went on in the black hole containing guilt. Two things became clear. One was that guilt is really self-hatred in some form. The second was that guilt was grounded in love: he felt guilty and responsible because he loved his father and felt thwarted in his desire to help him. Now he knew what Alice Miller once wrote regarding child-hood guilt: "Guilt implies a power and a freedom" an embodied soul doesn't have as child. From working with children, Stephen tied in his guilt with what he had learned from them; they often blame themselves for things over which they have no control such as parents divorcing. A session he had with an eight-year-old named Billy came to mind. Billy's response to the question, "Why do you think your parent's got a divorce?" Billy answered with, "because I threw paint in the garage."

Stephen knew that children will unconsciously opt for the pain of guilt over the fear of facing the truth that they are helpless and have no control. Children often hate themselves for being small and helpless. Stephen now knew this applied to him.

What a sense of relief and liberation Stephen felt! He now realized that his sense of responsibility and guilt was simply because he loved his father and wanted so badly to take away his pain, and, as a result, hated himself for not being able to help Earl. Somehow guilt being linked to love seemed to unmask guilt. He applied the mantra of compassion to dissolve childhood guilt as he once had used it to remove any regret he had in 1969 when he left college basketball. Silently he told himself, *I know in my heart, I would have done differently if I could have, but I couldn't at the time so I didn't.*

A decade later in 1995, Stephen uncovered the next insight hidden in the black hole of his hero-savior complex. It was a spiritual piece, in a spiritually-based hypnotherapy session. Nonetheless, he could feel that anger was fueled by his love for his father. Nothing more. Nothing less.

∗ ∗ ∗

FINALLY, IN 2005, AFTER ANOTHER DECADE PASSED BY, another insight emerged from the black hole regarding that unnerving night in 1955. It was now fifty years later and he zeroed in on the question, *What do I need to see for my eyes to heal?* This time a new insight emerged. He awoke from a dream whose contents instantly vanished as soon as he opened his eyes. What remained in his awareness was that same clear picture from years earlier; he saw himself as eight-year-old Stevie kneeling on his bed praying. This time, however, he recalled some unexpected, emotionally-charged words that had been sucked into a black hole the moment they were expressed. The words preceded his prayerful pleas to God to take away his daddy's pain. Silently crying out to God, Stevie fearfully and angrily exclaimed, *How could You let me* see *my wishes come true!*

Instantly, upon silently saying these words, Stephen had a flashback to a scene when he was four years old. It was classically Freudian. Four-year-old Stevie was seated on the sofa with his mommy. They were playing checkers. Daddy came in, said nothing to him as if Stevie weren't even there and moved the checkerboard aside, knocking the checkers off their places on the board. With his back toward Stevie, Earl sat down and starting kissing Gerry passionately. Stevie was mad. He had patiently waited for Mommy to finish her chores so that they could have this time together in the afternoon. He was mad at the total disregard Earl had shown him. What did he do? And, more importantly, what did he wish?

Stevie clenched his little fist and pulled it as far back as he could—so far back that he touched the floor behind him. He then swung with all his might and landed his four-year-old fist squarely on Earl's right temple. Earl's head dipped forward as he exclaimed, "What the hell did you do that for?" Almost as soon as he had done it, Stevie was blinded by a flash of light emanating from within and not the environment. A black hole was created in that instant, and it swallowed up what was going on in the space between Earl and Stevie as well as in the space between the surface and depth of Stevie's personality in its early formative years: the blue-print years.

Now as Stephen awoke from the dream, he remembered and recovered what had been swallowed up in the black hole. During the wind up, he had envisioned knocking his father to his knees to to make Earl feel the sense of defeat and humiliation he felt staring at Earl's back. Immediately after he struck Earl, Stevie experienced emotional blindness. He was a small soldier experiencing the emotional blindness and paralysis of combat neurosis.

He was blinded by a flash of fear and guilt. These feelings were accompanied by the thought, *Oh my God what have I done!?* He thought of how Earl could kill him since he was so much bigger. And, when Earl did not punish him, Stevie felt himself consumed with guilt and punished himself. The wish to defeat and humiliate Earl by bringing him to his knees lay buried.

The sentence, *How could You let me* see *my wishes come true!?* revealed how the painful feelings of anger and guilt over that anger can get rapidly repressed by a child. The painful feelings that arise in the space between children and their parents are redirected into the space between surface and depth within children. And within the depths of inner space, these feelings can become so twisted up that they collapse in on themselves and create black holes in a child's awareness.

There were many incidents of Earl being hard on Stevie in the four years from Stevie's round-house right cross to Earl's temple to Earl being brought to his knees. In reaction to his father disregarding him at four to being hard on him in the intervening years, Stevie had wished he could hit him hard enough to bring him down to his knees. Defeated. Beaten. Yes, on the one hand, Stevie had wished to retaliate against his father constantly criticizing him.

As happens in all families, Earl loved and hated his son, and Stevie loved and hated him in return. Within the black holes in

166

Earl's awareness, Stevie symbolized Vinnie. Stevie's birth was the birth of a competitor who threatened to take away Gerry's time, attention, and love as Earl felt Vinnie had done when they were kids.

Whereas Earl was engaged in a sibling rivalry with Vinnie for their mother's affection, Stevie's rivalry was clearly oedipal. When Stephen finally saw this so many years later, he felt embarrassingly stereotypical. What did he need to see? He needed to see how he had suffered the fate of Oedipus in the GreeK myth. In his imagination, he committed the crimes of Oedipus. He killed his father and married his mother. Upon realizing this, he blinded himself. Oedipus literally sticks needles into his eyes and blinds himself. That his glaucoma had its early roots in oedipal feelings he had buried in a black hole was staggering to him. . . .

Therefore, beyond his anger being a reaction to Earl having been hard on him with disparaging criticisms, Stevie also resented Earl as a competitor. Stevie simply wished to bring Earl to his knees because he took away Gerry's time, attention, and love.

There was another surprising element to this insight besides the simple oedipal wishes to defeat Daddy and have Mommy all to himself. This new insight clarified Stevie's anger at God. Stevie had been angry with God for allowing him to *see* his angry wishes come true. It wasn't simply that he was angry that God hadn't eased his daddy's pain; it was that Almighty God Who could have prevented the whole thing since He is All-Powerful let it happen. Stevie was angry at God for acting like a genie in a bottle and fulfilling Stevie's wishes. And, not only did God do that, He made sure Stevie got to *see* his hostile wishes come true in an up close and personal way just a few feet from his bed. He didn't think his wishes leveled his father; he blamed God for allowing his angry wishes but not allowing his wishes to undo them and ease his father's pain. As little Stevie, he might say to God, *You sided with my angry wishes . . . couldn't you have sided with my love wishes instead of leaving me with all the guilt?* Of course, adult Stephen knew these seemingly irreconcilable feelings are easily resolved when seen from my higher and wider perspective. Embodied souls love and hate those closest to them. Those closest mean the most. Working with children, Stephen knew that it all begins with parents: they are a young child's greatest source of joy and frustration. The Grail of an embodied soul's true self includes these authentic feelings of love and hate arising in childhood. Uncovering these feelings and lifting them into the light from the black holes of inner space is part of an embodied soul's quest for the Grail. All that once seemed irreconcilable is reconciled in the elixir of unconditional acceptance and love found in the Grail—the containing cup of consciousness.

* * *

THE LONG ISLAND TRAIN WAS NOW ENTERING THE DARK tunnels leading into New York's Penn Station. The dark tunnels mirrored Stephen's thoughts. He was thinking of how emotional black holes created by repression had contributed to what his first doctor had called advanced-juvenile-variant glaucoma. This diagnosis meant that his glaucoma had an early onset, possibly beginning in his childhood or adolescence. If so, it meant that the condition had gone undetected and untreated for over two decades.

What was too unbearable to be *seen* by little Stevie was totally natural, acceptable, and understandable to adult Stephen. How tragic it was that these *foundation feelings*, as he labeled them in *Love, Stress & Sex*, had to be repressed. Here was another source of his sense of the desire to rescue his father: guilt over his normal childhood wish for love and attention and the natural anger that arises when fulfillment of this simple desire is threatened. He couldn't believe these foundation feelings from his formative years had been buried in a black hole for fifty years. Stepping off the train to catch the next train to Trenton, he slowly shook his head in disbelief. He found it hard to fathom that this seminal scene was still impacting his life like a pebble tossed into a pond sends forth ever-widening ripples.

Stephen now understood what former psychoanalyst Alice Miller meant in her recently released book, *The Body Never Lies*. Examining the lives of famous artists and writers, she demonstrat-

ed how repressed and denied emotional pain originating in childhood can lead to more than unhappiness in adulthood. Disease
and premature death can result from painful childhood emotions
that remain unacknowledged. He then thought of the lives of two
men, discussed by Miller, whose writings he admired. Author
James Joyce and philosopher Frederich Nietzche suffered from not
being able to acknowledge the fear and anger they felt toward their
parents.

It gave Stephen an eerie feeling to think that Joyce went blind.
Nieztche went mad. And he felt a sudden shiver at the thought
that both died prematurely. Stephen had now acknowledged the
early emotional blindness to his childhood pain. Emotional insight
would not instantly restore his severely damaged optic nerves but
at least there was no need to keep unconsciously tensing the small
muscles around the blood vessels and capillaries within his eyes.
Today, when he saw Dr. Jindra, the blood flow test confirmed that
he had a significantly increased blood flow in his eyes.

✳ ✳ ✳

OVER THE NEXT DECADE, STEPHEN WOULD REALIZE HOW the space
between therapist and patient can help an embodied soul find the
Grail. David Hart's acceptance, compassion, and empathy helped
him develop acceptance, compassion, and empathy for himself.
Acceptance, compassion, and empathy sum up the goal of the
Grail of one's true self and the key elements of the way to the goal.
In other words, acceptance, compassion, and empathy for oneself
and others helps get an embodied soul to the Grail and it is found
in the containing cup of accepting awareness embodied in the
image of the Grail. Being able to witness whatever emerged within himself enabled him to be an empathic listening presence for his
patients in the same way David Hart had been for him.

David Hart would appear in dreams long after formal analysis
had ended; his appearance illustrated the powerful impact that
David Hart's listening presence provided. Stephen had internalized
the witnessing and nonjudgmental attitude David Hart had taken

toward whatever dream images, fantasies, and emotions emerged in the container of analytic sessions. When David Hart appeared in dreams as a silent listening presence, Stephen would find himself having deep emotional releases.

The legacy of David Hart was to put Stephen in touch with my silent listening and witnessing presence. David Hart had mirrored my function as a non-intrusive and supportive presence. This listening presence for himself would allow him to illuminate and eliminate on his own the black holes. He was then able to feel and release the hidden hurts of the past.

Eventually, he came to see that good and effective therapy and analysis simply put reunites an embodied soul with his or her sidereal self. Then therapy can help embodied souls achieve the goal for which they came to Earth: to experience the full range of human emotions, and learn to transform the negative ones back into love.

Stephen was now recalling how he found a new impetus to face the twin fears of his childhood: *Daddy's gonna die and Mommy's gonna leave.* Both fears added up to one fear: a fear of abandonment. Pleasing his parents was not so much accomplishing the positive goal of pleasing others and making them smile. Pleasing was to avoid and stave off the negative outcome of being abandoned. He had uncovered the layers of feeling related to his father. But now he had to explore the scary depths of the black hole related to his mother.

As I mentioned earlier, finding the Grail for any embodied soul meant uncovering and recovering one's true and real reactions from those early years of life. For Stephen, this meant also recalling what must have happened in the space between him and his mother. The answer came in a dream.

* * *

IN THE DREAM, STEPHEN WAS SEATED ACROSS FROM David Hart in an ice-cream parlor. He was about to discuss Annie, a twenty-year-old college student who was in therapy for an eating disorder. The next thing he knew, he was a small child seated somewhere in the dark. As this small child, he cried out, "Mommy, don't leave me! I won't be bad! I'll be good!" The emotion was so intense he woke himself up. There were tears in his eyes as there had been in the dream. He realized that he was reexperiencing the day his mother had taken him to nursery school for the first time.

He remembered crying and then sniffling all day. He recalled being inconsolable. He hated himself for not being able to stop sniffling after lunch when the young, pretty teacher was reading to the children. Even with the warm sunshine streaming into the room, four-year-old Stevie still felt the residue of the cold darkness of the morning when Mommy left him in this strange place. The sunshine and the warmth and kindness of this pretty teacher with long reddish-brown hair made the little room even cozier. He hated how he was unable to be soothed by her warm smile and the soft, reassuring touch of her hand on his little shoulder.

He was sure he was annoying everyone. From before seven in the morning until after five in the evening, he was crying. It was only when he saw his mother returning to pick him up that he finally stopped.

Actually, Stephen did not recall until shortly before Gerry died what actually happened that morning. Gerry told him, "You were putting up such a fuss about having to go to nursery school until finally, I had had it. I reached over and backhanded you so hard you flipped into the backseat." Gerry told Stephen this in a mat-ter-of-fact way. No sign of remorse. She did say that she felt she and Earl had been "too strict" since he was "such a good kid, per-haps, too good." She had said this at the last dinner he had with her before she died five days later.

As an interesting aside, the next session with Annie, the female patient he started to discuss in the dream, he asked her if she had gone to nursery school. (He did not tell her why he asked.) "Oh, yes!" she exclaimed. "When my mother left me off the first time, I cried all day. No one could console me, and I didn't stop until my mother came to pick me up." During the spiritual phase of his life, he would see this as simply another example of how all souls are connected. It was just one of many examples of how all embodied souls are here on Earth to help each other learn to love and forgive.

His dream illuminated one source of his fear of Gerry leaving when he was little. But what had he concluded from the experience? Don't express how you feel. Don't protest. Don't disagree. Don't displease others. This set up a pattern of pleasing others at the expense of his own desires. Of course, he was not even conscious of denying his own needs apart from the primary need to please which was really driven by a fear of being abandoned.

Reflecting on the dream, he recalled the story of *Little Bear* that Gerry used to tell him when he was between two and three years old. The story had a deep and lasting impact on him by feeding into the black hole containing his fear of abandonment. In a nutshell, Little Bear kept saying no to his mother's request to do his various chores. So later in the story as night approaches, the Good Fairy decides to teach him a lesson. She transports him deep into the forest. Darkness fell and he was getting cold, scared, and hungry. When the other animals attempted to help him by asking him if he was lost, all he could say was a surly, "No!" Inside he desperately wanted to say yes. He grew colder and hungrier but kept driving away any help by saying no to all attempts to help him.

Finally, the Good Fairy returns him to his backyard. He saw his mother standing in the lighted doorway. Stephen had a vague recollection of how Gerry ended the story with the words, "He ran as fast as his little legs would carry him, and when he reached his mother, he cried out, 'Mommy, I'll never say no again!'" Gerry told Stephen, "You always cried and cried at the end of the story."

When Stephen told the story to David Hart after Gerry died, he was surprised at how the story elicited a strong sympathetic response that brought tears to Stephen's eyes. "What a harsh thing to do to a little child putting up a protest over doing his chores." David Hart's comment had for the first time allowed Stephen to feel empathy for the scared little boy he once was. Prior to that session, Stephen had always laughed about the story. But now he was in touch with the deep feeling of fear expressed in the dream, "Mommy don't leave me! I won't be bad! I'll be good!" Deeply buried in a black hole of inner space. And this fear of abandonment exerted a strong gravitational pull on his life.

Just before Gerry died, Stephen had discovered *The Drama of the Gifted Child* by Alice Miller. The subtitle included the words, *The Search for the True Self*. Below is an excerpt from *Words Become Flesh* of what Stephen had to say about the book and its impact on him. What is missing is the fact that the part of her book which he read that moved him to tears was read just days before his mother died.

"The child learns to develop an acute sensitivity to the needs of the mother or to both parents. These children become their mother's confidantes. And when they grow up they may become analysts or therapists." The part where I cried, probably because I felt seen and understood, was when Miller said something to the effect that: *Who else without a history of having killed themselves to please their parents would want to pursue such a strange profession? Who else would muster sufficient interest to spend the whole day searching for the signals coming from the unconscious of others?*

The very thing that makes for an excellent therapist contained the "narcissistic disturbance" [lack of self-esteem] found in candidates for psychoanalytic training. Miller later extended her findings to the profile of therapists in general.

Now Stephen saw into the depths of the black hole that drew him to psychology. He now knew the deeper source of why he became a clinical psychologist, and when he did, he cried. The moment he read this passage and began to tear up, he spontaneously pictured his mother and then his father. It was at this moment when he imagined speaking directly to both of them. From the buried pain of the eight-year-old in him that he had just unearthed, he expressed his sadness and released his guilt and sense of responsibility for his parents' happiness. "Mommy, I'm sorry you're unhappy, but it's not my fault! Daddy, I'm sorry you're in pain, but it's not my fault!" And then from the adult Stephen, he proclaimed, "I now realize that I am responsible for my own happiness and you are responsible for your happiness." It was at this very moment that he began to think of ways to help others gain emotional insight into their personal emotional history much more quickly than he had been able to do.

* * *

IN ORDER TO MAKE IT EASIER TO ACCESS AND EXPRESS the hidden hurts of early childhood, Stephen developed what he called the *look through technique.* Alice Miller had helped him *see* and *feel* how these early hurts will continue to wreak havoc on adult happiness. Looking back over his life and the lives of his patients, he saw one continual threat to happiness: the *compulsion to repeat.* The look through technique was a way to help people uncover and feel the painful *foundation feelings* of childhood that will just keep coming up in disguised form in current relationships at home or work. It came to him when in the presence of his wife one morning at breakfast at the end of the first year of graduate school.

He and his wife rarely saw each other. She worked at night when he was home, and he was in class during the day when she was home. He had just finished final exams for the semester. As he began to express his frustration over the first year, he found himself filled with strong emotion as he said with some surprising intensity, "I needed you to be there."

Almost as soon as he said the words, he spontaneously looked through his wife and saw his mother standing in the kitchen when he was a toddler. He felt how the words were *really* meant for his mother, and only partially for his wife. He was able to see how he was unconsciously wanting his wife to make up for what was missing in the toddler phase of his life. Sure he was in a kind of toddler phase; he was in transition from teaching high school to becoming a psychologist. He was a toddler in the sense that he was in his first year of graduate school, taking his first steps toward getting trained in a new profession.

Looking through the present to open the door to the past, he was able to empathize with his wife feeling he was just as emotionally unavailable to her since he was so caught up in his studies. Looking through to feel the repressed frustration from childhood,

174

he was able to drain the intense pain from early childhood. This paved the way for a more loving sharing of their mutual frustration. Steps could then be taken to rectify the situation rather than cast blame at each other.

Seven years later, Stephen was in his private practice working with a couple in marital therapy. This was the first time he used the look through technique with a patient. Certainly, he had helped people gain insight into how their past was interfering with their present happiness. More specifically, he often helped patients uncover how their current conflicting feelings about a spouse or boss may be related to unresolved feelings about a mother or father.

The difference with the look through technique was that he would encourage patients to *intensify* their feelings about someone in their current life. This had the effect to weaken their defenses against feeling childhood pain. People had no problem expressing their current unhappiness with spouses or bosses. As soon as patients were fully feeling their present upset, he would ask them to look through to the past. The intensity of their feelings burst through the barrier to feeling buried upsets from childhood.

In this marital session with Lois and Cliff, he heard Lois scream, "You're never there for me!" Upon hearing this, Stephen asked Lois to look through Cliff and see who it was in her family that she could say those words to when she was growing up. She saw both her mother and father. Once she made this connection, the intensity of her anger at Cliff lessened some. Looking through Cliff helped her drain the early pain burdening her expectations of her husband. She needed Cliff to be more emotionally available but she could express her upset more lovingly. Cliff was also better able to empathize with his wife's concern when he heard and saw how she had not had anyone there for her when she was a little girl.

The look through technique enabled Stephen to help patients cut through current pain that kept being repeated in relationships. He came to call the effects of the compulsion to repeat, *repeated relationships stress.*

It was as if there were an emotionally injured child in adults who sought every opportunity to tell his or her story. The story was from the embodied soul's early experiences as a child growing up. The early experiences of hurt were disguised by being clothed in the details of current circumstances.

In almost all human interactions, Stephen saw an inner play being reenacted. Even though the roles assigned were always the same, the players were new. The persecuting parent of the past resurfaced as the critical spouse or boss. At other times, the roles were reversed. A victimized child now became a victimizing adult: doing to others what was done to him or her as a small and vulnerable child. The look through technique was a way to demonstrate to people how they were reenacting the unhappiness of the past in the present. By fully feeling and expressing their repeated relationship stress, embodied souls could break free of the prison of past hurts. Hidden hurst could be felt and released.

What people were saying to their spouse or boss or even their children was something they had been unable to feel and express to the early people in their lives: parents, siblings, teachers, and so forth. Stephen learned to hear these cries of the hurt child seeking disguised expression in the language of the adult. "You never listen. You always ignore me. You don't see my gifts. You always put me down."

In session after session, Stephen would encourage expression of the repressed feelings from early childhood and adolescence. "Now as you are feeling this hurt and anger, look through_____(the current person) and see who it is in your family when you were growing up that you could say those same or similar words to. Now picture this person and say the words to him or her." Hidden hurts buried in black holes were driving embodied souls to repeat the unhappiness of their childhood until uncovered and released. Instead of feeling like a powerless five-year-old in an adult body, an embodied soul could find the power to articulate their desires fully and effectively. Using the look through technique helped embodied souls find the power to defeat their inner demons of the past.

* * *

ATTAINING INNER FREEDOM IN THE SAFE SPACE BETWEEN therapist and patient was one thing. But maintaining the freedom to be and to express one's true self in the space between the embodied souls born into the same family was another thing altogether.

He saw so many individuals trapped in dissatisfying roles originally assigned to them in their families. Some of these are the scapegoat, the overburdened oldest or only child, the irresponsible youngest, the clown, and the hero, to name a few. No matter how deeply rooted an embodied soul's emotional problems, he or she can get free of the grip of the past. One simply has to change what one *says* or *does* in interactions with family members.

During his post-doctoral studies, Stephen came across a little-known paper by Dr. Murray Bowen, considered by many to be the father of family therapy. The paper was entitled, *Toward a Differentiation of Self in One's Family*. Stephen found the tips for talking to family members useful for his visits with Gerry and Earl. He also taught the tips to patients, telling them, "You can greatly accelerate your therapy by using these guidelines for communicating with your parents and siblings." Bowen recommended defining what he called an "I" position. The important thing was to fill the space between you and your individual family members by *stating* and *defining* your thoughts, feelings, and opinions. "I feel . . . I think . . . I believe. . . ." By simply stating and defining who you are and what you feel, think, and believe. This is your "I" position.

You avoid *pleading* or *attacking* statements. "You never hear me . . . Why can't you understand me . . . You are wrong. . . ." You don't plead for them to agree with your position, nor do you attack and put down their position to prove you are right.

Essentially, you give up seeking the approval and validation of your parents and siblings. And you also avoid getting caught in family triangles, especially the one involving you and your parents. When one parent complains about the other, you can politely listen. But you do not, as Stephen had in the past, intervene on behalf of the complaining parent and attempt to influence the other parent. You encourage the complaining parent to talk directly to the other parent. In effect, these communication strategies helped individuals break free of the tendency to fill the space between themselves and their family members with endless arguments.

Bowen emphasized how hard it is to stay differentiated from the old unproductive roles assigned in families. He himself shared how he was happy if he could stay differentiated for a few hours on any given visit.

Still, the enviable goal was to stay emotionally differentiated and be prepared for family members to gang up on you and call you "mad" or "bad." Bowen warned that breaking free of your role would incur the wrath of family members. For example, Stephen coached a number of patients who had been assigned the role of scapegoat; their role was to be the brunt of the family's jokes, teasing, and sarcasm. This was especially challenging because often the individual in this role was used to setting himself or herself up to get attention that way. These individuals needed to replace the old role with stating and defining a new role, an "I" position. This new role and definition of yourself reveals who you are in relation to other family members.

For Stephen, the attempt to differentiate a new self was narrowed down to not rescuing Gerry from her unhappiness with Earl and vice versa. No longer would he get caught in the old role of rescuing. He stopped himself from getting caught in the middle of the space between Earl and Gerry. Bowen explained how couples form a triangle to shift the tension in their relationship onto a child or some other third party such as a neighbor or extended family member. This had the effect of reducing the tension building up like steam in a tea kettle. Focusing on a common enemy brought them together. Stephen saw the idea played out in those old science fiction films when he was growing up in the 1950s. Russia and the USA stopped being enemies and joined forces to battle alien invaders from outer space.

Even with his thorough understanding of Bowen's concepts and tips, Stephen could still get caught up in trying to rescue Earl from his negative outlook on life and others. If he wasn't careful,

Stephen would get caught up in arguing with Earl to change his attitude. One time during a Christmas visit, Stephen gave Earl a set of relaxation tapes. They were recorded by Dr. Charles Stroebel, one of Stephen's mentors. Stroebel's work on the quieting reflex would become a launching point for Stephen's books on ways to effectively manage stress. Earl was resistant to using the tapes.

Finally, Stephen gave up as he prepared to leave for the airport. He hugged Earl and Gerry good-bye. On the plane, he remembered what Bowen had said about giving up the need to change one's parents. You simply *redirect* the energy you would use to change you parent into changing yourself. He did this on the plane. As soon as he unlocked the door to his apartment in Connecticut an amazing thing happened. The phone was ringing and when he answered it he heard Earl's voice saying that he had started using the tapes. He thought they were great.

Immediately, Stephen recognized the fact that it was only after he had given up the need to rescue and change his father that his father was free to change. Later on, this would be but one example of slaying the dragon of dependency. Without realizing it yet, he had inwardly affirmed, "I AM not dependent on you feeling good and being at peace for me to feel good and be at peace. I have everything I need within myself to feel good and be at peace."

Stephen was starting to see that there is a need for the embodied soul to hear with the heart and affirm his or her inner freedom to feel good and be at peace and thereby allow others that freedom.

∗ ∗ ∗

NOT LONG AFTER HIS PARENTS HAD DIED, STEPHEN HAD a tightness in his throat. He felt it had an emotional source but he was unable to discern what it was. He went to sleep one night, asking for a dream to shed light on this subtle clenching. He dreamt that he was on a desert landscape set somewhere in the American Southwest. It was night and far from any signs of civilization. An unknown man was kneeling by a fire. He was about to place in the fire a pre-Columbian clay sculpture of a man with his hands raised to the starry heavens. The clay was still wet and as the man started to put the sculpture in the fire, Stephen gasped in fear that the wet clay would extinguish the fire. Instead, Stephen was astonished to see that the fire was intensified and, with the force of a blowtorch, flames shot up through the feet into the legs and torso and out of the mouth of the clay man.

When Stephen awoke, I gave him a clue as to the meaning of the dream: *matter does not extinguish spirit.* As long as embodied souls choose to express rather than repress their true feelings then the inner fire of their spirit will not be extinguished by the stress of everyday life. Instead, their spirit will shine through, and they will experience the joy of inner freedom. This is the joy that comes from expressing the Grail of their true self in and through the material existence of everyday life.

At first, Stephen did not realize that his fearful gasp in the dream reflected a resistance to being fully embodied, that is, fully committed to life. He was holding back from being fully embodied. His soul was holding back from being rooted in relationship, whether the relationship was with a beloved, friends, or with a specific time and place. Up until then, he had moved about a lot, living in many different places before, during, and after his training.

Now he had a mortgage. He had settled down in the small New England town where he had his private practice. He did not realize it, but, underlying his fear of being fully embodied was another fear. It was a fear that being fully in the body meant he would eventually have to die as his parents had. It was as if he had the silly idea that if I don't fully inhabit my body and experiences on Earth then I can avoid dying. Embodiment equalled death until his encounters with me helped him realize that the soul does not die.

As an interesting aside, it was seventeen years later when he was fascinated to find confirmation of his interpretation of his dream as being related to the soul becoming embodied. Without him knowing it, I led him to a Sufi story when he was writing about his dream in *A Matter of Love.* The lovely little story describes the process by which a soul becomes embodied.

God sent the individual soul down to the material world, and

immersed it in each of the four elements of creation. First it
passed through water and became wet; then it passed through
earth and became clay, and finally it passed through fire and
became baked clay. Thus the nonmaterial soul passed through
all the basic material elements that generate the material world,
and the soul of light became embedded in a pot of clay—the
physical body.

Like this story, the dream signalled an initiation process whereby
Stephen was choosing true self-expression over true self-repression.

He was beginning to find the Grail of his true self hidden within the black hole of his *assumed* identity as his parents' hero-savior
son. He began to develop a technique to help himself and his
patients choose expression over repression. Stephen loved visualizing the image of screen icon Anthony Quinn in his role as Zorba
dancing on the beach at the end of the film *Zorba the Greek*.
Earlier in the film, Zorba proclaims, "They say that age kills the
fire inside. That's a pack of lies! I have enough fire in me to devour
the world!" To Stephen, these words and the image of Zorba dancing on the beach became the symbol of true Self-expression.
Zorba's passionate proclamation became Stephen's motto as an
aging Baby Boomer:

Borrowing from Bowen's guidelines for true Self-defining
communication, Stephen developed a technique he called the left
hand/right hand technique. Before describing this technique, I
want to share with you the moment of its inception. It came to
him during a conversation with his wife just months after Earl had
died and just weeks after the first anniversary of Gerry's death. He
was attending a weekend conference on Psychoanalytic Self
Psychology. All day he heard analysts talking about a new, more
human and positive paradigm for understanding human beings
and for doing therapy and analysis. It was to replace the mechanis-
tic and negative view found in traditional psychoanalysis. Stephen
was excited by what each presenter had to say; what they said confirmed what he was finding in his work with people. He was eager
to share what he was learning with his wife who was also a therapist.

The analysts of the old paradigm would share nothing of themselves in a session. His wife had told Stephen of her experience with such an analyst. She would excitedly ask her analyst if he had seen a particular movie that really touched her. Whether he did or not, and sometimes she suspected he had, he would invariably say no. Then the focus would be on her reaction to the film. That is where the focus should be for the new or old paradigm. However, in the new paradigm, the analyst would admit if he or she had seen the movie or not, and then the analyst would be sure to place the focus back onto the patient's feelings. Other than this one example, he was like a fish out of water gasping for air as he tried to explain the sustaining sea of ideas he had been immersed in all day. Not able to adequately describe the significant differences, Stephen stammered when he tried convey what he was so excited about.

Consequently, his wife said something to the effect that the new paradigm didn't sound all that much different. At that moment, Stephen struggled with what felt like a wet blanket being tossed upon the fire of his excitement. Contrary to his tendency to drop the discussion, he decided to not minimize the differences he had just heard for over eight hours. Opening the palm of his left hand, he agreed that, on the one hand, it may seem that there is no real difference between the new and the old paradigm. Then, gesturing with his right hand, he emphatically affirmed that, indeed, there were big differences. Stephen felt good. He had addressed both his desire to please both the other person, in this instance, Kathy, and himself.

On the one hand (left hand), he had acknowledged his desire to stay connected to the other person (Kathy) and make room for her thoughts and feelings. On the other hand, he fully expressed his excitement and thoughts. In this way, he could learn to express his feelings and desires apart from the desire to preserve harmony in his relationship to others. In the spiritual phase of his life, he would refine this technique and add two others to help himself and others be more effective in handling general stress and the stress of conflict.

In essence, he would strive to teach people how to *express* and not *repress* or *aggress* their *stress*. And he was to say these very words on national television and radio shortly after the tragedy of September 11, 2001 in an attempt to help people begin to cope with the horrific event.

* * *

THE SUN WAS SETTING AS THE TRAIN LEFT NEW YORK for Trenton. Stephen realized that underlying all of his seeking in the halls of academia and beyond, in exploring the space between surface and depth in himself and his patients, he realized he was seeking the Grail. In this phase of his life, he interpreted the Grail psychologically as his true Self. Ironically, in the next phase of his life, he would discover the true spiritual depths of the Grail was to be found in the historical references to the Holy Grail which was reflected in his Christian religious roots in the Episcopal Church.

Concretely and historically, the Grail was the Holy Grail, the cup used by Jesus at the Last Supper with his disciples the night before he was crucified. It became the basis of Holy Communion in the Christian Church. The Holy Grail became synonymous with his innermost heart. In recounting his time with the Maya and his media appearances in *A Matter of Love*, he coined the phrase "the Holy Grail of my heart" to describe the goal of his psychological and spiritual growth.

He saw the Grail as a symbol of the open, non-grasping heart containing the light of pure love. In a sense, for any embodied soul, finding the Holy Grail is finding me, the radiant star of his or her divine sidereal self. But it is more than that. It is not only finding me, it is the *conscious* reunion of the transcendent spirit and embodied soul. It is an atonement in the sense of being a return to the joyful awareness of the original at-one-ment of spirit and soul.

Stephen now understood what Jung meant when he shared his clinical observation that patients later in life were never cured of their neurosis unless they returned to their religious roots. For

Stephen, this meant returning home to a deeper understanding of what he knew in his heart as a child: "God is love; and he that dwelleth in love dwelleth in God and God in him" (1 John 4:16). It was in this next phase of his life that extraordinary events in unusual settings led him home spiritually. Unexpectedly, he would rediscover his religious roots in strange places. The first occurred in his encounter with an Asian-based ancient healing tradition. The next would happen in Tikal, Guatemala when he was with the Mayan shamans. In *A Matter of Love*, he wrote about that magical time.

The obstacles on the spiritual path to freedom, peace, and unconditional happiness were gradually being identified and removed. I was proceeding as a *practical mystic*. No matter what sacred tradition the guiding messages came from, I remained open to them. Like the knights of King Arthur, I was following the signs. And I was receiving daily confirmation that I was on the path leading to the true treasure: the Holy Grail of my heart.

III

The Space Between
Heaven & Earth

Any mind which accepts its power completely and can focus thought can do profound things . . . (*Infinite Mind*)

—Valerie V. Hunt

Verily, verily, I say unto you, He that believeth on* me, the works that I do, he shall do, and greater works than these because I go to the Father. And whatsoever you shall ask in my name, I will do that the Father is glorified in the Son (John 14:12-13).

—Jesus the Christ

Truly I say to you, whoever says to this mountain, 'Be taken up and cast into the sea!' and does not doubt in his heart but believes what he says is going to happen, it shall be granted him. Therefore, all things for which you pray and ask, believe that you have received them and they shall be granted you (Mark 11:23-24).

—Jesus the Christ

* Note: A possible significance of the use of *on* instead of *in* will be discussed in chapter 8.

Seven

Gifts, Signs & Wonders

OCTOBER 1995

ORION REPLACES THE THREE STARS THAT COMPRISED the summer triangle on October 29th. In pre-industrial times, this date would herald the start of winter. By these standards from a bygone era, winter was underway, and November's Frost Moon was the celestial signal of the start of winter. It was now dark outside the train. The sun had set and the moon was low on the horizon and beginning its ascent.

This newly learned bit of astronomy and history regarding October 29th startled Stephen. *How incredible!* he thought, while watching the parade of passing lights as the train rumbled by the small towns on its route. That this date used to mark the start of winter was not known to Stephen when he wrote about the seasons of his soul in the passage below from *Words Become Flesh*.

> The snow stopped and the pale winter sun shining in the late-afternoon sky reminded me of the round, paper-thin communion wafer. Something about the pale light of the winter sun has always stirred within me a strange, sweet nostalgia. But why? My reflections returned to a quaint little art gallery in Woodstock, Vermont. Four particular paintings fascinated me with their subtle contrast of the way the light of the sun changes with each season.
>
> Each painting was of the same scene. A cluster of evergreens. The only difference distinguishing the paintings from one

another was the quality of the light. Each painting depicted the light of a particular season. This fact was reflected in their titles: Winter Light, Spring Light, Summer Light, and Autumn Light. . . . Still, why did these paintings, especially Winter Light, move me?

Then it hit me: the light of the inner sun of our soul mirrors the ever-changing sunlight of each passing season. As we journey through the seasons of our soul, the light of our soul changes. The soft light of spring, ever growing in its intensity, comes first. Then comes the harsh blinding light of summer. The harsh light of summer is followed by the softer waning light of autumn. Finally, comes the softest light of all, the pale light of the wan winter wafer.

Just what does this mean for our inner life and the growth of our soul? To me, it means that the young soul begins with a soft gaze toward others. A child can be so innocent and purely loving and accepting and so can the young soul. In summer, our capacity to love is tested. As we are hurt and betrayed, we may become cynical. Our gaze may take on the relentless harshness of the summer sun. We look at things straight on with a clarity that seeks out the flaws of others. We can burn them with our gaze. Or, in seeing things clearly, can we find it in our heart to be forgiving and accepting? If so, we can move on to develop the more accepting gaze of autumn.

The autumn sun shines equally on all the various colors of the changing leaves. Summer's green gradually gives way to reds, oranges, yellows, golds, and browns. Likewise, in autumn, our soul can gaze upon all the colors of humanity with an appreciative eye.

Finally, if we are able to move into winter, we can be as accepting as the pale winter sun; it softly shines on the all-embracing snow. Under the glistening white blanket, the seemly and the unseemly—dead leaves and grass, barren branches, the junk in people's backyards—are equally embraced. No harsh judgment.

Stephen didn't know it but he was referring to the stages of spiritual growth embodied souls go through. It was the beginning of Stephen becoming more conscious of me. You could say it was the beginning of returning home to his spiritual, and religious roots in the true sense of the original meaning of the Latin word *religio,* to link back to God. In a way, it was a returning home, not unlike the biblical parable of the prodigal son's return home. After this life-changing experience, he received other spiritual gifts. One was an ability to be granted occasional glimpses into the spirit realm. From his own direct experience, Stephen would begin to discover the truth of what he learned in Sunday School: angels and demons exist. He also learned that church rituals were not empty recitations. They mattered.

∗ ∗ ∗

ON OCTOBER 29, 1995 AS THE DIGITAL CLOCK READ 3:33 A.M., Stephen (he knew it was around 3:00) had a life-changing spiritual experience—the specific details of which we will delve into later in this chapter. This mystical event marked the very moment Stephen entered what he called the winter of his soul.

Stephen was staying at a seaside inn, a bed and breakfast set right on the craggy coast of Rockport, Massachusetts. Before drifting off to sleep, Stephen could hear the waves splashing against the rocks below. Later that night, he had a profound experience that left him with an ability to transmit a healing energy. The hot hands that once scored baskets in high school, college, and briefly as a professional, were now able to relieve the suffering of people and animals near or far.

Looking back now, he recalled how the view from his room on the second floor of the inn was significant. By day, the room afforded a picturesque view of the ocean and Thatcher's Island with its two lighthouses. At night, he could see the beacons of light flashing to ships at sea returning to port. With the benefit of hindsight, Stephen could now see how the lighthouses symbolized the turning point in his life. The lighthouse as a symbol provided a clue for understanding the gift of healing he had received that night. He prayed for insight and clarification. Then he heard me speaking as the still small voice within him saying, *Turn on the television.* When he did, he saw that there was a children's show on and it was providing information about lighthouses. There was actor LaVar Burton from the famous television mini-series *Roots*. LaVar had just finished asking the lighthouse keeper a question.

Stephen was about to change the channel since he was not seeing how this show might be an answer to his prayer. At the very moment that he started to switch to another station, he heard the lighthouse keeper say, "The lighthouse lamp is composed of the bulb and the lens, and the lens does all the work."

Instantly, he saw his role as a healer. He was a beacon of light, a lens for the ever-shining light of God's love. Like the bulb, the light of God's love continually shines. The lens, on the other hand, directs the healing light. He recalled wondering, *What then is the healer's job as a lens? What are the qualities a lens can have? It can be clear or unclear because it is covered with dust and dirt. A lens can be thick or thin.* He thought of the telescope he had as a child. The lens used to see the moon had to be replaced by a more powerful lens in order to see the rings of Saturn. He also remembered thinking of how, without the aid of a lens, the Andromeda Galaxy, even though immense, was just a wisp of light to stargazers.

Then he recalled how he had come to the realization that a lens can vary in how clear and powerful it is in its ability to magnify the light coming from God. Being clear meant being pure in the motive to relieve suffering. It was not to be glorified as a healer. He reasoned that to be clear as a lens was to keep it clear in one's own mind that God performs the healing. Jesus said it this way, "Verily, Verily I say unto you, of mine own self, I can do nothing. It is the Father within me, he doeth the works" (John 5:19).

Stephen saw his role was that of a revolving lens of the lighthouse lamp. He was to direct the almighty healing energy of God's light of divine love to those lost in the dark night of pain and suffering.

Now in retrospect, one lighthouse could be said to represent his healing role as a psychotherapist; he helped people find their way out of emotional pain and suffering. The other lighthouse might be seen as a symbol of an ability to help people near or far find healing and relief from physical and emotional suffering.

* * *

OCTOBER 29TH HAD ANOTHER SIGNIFICANCE: IT WAS HIS father's birthday. Earl had been dead for ten years. Stephen suspected there was something symbolic about the day he received the ability to perform healings being his father's birthday. Earl had been a spiritual seeker. One day, Earl crumpled up his last pack of Camels which still contained some cigarettes. Camels were an unfiltered, heavy-duty cigarette. Straight tobacco. Very addictive. With the crumpled pack in his hands, he prayed to God the Father for help. He told his young son how he said a prayer that involved surrendering his will to God's will. By turning to God as his Heavenly Father, Earl successfully went cold turkey after smoking nearly a pack of Camels a day for close to thirty years. This was quite a feat and an important lesson for Stevie since Earl used prayer power. Not will power.

Stephen now thought of the dream Earl related to him following the prayer for the strength to quit smoking. In his dream, Earl went into the attic of their small ranch house and found that it was huge and had many rooms. It was as if it were a large mansion. After discussing the dream, Earl made reference to the biblical passage in which Jesus said, "In my Father's house there are many rooms" (John 14:2). Stephen could still see Earl running his fingers through his thick black hair as he described the dream and the words of Jesus with a sense of awe.

There was also Earl's openness to the mysteries of life and his belief in forces beyond human understanding. When the well ran dry and Earl realized a new well needed to be drilled, he investigated ways to determine where to drill into the ground to find a steady flow of water. He discovered dowsing and met men who demonstrated the ancient art to him. Stephen smiled as he remembered the day Earl took into his hands a wish-bone-shaped set of branches from the cherry tree in their backyard. He began walking around with one branch in each hand; the short branch where the two branches were joined was pointing toward the sky. Earl was dowsing for water. He had walked over a good-sized area of lawn when the short branch suddenly shifted from aiming at the sky to aiming at the ground beneath Earl's feet. The bark twisted off as the branch in each hand moved forcefully. The dark bark of the cherry tree peeled off and fell to the ground forming rings that reminded Stevie of rings of peeled potato skins.

When the twisting stopped, the short center branch pointed toward the ground. That was where the well-digger drilled and sure enough he found an excellent source of water eighty feet below the surface. Unlike the old four-foot-in-diameter well that was twenty-five feet deep, this one-foot-in-diameter well never ran dry. Holding up the dowsing rod of branches from the cherry tree, Earl smiled at his ten-year-old son and quoted from John 15:5, saying: "Jesus said, 'I am the vine; you are the branches.'"

Then, handing Stevie the water-seeking branches, Earl added, "And Jesus also tells us that the branches are where fruits grow." It now seemed to Stephen that Earl's enigmatic smile suggested that he believed his son was getting the point: a man's power comes from being aligned with God. Earl rarely went to church with his wife and son, but he would quote the Bible from time to time. Then again, he would quote philosophers: Plato, Aristotle, and Epictetus were among his favorites. Sometimes he would recite a verse of poetry as well.

One of his favorite verses came from the Persian poet Omar Khayyam. Stephen fondly remembered Earl would display a touch of drama as he held his finger in the air while saying, "The moving finger writes and having writ moves on. Not all thy piety nor wit shall lure it back to cancel half a line, nor all thy tears wash out a word of it." When he heard his father recite this to him, he would think, *I guess he means there's no sense crying over spilt milk.*

The other verse Stephen recalled was either by an unknown author or one Stephen had simply forgotten. "I sit on a seat by the side of the road where the race of men go by. Some are weak. Some are strong and so am I. Why should I sit in a seat by the side of the road and cast the cynic's ban? Why not sit in a seat by the side of the road and be a friend of man?" Stephen loved how this little verse seemed to sum up the need to accept our common humanity.

How curious it was to Stephen that he had received a gift from his Heavenly Father on the birthday of his earthly father. But it was not until he met the Christian minister fresh from Scotland that Stephen would gain a deeper understanding of what happened on that night in Rockport. In retrospect, October 29th was, in effect, his *spiritual birthday*. And it was the day he took his first step on the snow-covered path of the winter of his soul and it marked the beginning of his spiritual awakening.

* * *

THREE YEARS LATER, STEPHEN MET AN ADORABLE ELDERLY couple: a ruddy-faced Protestant minister and his wife on a beautiful and breezy autumn afternoon. The meeting took place aboard a sight-seeing schooner out of Camden, Maine. The couple had recently moved to New England from Scotland where they both were born, raised, and spent the bulk of their adult lives.

Stephen felt a subtle inner prompting from me to share with the minister and his wife what happened in that inn off the rocky coast of Rockport, Massachusetts on October 29, 1995. He found it interesting that the schooner was just now sailing past the harbor of another Rockport: Rockport, Maine. For it was then that he felt me nudge him to address this lovely couple.

In talking with the couple, Stephen described in detail what happened that night. He began by telling them that on the afternoon of October 27, 1995, he was in a bookstore in Salem, Massachusetts. There he met Mercedes, a lovely woman originally from Guatemala. She had shiny black hair and mocha-colored skin. Her coloring contrasted with the loose-fitting, pure-white dress she wore with a matching scarf tied around her head. A dozen years later, Stephen would discover that in Spanish the name Mercedes is related to the word mercy and is the name given to *Virgen de la Merced* (the Virgin Mary). This proved to be very significant, given what was going to happen. Mercedes would be, in some sense, the Virgin Mother of the miraculous events about to happen in

Stephen's life.

Standing next to her in line at a cash register, he felt that she had a gentle angelic presence. She was purchasing a book on the ancient Tibetan and Japanese healing art of Reiki. He had heard of Reiki and he mentioned to the couple that all he really knew for sure was the Japanese word translated as universal (rei) life-force energy (ki).

Stephen told the couple how he struck up a conversation with Mercedes. She told him that on that very weekend she was teaching an intensive Reiki class. It involved all three levels: beginning, intermediate, and advanced. The level students reached that weekend depended on their readiness to advance. Some would only take the beginning level whereas others would go on to intermediate. A few would proceed to the advanced level of Reiki Master. He told the couple how he found the idea of the class interesting but he did not see how it would fit in with his work as a psychologist doing psychotherapy. That night, despite his interest in the class, he went to sleep deciding that he would not attend.

Then he told the couple that he was awakened on five different occasions by a purple light the size and shape of a reddish-purple plum pulsating in between his eyes and slightly above eye level. He felt it was somehow both inside and outside. At the time, he did not realize that the light was in the place where inner and outer space converge.

He related how he kept thinking that, on the one hand, purple was a positive spiritual color. But each time he focused on the color and thought of its as a positive color, it seemed to seize him from head to toe by radiating an energy throughout his body. Feeling as if he were almost being possessed by the light, he kept commanding it to leave. Each time, it would leave, only to return later after he had gone back to sleep. After he got up on Saturday morning, he decided that he should talk to Mercedes and find out what she thought about the purple light. She took it as a sign that he should take the class. So he did.

Stephen then told the couple the surprising thing that happened on Saturday afternoon. When he did the meditation that involved meeting his Reiki Master Guide, he was stunned by *who* appeared.

He told the couple, "In my meditation, I saw a large white, classical-style temple with a gold dome and a large thick gold door. When I opened the thick (it appeared to be a foot wide in thickness) gold door, I saw Jesus standing before me in a white robe. Instantly, I dropped to one knee and bowed my head as a knight does before his king."

Stephen then told the couple, "I was so surprised to suddenly find myself overcome by a deep and abiding love for Jesus. Tears filled my eyes. No words were spoken. Communication took place telepathically." He then related, "My thoughts burst forth from the wellspring of love I felt as I silently declared to Jesus, *I've served you as a soldier.* My mind flashed on an image of ancient Rome. Despite my reluctance to believe in reincarnation, I saw a man in my mind's eye with whom my heart felt a deep kinship. Somehow the man seemed to be me in a different body. The man was wearing a metal helmet with a tightly-cropped red plume that was more brush-like than feathered. He also wore a form-fitting breastplate; it resembled the armor I had seen in movies about Roman times. The men under my command as this Roman soldier had followed my lead and become followers of Jesus the Christ."

Stephen then told the couple how he continued the telepathic communication. "I then silently said to Jesus, *I've served you as a healer of emotional problems.* (I was referring to my current work as a psychologist). *And now, presumably, I can serve you as a healer of physical problems."* He then went on to describe his next thoughts.

"What was this? I was surprised. I had not thought of organizing my life around serving Jesus except on a few occasions. The first time was when I was in my early adolescence. It lasted for a few months before, during, and after receiving the sacrament of confirmation in the Episcopal Church at thirteen years old. Another time occurred when I was serving in the National Guard after I had returned home from basic training in the regular U.S. Army. Yet here I was spontaneously communicating these thoughts to Jesus from the depths of my heart and soul. Uncensored. Pure. Unqualified. No if's, and's or but's, as my mother would say. I may not have had the clear thought that I was serving Christ in my life as a psychologist; however, I loved my patients no matter how obnoxious the patterns of thinking and acting that brought them to therapy might be. I truly loved them unconditionally. In this sense, I practiced the commandment of love which Jesus gave us."

Stephen smiled as he told the couple how Karen, one of his adult patients once said to him, chuckling as she spoke, "Dr. J., I could come in here and told you I killed someone this week, and you would say, 'That's understandable, you were very upset.'"

He then told the couple, "As ludicrous as this comment sounds, it reflected her feelings. She knew I would not condemn her, but be understanding and validating of her feelings. She felt accepted by me no matter what."

He then described to the couple how his graduate-school-trained mind was questioning why he was seeing Jesus since Reiki was originally Tibetan and later Japanese. "I was puzzled. I thought, *Am I making this up? Why am I not seeing an Asian teacher? I was raised Episcopalian. Was that why I saw Jesus?* No. It was much more than that; I felt a deep love for and complete devotion to Jesus. I felt as if I really did know and love Him in the flesh during Roman times as deeply as one knows and loves the members of one's family. And it was a love and gratitude mixed with the devotion one feels for an admired and revered teacher whom one has gotten to know personally. Intermingled with these feelings was the loyalty as well as the readiness and willingness to die that a knight feels for his king."

* * *

THE MINISTER AND HIS WIFE WERE LISTENING ATTENTIVELY despite the distraction of the schooner's movement through the water. The stiff and steady ocean breeze made the sails so taut they seemed ready to tear in two, and the couple clung to the wooden handrail as the schooner tilted at nearly a forty-five degree angle. Even so, they kept their focus on Stephen as the craft sliced through the frothy waves as effortlessly as a sharp knife through freshly baked bread.

He went on to tell them, "After the meditation, Mercedes told all of us in the class to call on our Reiki Master Guide if we felt we needed help."

Stephen then told the couple, "I felt the need to call on Jesus as my Reiki Master Guide on Saturday night. I was again awakened by the plum of purple light pulsating between my eyes. I was not sure if the purple plum of light was beneficial or harmful. Therefore, I did as Mercedes had recommended. I called on my Reiki Master Guide by silently saying, *I call on my Reiki Master Guide Lord Jesus Christ. If this light is good for me I surrender to it. If not, I ask You to protect me from it.*"

Stephen then related what happened following his plea to Jesus. "A small dark cloud passed over me and I felt a coolness. It was as if I were at the beach lying in a lounge chair and a cloud briefly hides the sun."

With the boulder-lined coast of Rockport, Maine in the distance, Stephen told them, "After the tiny cloud passed, I opened my eyes to an amazing sight. I saw a white light with wings hovering by the ceiling in the center of the room about fifteen feet away from the bed."

He then told them, "Biased by being in an inn by the sea, my head instantly interpreted the light as the shape and size of a small sea gull. But my heart knew it looked more like a white dove with large butterfly-like wings. How appropriate that I thought of a butterfly, the perennial symbol of transformation, because what was about to happen was clearly transformative. With its wings fluttering slowly and rhythmically, the bird of light came toward me. It stopped a few inches above eye level, about a foot from my face. This radiant dove of white light just hovered there. As it did, it began emanating an indescribable love. It was an immensely loving consciousness that began communing with my consciousness.

"After a few moments of communing with this loving presence, I let myself simply soak up the love like a dry sponge suddenly immersed in the ocean. Then, with the speed of lightning, the winged-white light struck me in the forehead between my eyes."

He described how before the dove of light struck, he had craned his head forward to look directly at the winged wonder while he still lay motionless in bed. He then told the couple, "My head was knocked back and hit the pillow while my body became as stiff as a board. Instantly, I felt an electrifying energy surge through my body. It went from the top of my head down to the soles of my feet and back again. It was as if I were being bathed inside and out by the enlivening energy of the dove of pure white light. It was like an exhilarating electrocution.

"I awoke two hours later just in time to see the morning sun appearing on the horizon line. When I got out of bed, I felt both buoyed up and weightless. It was as if I had been bathed in bliss. And when I walked across the room, I felt like I was floating. My feet felt like they were barely touching the floor. I guess, because I felt like I was floating, the sun seemed to be floating on the sea. Looking at the sun, I thought of the big bubble of light that carried Glinda the Good Witch of the North to greet Dorothy after her arrival in the Land of Oz. Seconds later, there was a glorious sunrise as the sun blazed a wide golden highway across the waves.

"Later that day, after Mercedes finished the final procedure for preparing students to be transmitters of the healing energy of Reiki, referred to as an attunement, she asked students to share their experiences of what had just happened. Before I could speak, she motioned to me and indicated that she would like to meet with me during the break.

"After the other students were out of the room, Mercedes suddenly shifted from her professional demeanor to the uninhibited excitement of a child. She exclaimed to me, 'I didn't need to attune you. You were already streaming with healing energy. It was coming out of your palms and it was circulating all around your body.' I told her about the winged-white light, and she exclaimed, 'You were attuned in the middle of the night!'"

Stephen proceeded to tell the couple, "Since that wondrous night I have felt blessed because I have been able to help relieve the physical suffering of many people and their beloved pets." He was also excited to tell them how he had also felt blessed to help people restore their dying house plants with new growth. Because he was not so sure about the validity of reincarnation and knowing it was contrary to what he had learned growing up as a Christian, he did not share with the minister and his wife the other thing Mercedes told him. She told him that, during the attunement, something was revealed to her that he would probably not believe since he was a psychologist. She told Stephen, "You were a great healer in ancient Egypt and in Mayan times." He found this interesting but as a therapist he thought people had enough to deal with without adding past lives into the mix. What was important was *now*, not some supposed distant past, and he was now blessed with a new ability to help others.

∗ ∗ ∗

AFTER STEPHEN FINISHED, THE MINISTER AND HIS WIFE WERE both grinning. The minister spoke first. He excitedly exclaimed to Stephen, "Why Laddie, you were *anointed* with the *geeft* of healing by the Holy Spirit. This is one of the nine gifts of the Holy Spirit (I Corinthians 12:9)." He patted Stephen on the back as he continued, "You were anointed, Laddie. Not attuned." Then he pulled a Bible from his knapsack and read from Acts 10:38. He prefaced his reading by saying, "Saint Peter uses the term anointed when he speaks of 'How God anointed Jesus of Nazareth with the Holy Spirit and power, and how He went around doing good and healing . . .'"

The minister's wife interrupted and excitedly chimed in, "When you call on Lord Jesus Christ, and the Holy Spirit comes to you in the form of a white dove . . . why then you've been baptized with the Holy Spirit by Jesus Himself! Remember what the Bible describes about Jesus being baptized with water by John the Baptist, and then receiving the baptism of the Holy Spirit." She asked her husband for the Bible, and, after he handed it to her, she read aloud from Luke 3:22: "After all the people had been baptized, Jesus also was baptized. While he was praying, Heaven was opened, and the Holy Spirit descended on Him in bodily form as a dove."

Stephen responded, saying, "I can understand the concept of being anointed since I remember the Episcopal priest making the sign of the cross in oil on my forehead were the pure white light of the Holy Spirit struck me. But now, as I think about it, my experience of the light was like a baptism. I did feel inwardly and outwardly bathed by an all-embracing love."

"You were bathed in the pure white light of the Holy Spirit," she said, her face glowing with joy. The late-afternoon autumn sun gave her face and hair a golden glow. The excitement in her voice seemed to tickle her husband. It was a pleasure for Stephen to see a man married for over fifty years look admiringly at his spirited wife as she spoke. The typical competition Stephen had seen in many couples vying to speak was replaced by a delicate dance of cooperation.

The old Scot's eyes twinkled as brightly as stars on a moonless night when he interjected his words of wisdom. "The Holy Spirit came to the Samaritans when Peter and John laid their hands on them in the name of Jesus. You called on Jesus and then the Holy Spirit descended upon you. He opened his Bible and read from Acts 8:14-17: "When the apostles in Jerusalem heard that Samaria had accepted the word of God, they sent Peter and John to them. When they arrived, they prayed for them that they might receive the Holy Spirit, because the Holy Spirit had not yet come upon any of them; they had simply been baptized in the name of the Lord Jesus. Then Peter and John placed their hands on them, and they received the Holy Spirit."

"Yes, Dear," she said, gently interrupting her husband, "Stephen received the baptism of the Holy Spirit in the name of Jesus but something else happened as well." Then, addressing Stephen with a serious tone laced with heartfelt sincerity, she said, "Your heart was circumcised that night.. In Romans 2:29, Saint Paul speaks of the 'circumcision of the heart by the Spirit.' God knew your heart was true to His word of love even if your head had not yet caught up. And when the cloud passed, after you surrendered your will to Lord Jesus by asking Him to take over, a layer of fear covering your heart was cut away just as the foreskin is cut away in the circumcision of a male child. You were receiving what is called the 'circumcision of Christ.' At that moment the barrier to a direct experience of God in the form of the Holy Spirit was removed."

"Yes dear," the minister quickly added, "it was the great love Stephen felt and expressed when he met Jesus in the meditation that also led to the manifestation of the Holy Spirit!"

Stephen thought, *Yes, it's all about love.* Nine years later, he would hear these words of the minister echoed in a sermon given by Reverend Nicky Gumble from Great Britain. Gumble described how the "manifestations" of being filled with the Holy Spirit are a "by-product" of loving Jesus and through Him God the Father. Similarly, the "tingling" all over when embodied souls are in love is a "by-product" of being in love.

Stephen felt a tingling up and down his spine as the couple from Scotland spoke. The scriptural references were pouring out of them. They were enthusiastically sharing their wisdom with Stephen. He felt transported back in time. Stephen imagined it was the nineteenth century. He felt as if they were his adoptive spiritual grandparents from Scotland. He pictured the cuddly couple sitting next to him on a swing seat set on a wrap-around porch with pillars attached to one of those old-fashioned white-clapboard homes found in New England. With each quotation from the Bible, he imagined they were pouring him glass after glass of freshly-squeezed sweet-tasting lemonade.

Even though Stephen had called the name of Jesus in an unorthodox way, referring to Him as "My Reiki Master Guide Lord Jesus Christ," his prayer plea was answered. The minister and his wife were right, Stephen's heart was filled with love for Jesus and that was the important thing.

Deep down, Stephen knew what I knew as his innermost heart. Intuitively, he knew all along that it was the white dove of the Holy Spirit. So even if his head had not caught up with what his heart knew, Stephen always prefaced every healing session with the following prayer: "Thank You Beloved Holy Spirit for bestowing upon me the blessing that allows me to proclaim that I AM a beacon of Your light of divine love, a clear and powerful lens—becoming ever-more clear and ever-more powerful—through which the almighty healing energy of the light of Your divine love may shine into_____(the person in front of him or at a distance). May this person receive the healing You would have him or her receive, the healing he or she truly needs spiritually, mentally, emotionally, and physically."

He would always repeat this prayer (or some variation of it) no matter what the symptom. Being trained as a psychologist, he wanted to cover all the bases; the prayer addressed all the possible factors contributing to the symptom, whether a headache, back pain, or serious disease such as cancer. Yes, he had intuitively known in his heart that he had been struck by the pure white light of the Holy Spirit. The Scottish couple clarified what had happened to him in a traditional Christian framework. He was excited to be returning home to his religious roots.

Eventually, his head and heart would become unified in understanding the gifts that had been bestowed upon him on that wondrous, starry night in Rockport. He would come to fully feel the truth of what Reverend Bill Johnson wrote in his book *When Heaven Invades Earth*, "The hands that are surrendered to God can release the power of Heaven into a situation. In the spirit world it is released like lightning." Johnson extrapolated his beautiful and powerful words from the Bible. "He [God] comes with the brightness of lightning; light flashes from His hand, where His power is hidden" (Habakkuk 3:4).

* * *

STEPHEN WAS PUZZLED BY THE PLUM OF PURPLE LIGHT THAT came to him on Friday night and again on Saturday night. Neither the minister nor his wife had said anything about it. It was me but he did not know it. I came to him in a condensed form clothed in the purple light of Christ. I came to him to prepare the way for his baptism and anointing. The small cloud was not only his fear but his sense of being unworthy to receive God's love and blessings. It was his self-condemnation for not living up to his own standards.

On Friday night, I tried to come to him five times throughout the night. The last time was as the light of dawn was appearing over the Atlantic. Each time I was clothed in the purple light of Christ. He was unsure of me. Still, his thoughts were positive. He thought of how purple hearts are the medal given to soldiers when they have been wounded. Purple is also associated with royalty.

A few years later, a friend, a Reiki Master who was formerly a histologist in a local hospital, told him how purple is the color of blood before it is exposed to the oxygen in the air and turns red. Stephen heard that some esoteric writings claim that God's love can manifest as a violet flame that consumes all human negativity. Supposedly, it was helpful to proclaim the affirmation, "I AM the violet flame of God's all-consuming love in action now!" Saying this silently or aloud in daily life was said to be helpful to all embodied souls. It was supposed to burn away the accumulated layers of negative emotions and experiences as effectively as a hot blaze consumes a pile of dry brown leaves in autumn.

Pondering whether these claims about the violet flame were true, he whispered a brief prayer regarding the validity of the violet flame and whether it was connected with the pulsating plum of purple light.

Suddenly, he was jarred out of his prayerful reflection by the sound of a radio. The man seated directly in front of him on the train had taken off the headset of the portable radio clipped to his belt. A woman's voice blared out through the earphones, "Stars produce different energy based on their surface temperatures. This affects how we see them because we see them through our optical wave bands. Ultraviolet energy comes from the hottest stars. Infrared energy is radiated by cooler stars." Was this a message and confirmation from God? It seemed that the daily dialogue with the Divine was telling him that the violet flame has a counterpart in the natural world. The natural world teaches us about spiritual truths. The creation teaches about the Creator, God. This was something he would discover in the time he spent with Mayan shamans amid ancient pyramids in the jungles of Guatemala and Mexico.

∗ ∗ ∗

BY TURNING THE HEALING OVER TO THE HOLY SPIRIT unexpected things happened. For example, in *Love Conquers Stress,* Stephen describes a woman seeking relief from her arthritis. In her session, she recalled what seemed to be two past lives: one in ancient Egypt and the other on the dusty plains of the Old West.

Francine, a retired executive of United Airlines, was receiving Reiki from me for the arthritis in her hands and knees. I asked her to speak to the arthritis saying: 'Stop hurting me like this!'

She looked through the arthritis to see who it was in her current life that she could say this to. She saw a woman with whom she did volunteer work. Then she looked through and saw her mother.

When I simply asked her subconscious mind if there were any other experiences that might help with easing the pain of her arthritis, something totally unexpected happened. She suddenly saw herself as a young Cherokee child. The setting was a prairie somewhere in the West. Everyone was running. The U.S. Cavalry was bearing down on her tribe. Francine saw herself as a four- or five-year-old child with long braided black hair. There was an arrow piercing her blood-stained back. 'I've been shot by my own people! Why are you hurting me like this? What have I done to deserve this!' she cried out to her Cherokee mother.

As she saw herself die and felt her soul leave her body, she looked back and saw her little body lying lifeless on the ground. She then saw some of the soldiers raping and murdering not only women but little girls like herself. She instantly knew that she had been killed by someone in her tribe to spare her a worse death at the hands of the soldiers. She cried out, 'They killed me because they loved me! They didn't do it to hurt me!'

When the session was over, her hands and knees were free of the arthritis; she remained pain free for six months. The stress component of the disease was addressed but she has continued to need a Reiki session every so often. The arthritis contained a conflict between her desire to reach out for love and her fear of doing so. I have seen this with other people with arthritis. The nearly frozen state of the hands seems to fit Freud's description of symptoms as a compromise between a wish and a fear. In this case, there was a wish to reach out for love and a fear that doing so would lead to being betrayed by the ones you love. Her soul had remembered.

Even as Stephen originally wrote this, he was not sure whether what Francine recalled was a literal, documentable past life or not. Stephen searched for a way to reconcile having been raised as an Episcopalian with what seemed to be memories of past lives that he or his patients had lived. Nevertheless, what was clear to him was that recalling and reliving these dramas from the distant past led to profoundly heart-opening healings involving love and forgiveness. Now, on more than one occasion, he had called on the Holy Spirit in healing sessions and he found people like Francine recalling what appeared to be past lives. In addition, the immediacy of his own heart-opening experiences in reliving what seemed to be past lives was hard for him to ignore.

* * *

"THIS TIME I WANT TO KEEP ME HEART OPEN NO MATTER what happens!" cried out the red-haired Scotsman. Stephen's soul vowed these words as he began his descent to Earth. He could feel a part of him shrinking down to squeeze into the little fetal body about to be born. This is but one of a number of experiences he had of pre-birth and what seemed to be past lives.

From my transcendent perspective, I have looked on lovingly and joyfully when he has remembered and released hidden hurts from the distant past. Whether in this life or other lifetimes, these hurts buried in the black holes hidden in the space between surface and depth, were holding him back. He was captive to the gravitational fields of fear formed by the black holes. The tight orbits produced by the gravity of repressed fears were preventing him from the freedom, peace, and happiness of living from love with an open heart.

I watched while he pondered the question of past lives. I've appreciated his operating in the manner of William James who considered himself a radical empiricist, subjecting the varieties of religious experience to empirical and pragmatic investigation.

If reincarnation is true, Stephen wondered, *why don't most people remember past lives? Is it for the same reason that we don't remember childhood traumas? Is it simply that we repress and deny painful expe-*

riences? Is it because Christianity denies reincarnation? But then, Stephen once read that Buddha taught that people don't remember past lives so that they can concentrate on this one without distraction. And when an embodied soul becomes enlightened, he or she will remember all previous incarnations. Of course, Stephen eventually realized that all of the above are a factor in why people forget other lifetimes.

In college, he met Dr. George Ritchie, a psychiatrist and a devout Baptist. During the time he was pronounced clinically dead, Dr. Ritchie encountered Christ Jesus who took him to different realms. (For detailed descriptions of Ritchie's experience, see *8 Steps to Love* or Dr. Ritchie's book *My life After Dying,* also re-released as *Ordered to Return.*)

Given Dr. Ritchie's credentials, firm religious faith as a devout Christian, and his extraordinary near-death experience, Stephen found Dr. Ritchie to be an eminently credible source. Dr. Ritchie mentioned how the early Church held a council during which all references to reincarnation were deleted from the Bible. However, Dr. Ritchie showed him how the council overlooked a few passages in the Bible that reflected a belief in reincarnation.

One example involves the passage where the disciples ask Jesus, "Master, was this man born blind because he sinned or because his parents sinned?" (John 9:2). The fact that the disciples ask if the man sinned suggests that they believed in reincarnation. The very question presupposes the man must have lived before and sinned for how could a fetus sin? Of course, the answer that Jesus gives reveals that the reason the man was born blind was so that Jesus could heal him. And through the miracle of restoring the man's sight, many embodied souls could witness the power of God.

Another example Dr. Ritchie cited was from Matthew16:13-16. Jesus asks his disciples, "Who do people say the Son of Man is?" The disciples reply, "Some say John the Baptist, others say Elijah and still others say Jeremiah or one of the prophets." Jesus then asks, "Who do you say I am?" Then Simon Peter answers, "You are the Christ, the Son of the living God." The passage suggests that many believed in reincarnation since Jesus was thought to be one of the prophets returned. Still, Stephen was skeptical. Even if Jesus were alive in human form before incarnating as the Christ (described in the book *The Lives of the Master* by Glenn Sanderfur), Stephen sensed there was some significant spiritual reason for disregarding the idea of reincarnation. It was many years before he realized the reason. Meanwhile, he listened as Dr. Ritchie marshalled more evidence for reincarnation.

Dr. Ritchie also told him about the distinguished Dr. Ian Stevenson's impeccable research on reincarnation. Dr. Stevenson investigated over two thousand cases of children spontaneously remembering past lives.

Even with this eye-opening information, Stephen did not find himself fascinated by the prospect of past lives. He was open to the possibility of living many lives. Nearly four decades after Dr. Ritchie told him about the removal of reincarnation from the Bible, Stephen found confirmation of what Dr. Ritchie told him. Stephen read what religious scholar Holger Kersten discovered in his research. The early Christian Church fathers such as Origen and others espoused the doctrine of the soul coming to Earth many times. Saint Gregory of Nyssa (circa 334-339 A.D.) suggested the following (The Catechetical Orations VIII, 9):

> *The soul seems to undergo a kind of healing process in order to be cleansed of stains caused by sin in the present life; virtue is the remedy applied to heal these scars. If they remain incurable in the present life, then the healing treatment is continued in a future life.*

Kersten discussed how it was in 553 A.D. at the Council of Constantinople, attended by only a handful of people, that the doctrine of reincarnation was declared an anathema, a heretical belief.

Stephen was surprised to read that the wife of Emperor Justinian had been a courtesan. In today's terms she might be called a high-class hooker. Kersten claimed that, in an effort to separate herself from her questionable past and to appear moral, she ordered the death of hundreds of her former courtesan cohorts.

To save herself from the karmic consequence of being responsible for such a massive number of murders, Justinian's wife asked him to have the council declare reincarnation a heresy. She believed that an official church edict would spare her from suffering the consequences in future lifetimes. *What a capricious twist!?* Stephen thought when he read this information. He thought, *Perhaps there is a literal and historical truth to the past lives I've recalled.* Still, Stephen felt the important thing was to focus on this current life and not get distracted by the past.

In his work with people in therapy who recalled past lives and in his own memories, he felt the important thing was to *feel* and *release* the emotions triggered by the supposed past life memories. Even in traditional therapy, the forays into the past are to make the present better. So he concluded that it is important to honor the feelings even if they were only a symbolic psychodrama that, similar to a dream, was created by the unconscious mind for a person's healing.

Stephen's path also led him to the words of Jesus according to Glenda Green in her beautiful book, *Love Without End: Jesus Speaks*. In her book she reveals her dialogues with Jesus when he appeared to her daily from November 1992 until March 1993. When she asked Jesus about past lives, He did not deny the soul lives again in other bodies. Instead, He told her that all souls have "one life with many chapters." Stephen felt that this cryptic comment contained an important spiritual truth.

Eventually, Stephen would conclude that although recalling past lives can be healing, they were largely a distraction from the present and from what Jesus was emphasizing. In the Bible and in His comment to Glenda Green, Jesus was teaching a vital spiritual truth: embodied souls cannot find freedom, peace, and happiness by their own efforts. And the doctrine of reincarnation implies that souls can progress spiritually by their own efforts over many lives. An attitude that promotes the idea that embodied souls can *do* something defeats spiritual growth. Therefore, the removal of reincarnation from the Bible emphasizes the idea that salvation comes from *accepting* the grace of God's love and from loving oneself as well as others and not by *doing* good works. This shift of emphasis can serve to help embodied souls wake up to the truth of simply *being* who they truly are: the expansive energy and peaceful power of pure love existing both within and beyond space and time. Stephen smiled and thought, *Instead of doing good things to earn cosmic brownie points, we do good things out of an inner fullness of love. But then again, maybe it takes souls many lives to finally open their hearts and wake up to this truth of the spirit of love.*

The dramas an embodied soul experiences while living and loving in various historical-cultural contexts are like dreams. No effort *in* the drama of a dream ends the nightmare. Stephen was grateful for realizing this when he relived his experience in the womb. He simply stopped struggling, merged with me, and woke up from the nightmare of his little body's hellish hunger. He was now beginning to see the deeper truth that soul dramas end when embodied souls stop struggling and awaken to who they are: the unity of the one spirit of love hidden in the diversity of soul suits.

✳ ✳ ✳

Red ribbons of light stretched across the horizon as the sun was setting and the train pulled into Trenton. Stephen recalled something he had not thought of for many years. When the hand of the Episcopal bishop touched his head during confirmation, he felt a surge of energy shoot through his thirteen-year-old body. The bishop had said, "May you receive the blessing of the Holy Spirit from this day forward." Back then, he knew something special had happened but he was not sure what it was.

Now, in retrospect, he thought, *Could it be that those rituals in church really did have some true and lasting significance for the soul?* More than this, he began to see the ever-present and eternal reality of Christ Jesus. He was always showing up in the most unlikely places: the Reiki Master meditation, various books on Reiki, the Mayan pyramids in the jungles of Guatemala and Mexico, and on his trips to Mexico City, Puerta Vallarta, Athens, Greece, and the Greek isle of Mykonos.

Wherever Stephen's spiritual search led, Jesus appeared as the

Good Shepherd watching over His flock. Stephen's thoughts were drawn back to the question: What happened in the year of 1995 to prepare the way for this miraculous event of being blessed by the Holy Spirit with the gift of healing?

∗ ∗ ∗

THE YEAR OF 1995 BEGAN WITH ANGELS IN SUNNY MEXICO. It was New Year's Day and the plane Stephen was on was flying to the seaside resort town of Puerta Vallarta. As the plane was about to land, he finished reading a passage in a book entitled *Ask Your Angels*. In the passage, a man in England had climbed a stone tower. He sat atop the tower on New Year's Eve, reflecting over the past year. The man was listening to the instrumental theme to the film *Chariot's of Fire* which was composed by Vangelis. The composer's name and this piece of music would turn out to be significant a few days into the trip.

Stephen yawned and closed the book. The plane ride had been long and he needed to get his body moving. But then he felt a spark of excitement when he looked through the little window as the plane circled the city before landing. There atop the tall Church in the midst of the city, he saw large statues of angels. The angels were standing tall as if on guard. They faced outward, appearing sturdy and strong. Their arms above their heads, they were holding up a crown with a cross on it. Stephen counted eight angels.

Two days into the trip, Stephen walked into a hallway with a winding stairway leading to an open-air restaurant. The dining area was on the second floor overlooking the Sea of Cortéz. He began his ascent up the stairs when he was startled to see small terra-cotta sculptures of angels evenly placed on both sides of the stairway.

Once situated, he ordered a beer and chips in Spanish. He asked the waiter for a *Corona con limón* (a Corona beer with a wedge of fresh lime crowning the neck of the bottle) and tortilla chips with freshly prepared *pico de gallo* (salsa). Before sitting at his table, he caught a glimpse of a man in the kitchen with a knife in hand; his mouth began to water as he saw the man dicing the tomatoes, onions, jalapeño peppers, and cilantro leaves. He sat back and inhaled the ambience. A gentle breeze was coming off of the gorgeous aquamarine-colored sea. Upbeat Mexican dance music was playing while he reflected on angels appearing all around him. All his senses were sated by the sights, sounds, smells, anticipated tastes, and the cool touch of the sea breeze.

Suddenly the music stopped. Savoring the scene and the food and drink, he heard a completely different kind of music begin to play. *Oh my God!* he thought. *It's* Chariots of Fire *by Vangelis!* He remembered that the beautiful musical score was mentioned in the book on angels. Then it hit him, *Vangelis looks like the word angels with the letter "V" in front of it.* The very first word beginning with a "V" that came to mind was victory. His association was significant given what happened next. . . .

Strolling down the cobblestone street, Stephen decided to check out a few of the restaurants recommended by the *concierge* at the hotel where he was staying. It just happened that the restaurant he spotted held another surprise . . . a large sculpture of Archangel Michael graced the arched entryway. Thinking back about the word victory, he thought of how Archangel Michael was the one who led the legions of Heaven to victory over the rebellious fallen angels led by Lucifer whose name became Satan after his fall from Heaven. And, as you will soon see, eight months later, Archangel Michael would reappear as part of a spiritual form of hypnotherapy.

Stephen was stunned by being surrounded by statues of angels and then the music from *Chariots of Fire*. He wondered if there was any connection to the title of the movie? A tingling shot up his spine; he remembered the prophet Elijah was said to have ascended to Heaven in a "flaming chariot." A few hours later, Stephen was astonished to learn that out of all the stores, restaurants, and hotels, these two establishments were the *only* ones with angel sculptures.

God was sending His messengers. Jesus had not appeared directly as he would later on. Instead, He appeared in the form of the crown topped by a cross held up by the eight angels atop the church in Puerta Vallarta.

To top off his trip, Jane, the first patient he saw upon his return home, brought in a photograph in which he could see the misty apparition of three huge angels standing as tall as the forest in front of which they were hovering. To Stephen, these large winged figures seemed to be archangels.

Jane trembled with excitement as she began to tell him a story about her friend and her friend's husband and two daughters. It was a Sunday afternoon in late September. The family had finished a picnic and the father was about to take a family photo. There was a timer on the camera so the father could get everyone positioned and then he had thirty seconds to move to his place in the picture. During the seconds remaining, the raucous sound of motorcycles shattered the peaceful moment. But then, just seconds before the camera took the shot, the gang of bikers, their shirts featuring a skull and crossbones, suddenly looked spooked. The rough-looking crew sped off with the same rapidity with which they had arrived on the scene. Apparently, the menacing motorcycle gang was frightened off by the imposing appearance of the angels standing tall behind the family. In this instance, angels had been captured on film. A few weeks later, he discovered a weekly TV series in which angels intervened to help people as they had with the family of Jane's friend. The show was called *Touched by an Angel*.

In the years to follow, the gift of discerning spirits, bestowed upon him by the Holy Spirit, allowed Stephen to see angels. A female angel appeared to him during the writing of *8 Steps to Love*. She first appeared after he had spent the night hours from midnight until dawn writing. As though confirming what he had written that night, the female angel appeared across the room from his desk. He looked up from his lap-top computer to see her in the shadows of the foyer near the door to his home.

The sun was just peeking over the tree-covered hill overlooking the Brandywine River. She had no flesh tones. Instead, she was all aquamarine. Her face, gossamer body, and the lacy latticework of her wings all had an aquamarine radiance illuminating the shadowy foyer. Communicating telepathically, she told Stephen, "Your book has a message and a method the world desperately needs." Stephen felt his body quiver with delight as his eyes locked onto her eyes which resembled two aquamarine gems. Her eyes glistened with love. It was not a romantic love but an unconditional love that extended to all humankind.

Stephen had no idea that the angels were sent to prepare the way for him to begin following the thread of his divine destiny. He could hear Rod Serling from his childhood and adolescence speaking in his mind, "You're about to enter the Twilight Zone."

∗ ∗ ∗

SAINT GEORGE KEPT SHOWING UP ALL OVER THE PLACE, both with and without the dragon. Once again, as had happened four months earlier on the flight to Puerta Vallarta, Stephen was reading something that would keep appearing in various ways. Just before the plane was about to set down in Athens, he read about Saint George slaying the dragon being a symbol of rebirth. The book was *The Holotropic Mind* by psychiatrist Stanislov Grof.

Two months later in June of 1995, this book would provide a framework for understanding one of his most vivid experiences of me mentioned at the very beginning of chapter one. *The Holotropic Mind* described Grof's use of a therapeutic breathing technique that helped people heal buried birth traumas. Drawing on over thirty thousand cases, Grof discovered four stages of the birth experience. Suffice it to say, the fourth stage involved finally emerging from the struggle through the birth canal into the world. And Saint George triumphing over the dragon would sometimes spontaneously appear as embodied souls reexperienced the moment they exited their mother's womb. They often reported feeling a sense of triumph. Relief. Liberation.

Prior to reading about Saint George, Stephen read of other universal images accompanying the different stages of birth. Stage one involves the symbiotic oneness of fetus and mother where all needs are met effortlessly. This stage is associated with images of comfort and bliss. Pictures of a paradise or the Garden of Eden may emerge into the consciousness of people reexperiencing stage one. Of course, this is the stage of Stephen's birth when he met me, and, far from bliss, he experienced a painful, inescapable hunger. Similarly, Grof reported unpleasant experiences in the womb: he tasted tobacco and alcohol. One's womb experience depends on one's mother. By August of 1995, Stephen would reexperience all four birth stages.

Having been a fan of existentialism in his early twenties, he was fascinated by the correlation between John Paul Sartre's play *No Exit* and Grof's report of the philosopher's trauma during stage two of birth. Sartre was not made aware of his trauma until well after he had penned *No Exit*. In stage two, people describe images of being tortured in a prison cell when reexperiencing stage two. Feeling trapped with no escape is due to the fact that in this stage the cervix is not open and the mother's labor contractions have begun. The fetus is literally trapped. No exit is available. The title of Sartre's play captures the feelings of people who had traumatic experiences in stage two where they longed for liberation from the crushing contractions. It was clear to Stephen that Sartre's view of life had been colored by his birth trauma.

Stephen read how stage three occurred as the fetus made its way through the birth canal. The fetus experiences the narrowing and expanding of the canal caused by the mother's labor contractions. The fetus alternates between feelings of relief with expansion and fear of dying from the contractions. This led Grof to call the stage the death-rebirth struggle. *No wonder Saint George defeating the dragon is associated with emerging from the struggle in the birth canal,* he remembered thinking at the very moment when the plane landed and the squeal of rubber on the runway startled him out of his reflections on the stages of birth.

When he arrived in Athens, it was three months since he had felt the presence of angels on the coast of Mexico. Busy with work, Stephen did not really know what the travel agent had booked. He only knew the trip had three parts: Athens, Mykonos, and Santorini. Stephen was surprised to discover that the time in Athens would be spent at the Saint George Hotel. The hotel was at the bottom of the hill boasted to be the highest point in Athens. And atop that hill, overlooking the city, sat Saint George's Chapel. Saint George and the dragon appeared when Stephen strolled through the streets of the Plaka, the old city surrounding the base of the Acropolis.

From the balcony of his room near the top floor of the Saint George Hotel, he saw the majestic remains of the Acropolis (high city) set on the elevated plateau of ancient Athens. There were the Parthenon and other recognizable stone structures.

Nonetheless, it was on the streets below the Acropolis where Saint George appeared again. There amid the wares of one of the many street vendors, Stephen found an antique wooden plaque. He stood there for a few minutes just admiring the small square piece of varnished wood that had darkened with age. It featured a hand-painted picture of Saint George triumphing over the dragon.

After Stephen returned home to Connecticut, he placed the plaque of Saint George in his office. He found the perfect place for it: on the table by the sofa next to the bronze Tiffany lamp with the rounded shade composed of multi-colored pieces of stained glass. Both the plaque and lamp appeared to be from an earlier era in human history. When a teenage boy named James arrived for his session, he noticed the plaque. His voice elevated with excitement when he spoke, "I have the exact same picture of Saint George and the dragon on the visor of my V.W. Beetle!"

Two weeks later, David Hart came to town to give a talk to the Connecticut Society for the Study of Jungian Psychology. Stephen had never been to the location where David Hart was to present. Guess what? On the stage where David Hart stood, a few feet to the right of the podium, there was a good-sized wooden sign. It was old and varnished like the plaque in Stephen's office. And yes, the hand-painted picture on it was of Saint George and the dragon. The words on the sign read, Saint George's Tavern. It was brought back from England where it had hung outside an old English pub. The sign became available after the building housing the pub was torn down.

Still, Stephen wondered why Saint George was showing up. It would be nearly ten years before he would see the true significance of Saint George appearing in 1995. In 2005, I quietly guided him to research the story of Saint George and the dragon while he was just finishing up *Slay the Dragon—Not Each Other*. He found a reference to the power that enabled Saint George to slay the dragon and he placed in the epilogue of his new book.

According to the legend of Saint George and the dragon, Saint George slew the dragon and saved the princess Sabra 'with the help of Christ.' Aside from the literal understanding that Jesus appeared to help George, what can the slaying of the dragon by the power of Christ symbolize for the inner psychological and spiritual life of everyone? What does the power of Christ mean as a fundamental human experience no matter whether you are Christian, Buddhist, Muslim, etcetera, or profess no religion at all?

The power of Christ points to the power of love. The core of Christ's teaching involves love and forgiveness. He taught us to "love thy neighbor as thyself." The dragon in us desires to receive for the self alone. This is the core of what the Kabbalah calls the Evil Inclination. And the essence of all 8 steps [*8 Steps to Love*] is to replace a selfish, reactive fear focus with a love focus that honors self and others.

Shifting to a love focus involves focusing on loving and accepting others as they are instead of trying to change them. In effect, we slay the dragon in us with the sharp-focused awareness that is our sword of love. This is the love focus fostered by the four inner steps and extended to others in the four outer steps. With the four outer steps conflict becomes a dance of love instead of a battle of fear and anger.

The princess saved by Saint George is our innermost heart, our very soul, where love, the ultimate power of the universe, resides. By slaying the dragon, we release our capacity to love freely without the sticky fingers of trying to control others. We realize that our feeling good and being at peace do not depend on anything external to ourselves. When we take the letter x out of external, we have the word eternal. What is eternal is not the stuff of the world but the stuff of our heart: love—the energy animating all of life.

It was interesting to him that on the flight to Greece he was reading about Saint George slaying the dragon being an image associated with rebirth. It was interesting, given the fact the first week of the trip ended on the island of Mykonons with Greeks shouting *Christos anesti! Christos anesti!* (Christ is risen!) Just by chance Stephen's trip to Greece had coincided with the festive experience of Greek Orthodox Easter. Then again, it did not seem that it happened by chance. The invisible thread of his divine destiny was guiding him. Two years later, he would revisit this passage and see that calling out anything in the name of Jesus is a key to releasing the power of triumphing over evil and sickness. The power of using the name of Jesus had been stated in the scriptures, especially in the books of Matthew, Mark, Luke, and John. Stephen would eventually discover that using the name of Jesus could work miracles.

* * *

IN AUGUST OF 1995, STEPHEN NOTICED THAT THERE were three different hypnotherapists who were reintroducing the age-old phenomenon of possession as an underlying problem of their clients. These therapists had developed a modern clinical way to approach it. They were presenting classes on clinical depossession at the annual National Hypnotherapy Convention held in Nashua, New Hampshire. Stephen was intrigued by what the presenters had to say. He was amazed at the results they reported getting with regard to emotional problems; but what was especially impressive were the results with cancer and the Gulf War Syndrome.

As an empiricist and pragmatist in the tradition of William James, Stephen was open to explore these unusual approaches. In his clinical work, he defined truth as what you see (empirical/observable) and what works (pragmatic/useful). It was in this spirit that he decided to take a class. Even though, it seemed like a throwback to ancient times and conjured up scenes from the film *The Exorcist,* he decided to investigate these classes on clinical depossession.

One class was called Spirit Releasement Therapy (SRT). It was being taught by Dr. William Baldwin and his psychically-gifted wife Judith. This therapy had one primary premise. Just as unseen bacteria and microorganisms can attach themselves to human bodies without people's knowledge, so can various kinds of unseen energies or entities attach themselves to people without their awareness. The claim was that earthbound spirits of deceased human beings and what Baldwin called dark-force entities (demons) could attach to a person. Drawn to a person's fear, rage, or depression, these spirit energies or entities form a *parasitic* attachment to a person as its host organism.

Contrary to the dramatic displays of possession depicted in the movies, Stephen learned that these non-physical-energy parasites present as physical, mental, and emotional symptoms that harm the health of their host. Given what he heard from Dr. Ritchie about his near-death experience where Christ Jesus appeared to him and revealed aspects of the spirit realm, Baldwin's premise was plausible to him. Regarding this aspect of Dr. Ritchie's near-death experience, Stephen wrote the following in *8 Steps to Love*.

Then Christ took his [Dr. Ritchie's] hand and told him: 'Come with me I have something to show you.' There was then what Dr.Ritchie described as a 'flash of light.' He found himself flying over 'the red-light district of a city.' There Christ took him into a bar and into a brothel. In the bar, Dr. Ritchie saw other beings like himself, hovering around the people drinking at the bar. He could also see the aura or electromagnetic-life- force field surrounding the people at the bar. These beings were like parasites trying to get into the body of the people drinking alcohol in order to experience the feeling of being intoxicated. Ritchie got the impression these beings had been alcoholics when they were alive.

These parasitic non-physical beings were really suffering. Dr. Ritchie noticed that with the people who were really drunk the electromagnetic field seemed to weaken and open up. He then saw these other beings appear to enter the body of the individuals drinking, but even as they did they did not seem to get the feeling of being intoxicated that they longed for. They continued to suffer. It was the same thing in the brothel except that instead of alcohol, it was the experience of sex that these other beings were trying to have through the bodies of the prostitutes and their customers.

Stephen decided to investigate further and see what Dr. Baldwin had to say. Baldwin indicated that he had developed steps to release the parasitic attachments and that doing so tended to relieve symptoms. Just as cleansing parasites from the body can restore a person's health, so can releasing non-physical-energy parasites help restore a person's health as well.

After witnessing a solid presentation of clinical material and case demonstration of SRT, Stephen considered having a session with the Baldwins. He did not have any particular symptoms but he felt it might be worth doing. Still, he was unsure so he prayed for God to give him a sign. As soon as he arrived in his motel room, he flopped on the bed and flipped on the television. Of all the things that might have been on in the middle of August, from sports to commercials to movies, Stephen could not believe his eyes. . . .

There on the screen was a scene from the epic film, *King of Kings*. Usually this is shown at Easter as it chronicles the life of Jesus as the Christ. And, of all the possible scenes in the movie, it was right at the point where a man falls to the ground next to Jesus. Seeing the man writhing on the ground, Jesus commands, "Come out of the man thou unclean spirit!" Then, addressing the unclean spirit, Jesus asks, "What is thy name?" The spirit replies, "My name is legion for we are many." Stephen was able to find the scene he saw referenced in the Bible (Mark 5:8-9). Stunned by the synchronicity, Stephen knew his prayer had been answered. He decided, *This therapy of Baldwin's dates back to Jesus, and yes I will have a session with Dr. Baldwin.*

The result: Stephen had an amazingly uplifting session. It was like *no* therapy or hypnosis he had ever experienced or practiced. The session started with Stephen reliving an anxiety he had felt when he was six years old. It was related to his parents arguing. Then he felt his body begin twisting and turning as if trapped. After a few minutes, he felt his body undulate as it moved through a tunnel until it went limp. Dr. Baldwin asked, "What just happened?"

"I feel like I just came out of something like a narrow cave," Stephen replied.

"Go back inside," Dr. Baldwin instructed. As an aside, after the session, Dr. Baldwin told Stephen that his lips turned blue for a few moments as happens when a baby is born and has not yet started to breathe. Stephen had reexperienced birth stages two, three, and four. He had gone from feeling trapped to reliving the struggle to move through the birth canal and out into his Saint George moment of freedom from the crushing contractions. He felt relief!

Immediately after Dr. Baldwin's comment, "Go back inside," he saw the scene shift. It was as if the curtain raised, and, as in in old movie theaters, a film began. Except with this film, Stephen was starring in it as a soldier. He could not see what he looked like since he was seeing through the eyes of the soldier. He was in a cell in a Russian prison from what seemed to be an earlier century. His body was in chains and he was enraged that his men were being tortured.

Then the scene shifted . . . he was eight-year-old Stevie and he was sobbing as he reexperienced that familiar, haunting memory. His father Earl was screaming in pain as he crawled across the floor. Stephen was again feeling the heartache of little eight-year-old Stevie. He was now reliving the moment he cried out for God to take away his daddy's pain.

In both scenes, Stephen felt rage when no help was forthcoming. Dr. Baldwin noticed his jaw jut out and his chest stick out while he was expressing rage at the men in robes who appeared to be monks. They were torturing his men in this Russian prison cell. Dr. Baldwin then said with an authoritative and stern voice, "You who juts out his jaw and sticks out his chest, what would you say to us?" Dr. Baldwin had identified and called forth a dark-force entity (what I prefer to call a demon). Once identified, the demon began to growl through Stephen, addressing Dr. Baldwin in a belligerent and derogatory manner. Stephen felt as if he were an onlooker and not the one speaking the hostile words. He was surprised by the deep and cavernous voice uttering guttural sounds through him.

From Dr. Baldwin's assessment, the demon had attached to little eight-year-old Stevie through the open window of Stevie's helpless rage. The rage was fueled by Stevie's desire for power to counter his powerlessness to relieve his father's pain and stop his father's scream-ing. As I mentioned in chapter six, he would later realize that he was angry at God but was not aware of this in this session.

Immediately upon hearing Stephen's growling and belligerence,

Dr. Baldwin called on Archangel Michael and the legions of Heaven to come and gather up this demon and lift it from Stephen's body. Dr. Baldwin then said to the heavenly messengers, "Wrap this one up in its own capsule of light, layer upon layer." Sealed in this divine light, the demon would not be able to escape. When the demon was released from him, Stephen saw in his mind's eye an inky-black shape with orbs of red light for eyes. It was hovering on his left side up near the ceiling.

A few years later, Stephen found the position of the demon interesting since he experienced me on his right side. He thought of old Bugs Bunny cartoons with the devil on Bugs Bunny's left shoulder, whispering "bad" thoughts into the rabbit's ear; while on Bug's right shoulder stood an angel with her cherubic lips whispering angelic advice into Bug's right ear. When Stephen thought of this, he had been studying the Kabbalah: the right arm was associated with the desire to share, and the left arm was linked to the desire to receive. And, as previously stated, the Kabbalah sees the essence of evil as the desire to receive for the self alone.

The inky-black shape resembled the irregular shape of the inkblot on the card of the Rorshach Inkblot Test that people often associate with power and authority. It was set against a ball of light like the sun. This, too, was interesting to Stephen years later when he was reflecting back on the experience. He thought to himself, *Hadn't Lucifer and a third of the angels rebelled against God? And hadn't this act of rebellion led Lucifer and his band of rebels to be cast out of Heaven? Wasn't their motto "Better to rule in hell than serve in Heaven?"* Stephen knew the answer to all of the above was yes.

Toward the end of the session, Dr. Baldwin confronted the demon. The demon was shown that, contrary to what it had been led to believe by the dark side, the light of God existed in its core instead of darkness. First, the demon felt the comforting warmth of the light around and within it. The demon then transformed back into the light of God's love. The dark deeds done by the demon merely hide the light of God in its core in the same way that a black hole traps light so that it cannot escape or a smoldering pile of debris hides but does not put out the fire underneath.

Dr. Baldwin then gave the demon a choice. It could choose the light of God or choose to return to the pit of hell. After the demon chose the light, Dr. Baldwin told the demon that it must undo the damage it had done to Stephen and others. "One way," he outlined to the demon, "involves suffering in equal measure to the suffering you have caused. And the other way," he indicated, "involves calling out to other demons and showing them what you have learned this day about the light of God being beneficial and not harmful."

Following Dr. Baldwin's instructions, the demon expressed to Stephen its sorrow and regret for inflicting harm on him and his family. And then, right before ascending to the light of God, it was instructed to lift off all the spiritual, mental, emotional, and physical residue of any harm it had inflicted on him and his family. From my perspective, I would say the fallen angel is now transforming back into the angel it originally was before the act of rebellion.

As the session continued, the next release involved the soldier in the Russian prison cell. Even in his skepticism about reincarnation, Stephen experienced the scene in the prison cell as if it were a past life of his in Russia. However, Dr. Baldwin discovered that the soldier was another soul who attached to Stephen during Stephen's birth struggle. Dr. Baldwin did this by telling the soldier to look inside the baby body of Stephen and asking, "What do you see?"

"I see a tiny dot of light," the soldier answered.

"That's the soul of Stephen," Dr. Baldwin said. "It's not your body. One soul to one body. That's the law of the universe. Now it's time for you to go to the Light. Call out to the soldiers under your command who were with you in the Russian prison. Now look up and see if you can see the Light. See if there are any of your loved ones waiting for you in the Light."

The soldier was an earthbound spirit who was being released to the light. He was now free of his attachment to Stephen. After the session, Dr. Baldwin explained that the soldier had been drawn to Stephen's birth struggle against feeling trapped because it resembled the soldier's struggle against feeling trapped in the prison cell where he helplessly watched his men being tortured.

Still identified with the soldier, Stephen saw himself ascending to the light of God as the soldier began his ascent. Stephen also saw the monks and the other soldiers all ascending *en masse*. He noticed that he could see inside of the monks and the soldiers as well as the soldier with whom he was identified. Every one of them had a jagged piece of light in the core of their being. Stephen wondered why they were jagged. *Jagged*, he decided, *probably because they were all part of one huge jigsaw puzzle, each with its particular place in the scheme of things.* It was a glorious apotheosis as all ascended, both enemies and comrades; he also heard a loud chorus of unseen angels singing the hymn *Onward Christian Soldiers*.

After the session was over, Stephen was not sure of what to make of it. He decided it didn't matter whether the session was viewed as the unconscious mind providing a creative healing imagery like a dream does or whether it was seen as an *actual* encounter in some objective sense. Whatever it was, he was left with what the Bible called the peace that "passes understanding." He was also left with a feeling of an unsurpassable love.

Stephen concluded that worrying about the possibility of non-physical energy parasites, whether demons or earthbound spirits, is not what embodied souls need to do. Eliminating parasitic relationships by slaying the dragon of dependency and loving freely is what is important. Embodied souls need to focus on the light of God's love that they are in their core and not the darkness that obscures it. Embodied souls are then less likely to attract interfering intruders. Stephen decided his experience simply confirmed what President F.D.R. said during the Great Depression of the 1930s, "We have nothing to fear but fear itself." To Stephen, the job of embodied souls is to keep transforming the contracted energy of fear, anger, and depression back into the expansive energy of love. By living from love instead of from fear and anger, embodied souls *strengthen* their spiritual immune system. They become like those electric-light bug zappers used in the summertime to eliminate annoying insects.

The other thing Stephen found interesting with Dr. Baldwin's approach was that the steps Dr. Baldwin used to release these dark-energy beings reminded Stephen of how Carl Jung recommended dealing with the shadow side of the personality of every embodied soul. The shadow was not to be repressed but needed to be transformed with the light of consciousness. Similarly, Stephen had heard one of his teachers paraphrase Freud by saying, "Fears grow like mushrooms in the dark but when exposed to the light of consciousness, they whither and die like mushrooms exposed to sunlight." Through my guidance, he was led to compare Jung and Freud with Baldwin's steps of capturing the demon in light and transforming it. Three years later, Stephen began developing his own technique for transforming the dark, contracted energy of the negative emotions of anger, fear, and depression back into the expansive energy of love.

Shortly after the session with Dr. Baldwin, he came across a book on hands-on healing in the Episcopal Church. It was written by a reporter who was a skeptic but became a believer after witnessing the effectiveness of it. In her book, the reporter referenced the passage in the Bible where Jesus told his disciples that they would have the ability to release parasitic attachments and the ability to heal. "Then He called His twelve disciples together and gave them power and authority over all demons and to cure diseases" (Luke 9:1-2). There was Jesus as the Good Shepherd once again; He who made the lame walk and the blind see had bookended the bizarre experience with Baldwin. Jesus showed up before the session in the film that followed Stephen's prayer and after in this passage from the Bible.

* * *

ON A STORMY NIGHT IN SEPTEMBER OF 1995, STEPHEN WAS staying in an inn on the Peninsula of Inch in Ireland. He was suddenly awakened from a sound sleep. He felt what turned out to be the energy of the earthbound spirit of a woman coming into his body. Stephen got the impression she was in her thirties when she died. She would enter and leave him. Each time, she seemed to enter him in the middle of his back, what he called the back door to his heart. She came to him at different times during the night. Following Dr. Baldwin's advice on such matters, Stephen kept refusing her permission to stay and she would immediately exit.

He was not in touch with anything like this as a traditionally trained psychologist. From my perspective, I knew that this event was an extension of all that had been happening spiritually in 1995. Beginning with the angels coming to him on New Year's day and continuing right up until his heart-opening experience with Dr. Baldwin, Stephen's heart was becoming wide open. One month later in Salem, Massachusetts, he met Mercedes. The way had been prepared for the Holy Spirit to come to him. His heart was ready, open, and willing.

Now, in addition to healing, the other gifts bestowed upon him by the Holy Spirit were about to be revealed. The first gift appeared in a series of sessions spanning the last two months of this life-changing year of 1995. Stephen was stunned by what happened when he engaged in his very first healing sessions using the Christian—inspired and guided by the Holy Spirit—form of Reiki healing. The veil between life and death was lifted. . . .

* * *

KAREN, A WOMAN IN HER MID-THIRTIES, HAD HER HUSBAND call Stephen's office to cancel her therapy session for that night. She couldn't make her session because of a painful migraine headache. After he heard the message left by her husband, Stephen called Karen and asked her if she would like to try an experiment by lying down for a few minutes and simply preparing to receive a healing energy. She said, "I don't believe in that kind of thing." Stephen told her she didn't have to believe and there was nothing to lose. Before they hung up, Stephen told her he would call her back in ten minutes.

He imagined her sitting in his office in the chair where she usually sat for her sessions. He then imagined her sitting there and he proceeded to place his hands on her head the way he would if she were in his office. Before ten minutes were up, she called Stephen and told him, "My headache is all gone and my back, which has been killing me for two weeks, feels better as well. When I laid down, I felt a cool river of energy flowing under my skin." Stephen did not know about the back problem so no suggestion was made.

He then asked her to describe where she felt the pain in her head; he wanted to see if it correlated with where he felt it in his hands. Sure enough, the pain had been in two spots: the back of her head on the upper right side and the left upper right of her forehead. They were exactly the areas that the Holy Spirit had revealed to him kinesthetically; he felt the information through his hands. Stephen was as amazed as the woman was by these results. The gift called word of knowledge can come verbally in words or by pictures, or, as in this case, by a clairsentience of sensations in his body corresponding to where the person receiving Reiki feels pain.

One other time, Stephen was doing Reiki on Cindy, a woman in her twenties. Cindy had been in a car accident. The car had been struck on the driver's side and she was driving. Stephen's mind concluded that her pain would be on the left side but his hands felt pain on her right side. He ignored his confusion. Standing behind her while she sat in the chair in front of him, he held his left hand over her left shoulder and his right hand over her right side. After the session, Stephen asked Cindy, "Which side hurt the most from the accident?"

She answered, "My right side because the impact of my car being hit sent me into the gear shift. My left side was not touched." Stephen began to trust the wisdom of the Holy Spirit. Any time the logic of his mind conflicted with what his hands felt, he trusted his hands over his head. His hands took precedence because he was beginning to trust the information provided by the Comforter, the Holy Spirit by way of the sensations in his hands. However, Stephen began to discover that the Holy Spirit had also bestowed upon him another gift: the gift of discerning spirits.

* * *

SUDDENLY STEPHEN WAS SURPRISED BY A STRONG FEELING OF love and a configuration of sensations flowing into the middle of his back: the back door to his heart. The sensations were accompanied by the vague image of a medium-sized woman jumping right into his back. The love he felt was for Bonnie, the thirty-six-year-old mother of three seated before him receiving Reiki. He had been holding his hands a few inches in front of Bonnie's eyes when this love from beyond began to surge through him but was not from him. Sure he cared for Bonnie but he did not feel this strongly about her. A clearer picture of a woman and words came into his mind.

Stephen then said, "I'm getting the picture of an elderly woman wearing white Bobby-Socks and a long blue dress with white dots on it. And she wants you to know that she loves you very much and she wants you to start believing in yourself."

Instantly, Bonnie identified the woman as her deceased grandmother. Bonnie told Stephen that she had experiences of not only feeling the presence of her grandmother but she could often smell her perfume. At that moment, she said that she could smell that same perfumed scent in Stephen's office.

Next to the picture of Bonnie's grandmother, Stephen saw the clear picture of a man in his mid-thirties. He was wearing bib-overalls. Stephen assumed it was Bonnie's grandfather at a younger age. It wasn't. Somehow Bonnie knew it was a friend from high school who had committed suicide. A message from the man came through to Stephen, "It wasn't your fault." This was followed by, "I never blamed you for not calling me back that night. I want you to stop blaming yourself and forgive yourself." Seconds later the message was, "I know you would've called me back if you knew what I was feeling."

Stephen told Bonnie to talk to the man. Stephen often used the therapy technique called the empty chair. The individual talks to the empty chair as though the person with whom the patient has unfinished emotional business is seated there. The empty chair could be used with someone in a person's life currently or from the past.

Stephen instructed Bonnie, "Close your eyes, visualize the man, and speak to him." She sobbed as she expressed her feelings of guilt and regret over not calling him back the night he took his own life. Each time Bonnie spoke, Stephen would immediately receive and repeat the words, "I know." These words were accompanied by a warm feeling of an all-knowing compassion which felt like it was coming from her long-lost friend. Finally, after all these years, she was able to release these feelings that would return to haunt her from time to time.

Four weeks after working with Bonnie, Stephen was doing Reiki on Ronnie, an eighteen-year-old boy who had been having problems with drugs, and he had dropped out of school. His mother Jill was present for the session since they were having trouble getting along and were frequently arguing with no resolution. Ronnie had been able to stop using drugs for a few months and he was determined to remain drug free. Stephen held his hands over Ronnie's eyes, and, after a few minutes, placed his hands on the back of Ronnie's head.

The goal was to relax Ronnie and work on overcoming the addiction by transmitting healing energy into his head in the hope of addressing any brain damage from the drugs. Stephen decided to use Reiki on Ronnie since he had used Reiki three weeks earlier on Tom, another young man who was in recovery from drugs and alcohol. When he worked on Tom, Stephen had felt pulsating pistons of energy emanating from his hands into the back of Tom's head for approximately five minutes. Stephen stopped when the pulsations stopped and he felt a calmness replace the tension in his hands. When Tom came for his next session, he reported feeling better and more clear headed. Stephen was sure Reiki would help Ronnie as well.

When Stephen placed his hands over Ronnie's eyes, he felt a large wave of energy come into the back door to his heart. At the same time, he felt the surge of sensations through his body, Stephen got a picture in his mind. It was of a man about thirty five years of age. He had brown hair that was parted on the left side. This man was slightly overweight yet he was still muscular. He was wearing blue jeans and a plaid lumberjack shirt that was unbuttoned. His sleeves were rolled up and his undershirt was showing.

Stephen began to feel waves of love for this boy flow through him along with the words, "I'm sorry I had to leave you when you were so young. I don't want you to follow in my footsteps. Drugs and alcohol are no good. It hurts me to see you and your mother fight so much. I wish you would try to get along with her."

The words stopped and the spirit of the man seemed to leave. Stephen kept his hands on the back of Ronnie's head as he had done with Tom. He felt the same pulsating pistons of energy he had felt with Tom. When the tension left his hands, he stopped.

Jill broke the silence and said, "I could feel my deceased ex-husband in the room." She said, "We divorced before he died from alcoholism." Stephen decided to ask a few questions to verify the validity of what he had pictured.

When he asked Jill to describe her deceased ex-husband, she said, "He was thin with long hair." Immediately, Stephen started to question what he had seen. Then I, as the still small voice within him, nudged him to ask, "Did your ex-husband always look that way?"

Jill quickly responded by saying, "No. He was much heavier when he died and his hair was shorter like Ronnie's hair. Only unlike Ronnie's, which you can see is parted in the middle, his hair was parted on the left side."

Stephen asked, "What did he tend to wear?"

She replied, "He usually wore jeans and long-sleeve plaid shirts with the sleeves rolled up on his forearms." Jill then pointed to how Stephen's sleeves were rolled up, saying, "Like yours." She went on to describe how he was often very casual. "He would wear his shirt with the shirt tail out, unbuttoned, and open so that the undershirt was showing." Jill's description matched the picture in Stephen's mind.

While Stephen was listening to Jill, he noticed that the slight pain he had on the right side of his head and running down into his shoulder was still there. Stephen had attributed the pain to the longer-than-usual period of time that he had held his arms up in order to keep his hands over Ronnie's eyes. Again, I, as the still small voice within him, prompted him to ask, "Did your ex-husband have any physical problems when he died?"

"Yes," Jill answered. She pointed to the right side of her head and shoulder, saying, "He had a pain in that area from an injury he received from doing some carpentry before he died." Stephen said a silent prayer for the deceased man to return to the light of

God's love. Then Stephen silently asked the spirit of the man to remove from him any physical, mental, emotional, and spiritual residue the man may have left by entering into Stephen's body. The pain instantly vanished.

These initial glimpses into the spirit realm did not stop there but continued on an as-needed basis. Stephen didn't know it at the time but the need to make contact with the spirit realm was always determined by the Holy Spirit. Somehow his heart knew this since he would issue the caveat, "With the Holy Spirit as the gatekeeper, may _____ (a person's deceased loved one with whom he or she had unfinished emotional business) be allowed to come through for the purpose of healing." The gift of the discerning of spirits was not limited to seeing or feeling the welcomed presence of a person's deceased loved ones bringing messages of love and forgiveness. Sometimes there were malevolent intruders. . . .

* * *

LIKE A CHILD JUMPING FOR JOY IN A SUMMER RAINBOW of droplets falling from a pinched garden hose, Stephen was awed by all of his spiritual experiences. He was being showered with all kinds of signs and wonders in the years following the magical year of 1995. And by the dawning of the new millennium, Stephen was even more awed and filled with gratitude for the gifts bestowed upon him on that blessed night in the Fall of 1995.

The Holy Spirit had blown open the doors of Stephen's spiritual perception. He began to see how the space between Heaven and Earth was not only populated with angels and demons but with what the Maya called "our space brothers and sisters," or what the Native Americans called the "star nation people." He would also discover that just as there are angels and fallen angels or demons so there are both benevolent and malevolent visitors from the stars.

* * *

ON A FEBRUARY NIGHT IN THE WINTER OF 1996, A STRANGE visitor appeared. Stephen had just completed the next phase of training with Dr. Baldwin and his wife Judith. But before going into that night, a little background might be helpful.

The Baldwins had incorporated the key concepts from the several-hundred-page text entitled *A Course in Miracles*. In a nutshell, the concepts from the course presented by the Baldwins boiled down to having no fear since as the course teaches, "Only love is real," and, "Nothing real can be threatened."

The powerful reality of love was brought home dramatically in a case reported by psychiatrist Dr. Brian Weiss in his book *Only Love Is Real*. Weiss was doing a past life regression with a patient. Contrary to anything he had ever witnessed with previous patients recalling past lives, the man under hypnosis saw a fiery landscape populated by demonic figures. Stephen thought of the third panel of the famous three-paneled painting by Hieronymous Bosch: *The Garden of Earthly Delights*. This third panel graphically portrays hell. The painting with all its gruesome images had been before his eyes for the entire year before he left for graduate school. Stephen had rented the small cottage of an English professor set in the rolling hills of Southern Pennsylvania. The professor was on sabbatical overseas. The painting with its disturbing images had hung on the wall over Stephen's bed while the outside of the cottage was bordered by a beautiful meadow.

Suddenly as Weiss' patient was looking at the hellish landscape, Jesus appeared and spoke to the man, saying, "Don't you know that all this is an illusion. Only love is real." And with that the fiery landscape changed into a beautiful meadow. Thinking back to that time in his life, Stephen now saw the peaceful pastoral scene of a soft meadow embracing the cottage containing Bosh's painting as a curious kind of presaging of this insight into the reality of love.

The training with the Baldwins reinforced his connection to the Holy Spirit. Armed with the awareness of the Holy Spirit, Stephen felt no fear in the face of evil spirits, what he called dark-energy beings. When facing apparitions of evil in healing sessions, he was fearless since he focused on the light and love of the Holy Spirit within him.

In reading the preface of *A Course in Miracles*, Stephen was astonished to discover the unusual origin of the text. The story of how the course came about dated back to the early seventies, when Stephen was just out of college. The preface indicated that the course was the result of a collaboration between Helen Schuchman and William Thetford. Both were professors of medical psychology at Columbia University's College of Physicians and Surgeons in Manhattan. Stephen was familiar with this college at Columbia since he received his training in basic medical hypnosis there in the Fall of 1981. His curiosity was piqued when he read in the preface that the origin of the course reveals how, indeed, "with God all things are possible" since these two professors were described as "anything but spiritual." In fact, Helen described herself as an "atheist" and both she and William were caught up in the competitive world of academia. They were interested in advancing in their field and in receiving recognition and acclaim. Stephen then read how the impetus for the course came one day when the chairman of the medical psychology department expressed his dismay with the hostile-competitive attitude of the department. He stated his belief that, "There must be another way."

Helen agreed. Stephen then loved how it said that Helen's "willingness gave the Holy Spirit a small opening to allow His power to go to work and create another way."

Given his work with dreams, Stephen understood how Helen kept having strange dreams. The next thing he read was startling to Stephen; Helen reported hearing what she referred to as the "Voice" which was said to be the voice of Jesus. Stephen was fascinated by what Helen described as a rapidly delivered "inner dictation" that would take place each night. Helen would write down the teachings she was receiving, and each day William would type out what Helen had been given in the night. "The special assignment" took place over seven years during which three volumes were produced: a lengthy text, a workbook for students, and a manual for teachers.

Jesus had shown up again in Stephen's association with the Baldwins. He appeared before Stephen's session with the Baldwins and now His teaching on love from *A Course in Miracles* was part of this next level of training with the Baldwins. For two weeks students taking the training learned to keep turning over any fear that may arise to the Holy Spirit. Stephen was not unprepared for what was about to happen . . . an unplanned final exam, a true spiritual test. . . .

Following the last night of the two week intensive program in in learning how to clear clients of unseen attachments, Stephen was awakened at four o' clock in the morning. Something strange was happening to his body. He described the event in *A Matter of Love*.

The molecules of my body seemed to be changing. I was excited as I felt like I was going to levitate right up through the sheets and blanket covering me. The large figure standing in the darkness was unimportant to me. I was more focused on how much fun it would be to float up to the ceiling and see if I could touch my toes to the ceiling. I had never been able to float in a pool without my legs sinking so that only my face remained above water. I got the impression that an energy was lifting me up.

At the same time that I felt an energy lifting me, I also felt as if a large palm, presumably the palm of the dark figure to my left, was lifting me. I started to slip off this palm. As I lost my balance, I was suddenly afraid of falling.

As soon as I felt the fear of falling, I reacted by visualizing the Tibetan Reiki Master Symbol and I [silently] said, *With this sacred symbol, I attune myself to the light and love of the Holy Spirit.* I visualized the sacred symbol as part of my commitment to shift negative emotions like fear and anger back to love. I had been making it a spiritual practice to use my own steps, the ones I outlined in *8 Steps to Love*, to shift all negative emotions to love.

Instantly, my body went back to normal. I then noticed the large dark figure race out of my room. It moved so fast, there appeared to be a trail of streak lines behind it; it seemed terrified!

Then the room lit up. It was as if everyone in the motel went into the parking lot, turned their car around, and shined their headlights into my room. Not likely at four in the morning! I then heard a soft-sounding, whoosh. It seemed that a spacecraft of some kind had just taken off into the night sky.

He lay there wondering if he had thwarted an alien abduction.

The next morning, he spoke to a woman who was also in the training. She was considered a naturally-gifted trance medium. She went into trance and began to tell him about the shadowy, dark figure. She described the figure as a demonic male energy with the classic extraterrestrial appearance of a large oval head with almond-shaped eyes. There was no trace of kindness or benevolence about his energy—he was malevolent and arrogant.

As the medium made contact with this alien infested with demonic energy, the being became more puffed-up and arrogant. As soon as that happened, Stephen again visualized the Tibetan Reiki Master Symbol, and he silently repeated the phrase: *With this sacred symbol, I attune myself to the light and love of the Holy Spirit*. Immediately, the medium's head snapped back and she came right out of trance, exclaiming, "Something scared him! He just flew out of the room!"

Stephen was surprised at how silently calling upon the light and love of the Holy Spirit sent the demonic alien scurrying as it had the night before. Stephen jumped for joy, thinking, *What a beautiful gift and message! When we remember the Spirit of God within us, the power of love, we are invulnerable!*

A few years later, Stephen was stunned when he stumbled upon the work of Dr. John Mack, noted Harvard Medical School professor of psychiatry. Of course it was no accident, I guided him to Mack's work. When Stephen read Mack's *Passport to the Cosmos*, he found confirmation of what he had experienced and discovered both personally and clinically.

Nona and Abby, two of the abductees that Mack worked with, reported the same kind of thing that Stephen had experienced. Nona described a "vibration under my back," and "a sense of being lifted." Abby told Mack that she felt as if her cells were "coming apart." She went on to describe feeling that she was "becoming separated molecularly." Stephen had a similar sensation when he described feeling as if the molecules in his body were changing and he was going to levitate.

It was in the experience of another abductee named Isabel that he found confirmation for the power of love. Isabel reported sending love to angry aliens. Mack interpreted her experience, saying, "It seemed that as she sent positive love energy toward these angry beings, she could hear them shrieking and saw them running, then backing off through the wall."

In another instance, Isabel was approached by a hostile alien to whom she sent love, and this time she called on Jesus. Isabel indicated that the alien responded by making a "weird sound," and it then "went down as if it were in pain."

Stephen was excited by the similarity of his experience to what Isabel described. He saw the huge dark alien by his bed race the length of his motel room and pass *through* the wall. The alien Stephen encountered acted in a similar way when Stephen called on the light and love of the Holy Spirit. Calling on Jesus or the Holy Spirit seemed to neutralize the angry aliens. Stephen was grateful that he had been given the chance to experience firsthand the truth of what he had learned in his training with the Baldwins: "Only love is real," and, "Nothing real can be threatened."

* * *

AS HAPPENED WITH THE ANGELS AFTER HIS RETURN HOME from Puerta Vallarta, aliens invaded the confines of Stephen's clinical practice. In A Matter of Love, he described what happened to Kathy, a woman in her early forties. Kathy was seeing him for help with the painful loss of her mother. During her Wednesday morning psychotherapy session, Kathy related a dream she had on Monday night. Kathy indicated that what she was about to tell Stephen seemed more real than a dream.

> I was awakened in the middle of the night by a huge sphere of light glowing brightly in my backyard. The next thing I knew, I was in my backyard under what appeared to be a round spacecraft of some kind. Standing there in disbelief, I found myself being slowly lifted by a kind of tractor beam of light through open doors on the bottom of the craft. It was like I was being beamed up into the craft as used to happen in the television show *Star Trek*. But unlike the show, I was being beamed up intact instead of dematerializing and rematerializing.

Once aboard, Kathy saw these strange beings. "The beings were tall and thin with large oval heads and big almond-shaped eyes. She was a little unnerved with them standing over her. Kathy described them as wearing "silver space suits" but she found the light in the chamber was so harshly bright that it was hard for her to see the beings clearly. She then described being examined.

> I was strapped in a chair with my wrists bound by straps to the arms of the chair. It was a kind of metal recliner with my legs propped up. My ankles were strapped to the bottom of the chair, and my feet were in stirrups, like the ones at my gynecologist's office when he is giving me a gynecological exam.

She was visibly nervous as she seemed to relive the experience in telling Stephen about it. She continued her account of the exam.

> One of the beings drew my nightgown back, exposing my inner thighs. I was freaking out inside, but I was careful to keep still and not react. I didn't want to provoke them. The being gently scraped my inner thighs with a small and slender fork-like instrument. I got the impression the being was attempting to take a skin sample. The next thing I remembered was waking up in my bed after my alarm went off. I got up and got ready for work.

Kathy described feeling a little dazed and groggy when she got up. She felt as if she had been drugged. She reported feeling more normal after her morning coffee. Later that same day, she told Stephen that something even more strange happened:

> When I was having lunch in the cafeteria of the company where I work, I overheard a woman talking at the next table. I was stunned when the woman told the two women sitting with her: 'Last night I had the strangest dream. I dreamt that I was taken aboard a flying saucer by a beam of light. The aliens put me in a chair and scraped my inner thighs with a long thin fork.

The woman's dream stunned Stephen as much as it did Kathy. Stephen remembered thinking that two people with the same dream in the same town seemed more unlikely than the two women both experiencing something that really happened. Here was confirmation that the space between the stars and planet Earth is indeed populated with other intelligent beings.

* * *

FOUR MONTHS LATER, STEPHEN FOUND THAT NOT ALL encounters with aliens are negative. Now, years later, he looked up at the stars from the window of the train to Philadelphia. Stephen's thoughts drifted back to the strange visitation that happened on the night before departing to the sacred Mayan sites in Mexico in early June of 1996. Immediately after he had turned the lights off in his Connecticut home, the room suddenly shimmered with long wavy columns of greenish light about two-feet wide and stretching from floor to ceiling.

The light reminded him of the eerie green glow of Saint Elmo's Fire which sailors have reported seeing all around the mast and sails of their ship during storms at sea. The columns of light then coalesced into towering greenish-light beings. They were human-looking and they were wearing small green-light crowns that had a feathered and floral design. Sensations of energy flooded into the center of his back: the back door to his heart.

As he lay there, he felt his whole body quiver with a steady stream of loving energy. Then he felt another of the greenish-light beings step into the room through the wall and the headboard of the bed. One being stood to Stephen's left. Facing Stephen, he bowed slightly and extended his left hand from his waist in a grand sweeping gesture. No words were exchanged. But in his thoughts, Stephen heard the words, "Welcome back to the brotherhood." Stephen felt powerful energies surging through his body.

There were twelve beings radiating a love and warmth to him. Later on, the shamans would tell him that he had had a direct experience of our "space brothers and sisters." A sister did not appear until the second visitation that happened the first night he arrived home.

At the end of his trip, he had flown into Boston's Logan Airport and had driven back to Connecticut. The very instant he climbed into bed and flipped off the lights, the greenish-light beings reappeared. Only this time, in addition to the tall male beings, there was a small female figure. She looked like a priestess with a distinctive headdress. During the trip to the pyramids of Mexico, the Mayan shamans led ceremonies designed to integrate male and female energy.

A year later, Stephen got the chance to ask the Mayan shamans about the beings who visited him. He was told that the greenish-light beings were star beings from the Pleiades. The Mayan shaman don Serillo told him that four of these beings came from the stars of the Pleiades and they gave the Maya their astronomy and mathematics. The Pleiades, known as the seven sisters, is 400 light years away. That means that for a spacecraft to span the gap between Earth and these stars, it would take 400 years, traveling at the speed of light, 186,000 feet per second. Despite such a distance, the Mayan shaman don Serillo claimed that these star beings lived among the Maya until one day they returned to the stars. Stephen describes this in more detail in *A Matter of Love*. For now, suffice it to say, Stephen felt an energy flutter up his spine as he listened to the Mayan shaman don Serillo tell the story of these four lords that came from the stars to start the Mayan civilization. Such shivers came to be interpreted by Stephen as a spiritual confirmation.

Stephen found further confirmation in John Mack's interviews with two Native Americans: Sequoyah Trueblood and Wallace Balk Elk. Like the Maya, the tribe of Sequoyah Trueblood claim that they are descended from the star people that come from the Pleiades. It is common for his people to not only see the star people land on Earth; it is also common for members of his tribe to talk with them.

For Sequoyah, the star people have been spiritual teachers. He told Mack the following: "Every day the invisible ones, extraterrestrials, spirit—all the same—taught me and showed me how to be peaceful and loving in any situation, how to be thankful for all that has happened to me and to be thankful for all that was to come."

Regarding extraterrestrials and why the scientific evidence is scarce, Stephen found Black Elk's comments very insightful. Of the scientists, Black Elk had this to say, "They [scientists] have to catch one first. They have to shoot it down and see what it is made of, how it was shaped and formed. But their intention is wrong, so somebody is misleading those scientists . . . But the biggest joke is on those scientists, because they lost contact with those star-nation people.

Stephen found his thoughts shifting back to when he first saw the word sidereal. He thought of how he had discovered it meant "of or pertaining to the stars" while he was writing *A Matter of Love*. He was writing the section on the new paradigm described by Dr. José Argüelles in his book *Earth Ascending*. Argüelles argued that it was time to move beyond our competition and war-based world and stop ignoring what Native Americans such as Black Elk and others call the Star Nation people.

Stephen's spine tingled as he recalled Argüelles claiming that humanity is being prepared for a "galactic-link up." Given his own experience with the Star Nation people, Stephen loved the vision Argüelles was proposing for the future: an interplanetary civilization of harmony on the Earth and beyond.

In line with the new paradigm, Stephen remembered writing of the need to expand the vision of the future to include each person learning to access the radiant star of his or her divine, sidereal self. He thought of how humankind needs to relinquish the narcissistic delusion that humans are the only intelligence in this vast universe.

* * *

STEPHEN HAD EMERGED FROM THE COOL, DARK JUNGLE, flashlight in hand. The predawn darkness was beginning to recede and the air was chilly; he could even see his breath float across the space in front of him, lit by the beam of light cast by the flashlight. A sense of the sacred filled him as he stepped into the shadowy courtyard of the ancient Mayan city of Tikal, Guatemala and looked up. Before him stood the tall, imposing structures of the pyramids. He was there because of his Reiki teacher Mercedes. She had invited him to go to Tikal with her and some other students from his Reiki class. Once there, they would join with many others from all over the world: Australia, Europe, and from the East Coast, Mid-West, and the West

239

Coast of America including Canada and British Columbia. They were all there to tap into the ancient wisdom of the Mayan shamans and participate in sacred consciousness-raising ceremonies to help awaken the heart of humanity from a five-thousand-year period of darkness and usher in a new period of peace on Earth.

According to the Mayan calendar, that period was to begin on the Winter Solstice of December 21, 2012.

In the meantime, the shamans believed the Earth would be going through drastic changes. These changes would be reflected in an increase in extreme weather patterns such as more hurricanes, floods, and tornadoes as well as an increase in the number and magnitude of earthquakes, volcanoes, and tsunamis. The consciousness of humanity had greatly impacted the Earth, and the ceremonies were to help ease the transition from centuries of discord and war to a more peaceful and harmonious world.

Today was the Spring Equinox of 1998. The group began to climb the long stone stairway to the top of the tall pyramid called the Temple of the Moon. While the others awaited for the sunrise, Stephen entered the sacred chamber at the peak of the pyramid.

The sanctuary was dimly lit by the pale predawn light. The sun was not due to appear for a half hour. To his surprise, he found himself visualizing his ex-wife Kathy. He could see the light of love in her eyes.

Filled with sorrow and regret, he imagined saying to her, "Please forgive me for ever doubting your love, for not accepting it. I'm sorry I couldn't believe and trust that you loved me no matter what!"

All of a sudden, the light of love in her eyes expanded and intensified as if incinerating the whole scene. She was gone. The stone walls were gone. All that remained was a blinding light which he knew was God since it was emanating an immensely-loving Paternal presence. In his heart, Stephen could feel that he was in the presence of God the Father, the Creator of the universe and all the billions of stars and all the galaxies.

His heart cried out before his head could catch up and process what was happening. As automatically and as involuntarily as a knee responds to the physicians's rubber hammer, he began repeating the same words to God as this blinding light. Later that day, he would think of Moses standing awestruck before the radiant light of the Burning Bush on Mount Sinai.

Flooded with feeling, Stephen sobbed deeply as he continued speaking to the light of the Creator, "Please forgive me for ever doubting Your love, for ever doubting You were always and are always with me!" Then the words, "I never stopped loving You! I just kept trying to replace You!" flew out of his mouth. These were the actual words he had said to his ex-wife Kathy. He had turned to her, took her in his arms, and said these same words as they watched the sun set on the bay by the village of Stonington, Connecticut on Christmas Day. He remembered thinking, *Christmas Day is the Birthday of God as Love.* He was now saying to God as this blinding light, "Please forgive me for trying to replace You."

Just as his heart had silenced his mind when he had encountered Jesus in the Reiki meditation, so did his heart override his head. The light had a deeply loving and *personal* and paternal presence about it. His catharsis was not unlike the kind his patients had had in therapy when reliving a scene from childhood. In such scenes, they would find themselves overcome with emotion as they were finally able to express in fantasy to a beloved parent something they had not been able to express as a child. Similarly, the floodgates were open for Stephen as well—only he was speaking to the Creator of all that is, God the Father with Whom Stephen experienced a personal relationship. His head found it strange to be talking to this light but his heart felt it to be as natural as if he were addressing Earl—his own flesh-and-blood father.

Stephen was sobbing deeply as he said these words to God in the form of this blinding light of divine love. His heart and soul were filled with deep gratitude for feeling that he had always been loved by God no matter what. He also felt that deep in his heart he had always loved and been loved by this personal and paternal presence that was God.

How could this be happening? he remembered thinking and shaking his head in amazement. He was grieving over more than his separation from this woman he had loved and been married to when

Gerry and Earl died. He was grieving over his separation from God as the ultimate source of pure unconditional love. The insight struck him like a bolt of lightning; he was shaken to the very core of his being.

Stephen's whole body was trembling with a profound joy. He felt as if he had come back *home* after being away for far too long. At that moment, God, the Divine Beloved, became a real concrete loving presence to him. Stephen watched the light fade and the walls of the small sanctuary reappeared. He was left with a profound feeling that God loved him and so he could now love himself, and, he could let himself be loved. A core problem had been illuminated: he had never really trusted that anyone could love him apart from what he did (his profession and accomplishments) or had (his bank account and possessions). Why? Because he didn't love and accept himself apart from the external stuff. That had been his dilemma in all his love relationships since his first girlfriends in high school.

Then, through his tears, he spotted Christian, a man in the group who was from Australia, standing by the doorway leading to the platform at the top of the stairs. Stumbling slightly as he stepped out of the sanctuary, Stephen went over to Christian and shared with him what had just happened. "It's not about separation from my former love," he exclaimed to Christian with tears of joy in his eyes. "It's about my separation from God as Love and from myself."

The two men embraced. It was interesting to Stephen that Christian just happened to be the best one out of the whole group to be standing closest to Stephen at that very moment. Christian was the only other person on the trip that was the same size and height as Stephen. The symmetry of their shared size seemed to validate and ground electrical charge of Stephen's mystical experience.

Stephen wiped the tears from his eyes and, standing atop the pyramid, he looked across the courtyard to the Temple of the Sun. There in the shadows of the portal to the sanctuary, he had a vision of Christ Jesus. In the Temple of the Sun Stephen saw the Son after experiencing God the Father. Stephen was stunned by the synchronicity that he had literally embraced Christian, a man whose name had the name Christ within it and was also the name of the religion into which he had been baptized and confirmed. Here he was having deeply moving experiences related to his Christian roots.

Then, Stephen remembered how the words of Jesus had come into his mind as if to crown the moment and cement into his heart what he needed to learn.

> You shall love the Lord your God with all your heart, with all your soul, and with all your mind. This is the first and greatest commandment. And the second is like it. You shall love your neighbor as thyself. On these two commandments hang all the Law and the Prophets (Matthew 22: 37-40).

Stephen could now see clearly how he had failed to follow the part of Christ's commandment that included self-love, that is, loving our neighbor "as thyself."

A few hours later that morning, the Mayan shamans conducted a sacred fire ceremony. On four separate times during the ceremony, Stephen stood ten feet from the sacred fire, cupped his hands, and held them up to send Reiki healing energy to the sacred fire. Each time he called on the Holy Spirit to bless the group encircling the fire. He asked for each person to receive the healing that the Holy Spirit would have each person receive, the healing they truly needed, spiritually, mentally, emotionally, and physically.

Each time Stephen cupped his hands and sent Reiki to the fire, the flames of the fire shot up into a whirling vortex. He felt the presence of the Holy Spirit in the fire. Here he was amid ancient pyramids and he was experiencing the Trinity of Father, Son, and Holy Spirit. To top off the day, he went out with a group of people to find a restaurant in the area outside of Tikal. The very first one they spotted was called *Corazón de Jesus* (The Heart of Jesus).

What a surprise it was for Stephen to experience the Trinity amid the ancient pyramids of the Maya, the Native Americans of Central America. He was now experiencing firsthand what he would later hear Christian minister Arthur Burk claim about the Trinity. As first mentioned in chapter five, God the Father gave the Native Americans the task of bringing through the knowledge of Him, the First Person of the Trinity.

Now, sitting back on the train, he reflected on the implications of his mystical experience of the light of God's love. Stephen thought of the film *End of the Affair*. He had seen it at the beginning of the new millennium. A particular scene from the film slipped into his thoughts. The theme was that there is no separation from love. The two lovers, Sarah (Julianne Moore) and Maurice (Raif Finnes) are discussing love. Sarah's position mirrored what Stephen had discovered in the Temple of the Moon.

> Sarah says, "You think love ends when you don't see me. Love doesn't end just because we don't see each other."
> "Doesn't it?" Maurice asks.
> "People go on loving God all their lives without seeing Him."
> Maurice responds, "That's not my kind of love."
> Sarah says softly, "Maybe there is no other kind."

As Stephen reflected on the exchange between Sarah and Maurice, he identifies the shift that had taken place in him ever since that day in Tikal. Before that, he was Maurice. Love was not constant and unchanging. Since that day, he began to see love as Sarah does. There is no separation from love, especially God's love. And, similar to Sarah, he thought, *Perhaps, there is no other kind of love.* Shakespeare's Sonnet 116 came into his thoughts:

> Let me not to the marriage of true minds admit impediments;
> Love is not love which alters when it alteration finds: Nor bends
> with the remover to remove. Oh no it is an ever-fixed mark; That
> looks on tempests but is never shaken. . . .

Empowered by his encounter with the all-powerful and pervasive love of the Three Persons of the Trinity, he was met with two challenges right after he returned home. The first was from a colleague. Samantha was a clinical psychologist who was experimenting with brain-wave research and altered states of consciousness. One night she had an unsettling experience that left her feeling that she was not herself. She called Stephen for a Reiki session. Samantha was seated in the large chair in her office when Stephen was startled. . . .

* * *

THE FACE OF A GREEN-COLORED DEMON WITH SKIN LIKE slimy clay appeared next to Samantha's left foot. The ghoulish face had appeared to Stephen as soon as he began Samantha's Reiki session. Stephen was reminded of the comic-book character Swamp Thing. He had once seen this demon in a dream five years earlier. In the dream, he looked up and saw this demon sitting by a second-story window. In the dream, Stephen had looked straight into the demon's red eyes, saying, "Oh, it's you." Somehow, deep down, Stephen knew this demon but he didn't know how he knew. Then, he said, "I'm not going to take you on by myself." Then following what he had learned from Dr. Baldwin, Stephen forcefully proclaimed, "I call upon Archangel Michael and the legions of Heaven to come and gather this one up in its own capsule of God's light, layer upon layer."

Stephen had not yet gone back to the word of God, the Bible, to know that he could simply act on the authority given to all believers in Christ Jesus. Jesus gave authority to all who believe in Him. He gave all believers power and authority over all demons, saying: "And these signs will accompany those who believe. In my name, they will drive out demons" (Mark 16:17). Even without being familiar with the powerful promise of this scripture, Stephen felt no fear because he was filled with the Holy Spirit.

When Stephen spotted the red-eyed demon with the green-clay-like complexion, he used Baldwin's procedure and silently called to Archangel Michael and the legions of Heaven to wrap this demon up and carry him away. The demon disappeared, and Samantha reported feeling better even though Stephen had driven out the demon with a silent prayer.

He continued sending the almighty healing energy of the light of God's love (his definition of Reiki healing energy) by holding his hands over Samantha's eyes. The Holy Spirit then gave him a vision. This vision is an example of another gift bestowed upon him on that night in Rockport. Referred to as the gift of word of knowledge, it involves receiving information not available to the five senses. In his mind's eye, he was given a vision of Samantha at five years old. She was sitting on the side of her father on a sofa. Her father was looking straight ahead at the television. He seemed to be tolerating Samantha snuggling up next to him.

245

When Stephen shared with Samantha what he had seen, she said, "You know that's the only memory I have of my father being affectionate to me. And I'm not even sure it's a real memory or just a fantasy." The vision of the demon and of her father's coldness made Stephen think of the rumors he had heard about Samantha's father. Some suspected him of having Mafia connections. *Certainly*, Stephen thought, *such a gruesome demon epitomized the ruthlessness of the Mafia.*

A few days after this session with Samantha, Stephen received a call from Carrie, a distressed young woman who was a sophomore at New York University. She had been using drugs in her freshman year. From time to time, even when she was not on drugs, she experienced what she felt could best be described as "possessed." Carrie had seen a psychiatrist for psychotherapy and medication. It was all to no avail. The episodes of possession kept happening. During those times, Carrie's roommate described Carrie as appearing to be "another person."

Carrie told Stephen that multiple personality or dissociative identity disorder, as it is currently called, was ruled out by the psychiatrist. By the end of her freshman year, Carrie was discouraged and scared. Over the summer, she researched possession and she discovered a book by Dr. Edith Fiore, a psychologist in California. In her book *The Unquiet Dead*, Dr. Fiore described how she discovered that some of her patients, notably those with psychotic symptoms, were suffering from "spirit attachment." They were possessed by earthbound spirits and/or by demonic spirits.

Carrie felt hopeful when she read that Dr. Fiore successfully used a process of clinical depossession with those patients suffering from spirit attachment. Psychotic symptoms such as delusions and hallucinations disappeared. Carrie was disappointed when she called Dr. Fiore's office and was unable to get an appointment. Instead, Carrie was referred to Dr. Baldwin in Florida. Baldwin, in turn, referred Carrie to two men he had trained both of whom lived in New York. One was too expensive for Carrie; he wanted three hundred and fifty dollars for a session. Insurance wouldn't cover it as it had for the psychiatrist. The other man did not have the time to take her case and referred her to Stephen.

Carrie called Stephen. After listening to Carrie's story, Stephen agreed to help her *pro bono* since she was struggling financially as a college student. He explained that he would do a remote release of the spirit and a distant Reiki healing on her that night. At eleven o'clock, Stephen knelt beside the sofa, and he imagined Carrie lying down in front of him. Then he placed his hands on the air where he was imagining Carrie. In doing distant healings, he would place his hands in the air where he imagined the recipient of Reiki to be seated or lying down. Then he prayed the following over Carrie.

> I call upon You, Beloved Holy Spirit, to guide this release and healing. Thank You for bestowing upon me the blessing that allows me to proclaim: I AM a beacon of Your light of divine love, a clear and powerful lens through which the almighty healing energy of the light of Your divine love may shine to those lost in the dark night of pain and suffering. Tonight, may the light of Your love radiate into Carrie so that she may receive the healing that You would have her receive, the healing she truly needs spiritually, mentally, emotionally, and physically so that she may be set free of this pain and torment.

Aligned with the Holy Spirit, he boldly addressed the entity by saying aloud with a stern voice: "You, the cowardly being who would prey upon a young woman, I command you to come to me now!" Instantly, the whole wall of the room behind the sofa filled with an immense dark, shadowy form. Its head and shoulders loomed large in the darkness. The dim glow of distant street lights provided enough of a contrast to reveal the menacing dark being. A childhood memory of the scene from Walt Disney's film *Fantasia* flashed into his mind. He remembered that segment of the film being entitled *Night on Witch Mountain*. A huge dark figure rises up out of the mountain to fill the entire movie screen. Despite being a scene from an animated film with a cartoon quality, it had scared him as a small boy caught up in the powerful music of the film accompanying the scary image.

For an instant, Stephen was as scared as he had been as a child, and I had never seen this happen to him before. He was fearless all the previous times he had done clinical depossessions either with the person present or at a distance. This time I could hear him think, *Oh my God! Have I bitten off more than I can chew?!*

Then he snapped out of his momentary lapse. It was as if he had been mesmerized and forgotten the presence of the Holy Spirit and Lord Jesus Christ as his Reiki Master Guide. Calm, centered and completely confident in the almighty healing energy of the light of the Holy Spirit directing the session, he then commanded the demon, saying aloud, "In the name of my Reiki Master Guide Lord Jesus Christ, I command you and any other entities in or around Carrie out of her now!" Dr. Baldwin had taught that dark force entities (demons) often form networks. He continued, "And I refuse you and any of your network permission to ever enter Carrie's body or mind in an attempt to control her in any way!" He then did as Dr. Baldwin had instructed, he called on Archangel Michael and the legions of Heaven to come and wrap this demon up in its own capsule of the light of God and lift it away from Carrie. He also included any other entities associated with this one.

Then, abbreviating Dr. Baldwin's more detailed procedure, he had the demon discover the light of God in its core and gave it the choice to repent and return to the light of God's love or to return to the pit of hell. In his mind's eye, he saw and heard the demon repent for all the damage it had done to Carrie and others. It chose the light of God. With the fallen dark angel returned to its true nature as an angel of light, Stephen ended the session by sending Reiki throughout Carrie's body. He wanted to make sure she was filled with the power of the Holy Spirit.

Two days later, Carrie called and told Stephen that she felt free for the first time since she had been experiencing these episodes of possession. She had lost Stephen's phone number so she couldn't call him the morning after the session. She awoke feeling like her former self before the drug use and the periods of possession. She did not call again, and she knew she could should any problems return. She knew nothing of what Stephen had said or done; she only knew that she felt deeply different in the core of her being.

In the years to come, Stephen would be drawn back to God's word. And when he did, he refined his approach to bring it more in line with the Bible.

Stephen learned to pray before performing depossessions or healing by silently stating, "I accept the authority Jesus gave all embodied souls when he proclaimed, 'And these signs will accompany those who believe. In my name, they will drive out demons. [and] . . . they will lay their hands on the sick and the sick will recover'" (Mark 16:17-18). Stephen found another biblical translation of the first part of the above passage from Mark. He liked to proclaim the following version of the first sentence of (Mark 16:17): "Believers will be given the power to perform miracles." Then he would add the sentences about driving out demons and healing the sick.

Stephen was also led by me to read about the saint with the same name, Saint Stephen. In particular, I led him to the following words describing Saint Stephen in Acts 6:5. He felt a wave of energy move through him when he read the words describing Saint Stephen as having "an arm full of faith and full of and controlled by the Holy Spirit." He now knew what that meant for he had had moments of feeling that in his body not only on the night of his anointing but when sending healing energy when laying on hands. He felt the energy of the Holy Spirit whether laying hands on a person before or at a great distance. He was especially moved when he saw it written, "Stephen full of grace and power [from the Holy Spirit] worked great wonders and signs among the people" (Acts 6:8). He felt honored to have the same name with the same spelling instead of the more customary spelling of Steven.

Next, in researching healings in the Bible, he was inspired by the following, "Now by the hands of the apostles numerous and startling signs and wonders were being performed among the people" (Acts 5:12).

Reading the Bible also reaffirmed and deepened his understanding of the mystery of the Three Persons of the Trinity. Indeed, the Father, Son, and Holly Spirit were manifestations of one God. He then thought of *three in One Oil*, the words he had seen on a can of oil in the garage when he was a child. These words took on new meaning. The Three Persons are merged in one underlying substance: the expansive energy and peaceful power of pure love.

* * *

ALL OF HIS EXTRAORDINARY EXPERIENCES CONFIRMED THE truth of the view of reality that he learned in Sunday School: the realm of spirit populated by angels and demons (fallen angels) exists. It was mind-blowing. What a shock for Stephen as a highly-educated man. There was no denying his experiences, and he had the tools as a clinical psychologist to distinguish hallucinations from dreams, visions, signs (synchronicities) and wonders.

In the next few years, he would discover that on that miraculous October night in 1995, the Holy Spirit had bestowed upon him two more gifts. These two gifts were in addition to the gifts of healing, discerning spirits, and the occasional word of knowledge.

The first was the gift of faith in the impossible being possible. He was grateful that he had the heart of a child in spite of all his education and sophisticated psychological knowledge. He was so thankful that he truly believed in his flesh, blood, and bones that with God working in and through an embodied soul filled with faith, the impossible becomes possible.

The next gift was grounded in the gift of faith—the gift of performing miracles. He would have direct experience of the truth of the following biblical passage: "The things that are impossible with men are possible with God"(Luke 18:27). He loved how he was able to truly believe with the open heart of a child the words he once heard the colorful Louisiana-based preacher Jesse Duplantis say, "Believe the unbelievable and receive the impossible!"

In the last years of the twentieth century and into the dawning of the new millennium, he witnessed many miraculous healings which the Holy Spirit worked through him. Healings happened even when the person receiving the healing was thousands of miles away: India, Hungary, Italy, Africa, and Canada as well as all over the USA. Stephen was awed as he witnessed autism, cancer, pyogenic menningitus, and other serious conditions yielding to the healing power of the Holy Spirit.

The shifting winds of the Holy Spirit had cleared the cloud cover obscuring the spirit realm, and the light of God's love was shining through the space between Heaven and Earth. And, as awe-inspiring as his experiences were so far, he would be even more blown away by the miracles yet to come. . . .

Eight

Shifting Winds

SCIENTISTS SAY THE UNIVERSE IS EXPANDING FASTER AS it gets older. And in the ever-expanding universe, stellar nurseries give birth to new stars. One such nursery is the Eagle Nebulae which can be seen after nightfall near two other eagles of the night sky: the stars Altair and Vega. In Arabic Altair means "flying eagle" and Vega, "swooping eagle." Together they form two points on the summer triangle with Deneb the third. And the Eagle Nebulae lies in the space between these two stars. In late August of 1995, a famous photograph of the tall clouds of dust containing the eggs of new stars was taken by the Hubble Space Telescope. It was entitled *The Pillars of Creation*. Stephen was fascinated by the fact that new stars are born in the space between stars. Contemplating this period of his life, he recalled how dramatically it was demonstrated to him that miracles are born in the space between stars . . . between what is and what an embodied soul would love to have happen.

The train slowly pulled away from the platform in Trenton and headed for Philadelphia. There he would switch trains for the final train, the last leg of his journey home. Stephen considered how the universe expanding as it ages did not necessarily mean that getting older automatically equals expansion in awareness for human beings. Sure it can but, as one of his female patients once said, quoting her mother, "Some people grow up but others just grow

252

old." *Growing up seems to be a fitting way to describe spiritual growth. And surely spiritual growth involves gaining a more expanded perspective,* he concluded.

Then he thought of Jung's beautiful metaphor for maturity as involving viewing the storms of life from the top of a mountain instead of staying stuck in the storm in the valley below. For when embodied souls are caught up in the valley, they are buffeted about by the wild winds and pounding rains. When viewed from the mountaintop, the storm is not, as Jung put it, "robbed of its reality." It is as Stephen discovered in confronting the scary storm of hunger in the womb. By adopting my higher and wider perspective, embodied souls can be still and remain cool and calm as they experience the wild winds and floods of fear, anxiety, anger, and rage as well as the oppressive storm clouds of depression.

It was in these early years of the new millennium that Stephen came to see psychological and spiritual maturity as being able to *shift* the inner winds of emotional turbulence back to the cool and calm breeze of love. Showing embodied souls how to make this shift back to love in the heat of the moment of everyday life was his mission and the focus of his first book, *8 Steps to Love.*

It was also in the early years of the new millennium that the Holy Spirit kept steadily blowing many blessings into his life. With the power of the Holy Spirit inspiring him and teaching him how to shift and calm the inner winds of emotional turmoil, Stephen remembered how he glimpsed a new element to spiritual maturity: the ability to perform miracles. I led him back to take another look at *A Course in Miracles.* Stephen sensed the truth of the teachings of Jesus on love from the Bible being clothed in the dress of modern terms. Given his own experiences of the Holy Spirit, Stephen had no doubt that the Holy Spirit communicated to Columbia professor Helen Schuchman what later became the text of *A Course in Miracles.* Reflecting back over the last year and a half, he wondered whether the ability to perform miracles the way Jesus did was a part of maturing spiritually. And, if so, what is involved? From his own experience, he knew it had something to do with filling the space between the stars of what is and what one would love to have happen with love and not fear, anger, or despair. . . .

Looking at the silhouettes of trees and buildings while the train continued to speed along, he recalled listening to one of Marianne Williamson's recorded sermons. To him and many others, she was *the* foremost authority and clearest presenter of the key concepts of the lengthy, and, often abstruse, *A Course in Miracles*. Stephen loved her beautiful book *A Return to Love*. What she had to say in her sermon appealed to him both as a psychologist and as a healer.

The story of Easter is the story of the complete transcendence of the laws of this Earth. *A Course in Miracles* tells us that miracles reverse the laws of time and space—that miracles occur naturally as an expression of love. And that as an expression of love what occurs is an unfoldment in which all negativity, all lack, all scarcity, all darkness or pain of any kind is transformed into the energies of healing and correction. . . .

One thought kept reverberating in the chambers of his heart and mind, *Miracles occur naturally as an expression of love.* He knew that this was true. His reflections drifted back to the moment he witnessed a miracle on August 13, 2004. Friday the thirteenth. The miracle happened naturally as an expression of love at the very moment a great danger was about to strike. . . .

* * *

WHAT IS ABOUT TO BE SHARED REGARDING THE SHIFTING of winds and calming of storms do not follow the strict rules of research design. Stephen was well aware that there is no way that his experiences qualify as a controlled scientific study or experiment. All the variables are not controlled for so that the effectiveness of the interventions about to be discussed can be evaluated. Therefore, Stephen knows that no scientifically-valid claim can be made that Stephen's spiritual interventions were a key, if not, *the* key, factor to account for the miraculous results.

Stephen's doctoral level training taught him how to conduct sound scientific research. Thinking things through, he had to conclude that what happened was anecdotal. Nevertheless, he did employ the essential elements of the scientific method. In any scientifically sound experiment, the researcher relies on empirical observations of interventions and the immediacy of their effects on the events the interventions were intended to influence.

He made moment-to-moment observations of interventions and immediate feedback regarding their perceived impact. The immediate feedback involved the Weather Channel's reports based on reliable scientific equipment and sources. Such close observation of contiguous events suggested a *correlation* between interventions and their *immediate* impact on events. Reports made on the Weather Channel could justifiably be taken as a comment on the perceived efficacy of the interventions. The results of Stephen's interventions relate to a review of the *replicated* research literature on the efficacy of intercessory prayer.

Stephen was well aware of what was missing in his interventions in terms of research studies on prayer. He saw one glaringly absent variable not controlled for in his spiritually-based experiments: there may have been many thousands or millions of people praying for the same thing for which he was praying and using Reiki techniques. In addition, perhaps other Reiki practitioners were attempting to influence events as well. However, he was aware that there is a specificity in the evidence. The specific words used in his prayers would be repeated verbatim by the announcers on the Weather Channel. As you will see, the words Stephen used were not always the obvious ones weather reporters might use. Sometimes they were. Still, the specific nature of the correlation between what was desired and what happened was precise.

This precision that he observed was typical of his daily dialogue with the Divine. Essentially, his daily dialogue involves praying to God and watching the specifics of the synchronicities—*meaningful* coincidences—that follow the prayer request. In line with paying attention to the details of the daily dialogue, Stephen was fond of quoting actress Julianne Moore in the film *End of the Affair*, when she says to her lover, "Accidents, little things—God is in the details, Maurice."

Regarding the effectiveness of prayer, Stephen knew of the 1991 hospital-based study on prayer. It involved nearly four hundred hospitalized cardiac patients. The study found that the patients prayed for fared much better than those who were not prayed for, and the results were statistically significant. When Stephen was talking to the head of the research department at Sloan-Kettering Cancer Center in New York City in 2000, he learned that the study on prayer had been replicated in 1997 at a different hospital than the first study. The result was the same: prayer was effective. Both studies were double-blind. Neither patients (experimental subjects) nor the members of the treatment team (doctors and nurses) knew who was being prayed for and who was not.

Despite all his knowledge of research design, Stephen knew it only takes the prayer of one embodied soul for a miracle to happen. What Stephen was about to do with regard to hurricanes could be considered a prayer buttressed by the promise Jesus made when He declared:

> Verily, Verily, I say unto you, he that believeth on me, the works that I do, he shall do, and greater works than these because I go unto my Father. And whatsoever you shall ask in my name; that will I do, that the Father may be glorified in the Son (John 14:12-13).

And in another passage, Jesus indicates that faith the size of a mustard seed can move mountains (Matthew 17:20). In *8 Steps to Love*, Stephen discussed how Herbert Benson from Harvard Medical School described the tremendous power wielded by the *faith factor* in influencing the results obtained in research studies. What comes next is probably best understood as what a love focus can do when fueled by faith in the miraculous being possible. And again, Saint John's words echoed in his heart and mind: "God is love; and he that dwelleth in love dwelleth in God and God in him" (1 John 4:16). Then, he thought of his experience of God as the expansive energy and peaceful power of pure everlasting love in the Temple of the Moon. Holding that focus on God as love, he thought of a way to remind himself of love as God—the ultimate power operating in time and space. He placed the word love next to God, Christ, and Father in the following statements. The first

two are made by Jesus and the last one by Saint Paul.
With man this is impossible, but with God [love] all things are possible," (Matthew 19:26). Verily, Verily I say unto you, of mine own self, I can do nothing. It is the Father [love] within me, He [love] doeth the works (John 5:19). I can do all things through Christ [love] who strengthens me (Philippians 4:13).

The compelling power of the above biblical claims aside, Stephen knew the risk of disclosing what he believed to be miracles. To most embodied souls seeing reality with only their physical eyes, what is about to be described below is likely to seem ridiculous. Absurd. Laughable. Ludicrous. Nonetheless, Stephen was starting to see reality from my vantage point. And I have encouraged him to share his experience so that other embodied souls might reclaim their power to perform miracles. To be able to do what Jesus did when he healed the sick and calmed the winds is part of the path to spiritual maturity for all embodied souls should they decide they desire to fulfill their God-given divine destiny. In following the thread of his divine destiny, Stephen was about to discover that understanding miracles involves both science and spirit. Fact and faith.

＊ ＊ ＊

THE SUN WAS JUST APPEARING THROUGH THE TREES ON the ridge above the river. Stephen was appreciating this view from his balcony before sitting down at his computer to continue his work on *Love Conquers Stress*, the book he was finishing. The phone rang, disrupting his sunrise reverie. It was his friend Pat, one of his four Reiki Master friends. She was alarmed as she spoke, "Hurricane Charley is heading for the Florida Keys. . . ." Her only child, her daughter Melissa, had moved to Key West in the spring. "Winds are expected to be approaching 160 miles per hour," she said, her voice filled with concern and worry. She had already begun praying and sending Reiki. She then requested that Stephen send Reiki to help protect Melissa. He agreed and began to pray and send Reiki right away. He started using distant or remote Reiki healing techniques—the same he used when the person receiving Reiki was thousands of miles away.

His teacher Mercedes had taught him that it was helpful to imagine shrinking the person, place, or thing being sent Reiki. When turbulence happened on any airplanes he was on, he would picture the plane as small enough to fit under his cupped hands. Usually, within a matter of seconds, the shaking and jostling of the plane ceased. He now did the same thing by picturing Key West fitting under the protection of his cupped hands. It seemed appropriate to hold his hands in this position since he was actually praying as he intended enveloping Key West in a protective energy field. In some sense, he thought of his hands as an extension of the hands of God the Father.

After an hour, Stephen switched on the Weather Channel to monitor what was happening. He saw cars driving on a street with a minimal amount of excess water. The reporter indicated that Key West had weathered the storm well. The winds had not been as bad as expected. He was grateful and immediately said a prayer to thank God the Divine Beloved Father, Son, and Holy Spirit. The phone rang. It was Pat. She called to thank him—she was relieved.

Then came the next phase of his task for that day. His sweetheart Janet and her family lived in Sarasota. He also had dear friends at various points along Florida's West Coast from Sarasota to Tampa.

Stephen was now sitting at his computer writing while the television was on the Weather Channel in the background. He would take breaks from writing to pray and send Reiki to try to contain and slow down the storm's winds. He felt reassured that Sarasota would be protected as Key West had been. But then his hope was shaken. . . .

Suddenly, the reporter on the Weather Channel anxiously announced that Charley just became a category four with winds upwards of 150 miles per hour and was expected to slam into Sarasota and proceed on to the Tampa Bay area. Fear shot through Stephen. His beloved and her family were in danger! He was immediately galvanized into action. No more passive and peaceful Reiki. He sprang up and placed his hands over the orange area of doppler radar revealing Charley's whereabouts. Then, in a loud and authoritative voice, he proclaimed, "Father God, with Your permission, I AM an extension of Your Almighty I AM Presence in action now! And in the name of my Reiki Master Guide Lord Jesus Christ, I command you [addressing the storm directly] to turn right now! Do no harm! Dissipate, and do the *least* amount of damage possible!"

As he shouted these words, he felt flooded with a massive amount of energy coming into the back door to his heart and out through the palms of his hands. In his mind's eye, he had a vision of a wide wedge of white light streaming into the middle of his back. It looked like an upside-down triangle: wide at the ceiling and narrowing down to enter the center of his back, passing through the back door of his heart. The very instant he finished his prayer-command, something extraordinary happened—a miracle.

* * *

"IT'S WOBBLING! . . . IT'S CHANGING DIRECTION! . . . IT'S turning! It's not going to hit Tampa! It's going to hit Port Charlotte. It's losing power," the announcer on the Weather Channel exclaimed, as if in total disbelief.

The very instant that he heard the reporter's startling words, the following biblical passage became a reality to him: "I can do all things through Christ who strengthens me" (Philippians 4:13).

As thankful and relieved as he was, Stephen was upset when Charley struck Port Charlotte. He had intended for Charley to shift to the right, pass by the bottom of Florida, and then move into the Atlantic to dissipate and die out. But he started his intervention too late for that to happen.

Limited by his partial focus on physical reality, Stephen could not quite believe it was possible to have *no* damage. Later, with future hurricanes, he would not limit his command. Instead, he would command, "Dissipate and do *no* damage!" Stephen had faith in the unbelievable being possible—shifting the winds of hurricanes. But his educated mind was hampered by what he

259

believed was realistically possible.

In the aftermath of Charley, Sarasota did not even lose power and hardly any tree branches were down. In the area hit, the only people harmed were those who did not heed the warning to leave their mobile homes to go to nearby shelters or local hotels.

On Monday, Janet told Stephen that she heard experts on the Weather Channel spend the rest of the weekend seeking some plausible explanation for the sudden shift in Charley's course. The short explanation is to say that it was, to borrow the words from the title of Stephen's second book, simply *A Matter of Love*. It was as Marianne Williamson had said, "Miracles occur naturally as an expression of love. . . ."

* * *

STEPHEN RECEIVED A CURIOUS KIND OF CONFIRMATION on Saturday, the day after he intervened to shift the winds of Charley. The confirmation of the effect of his efforts was preceded by a series of synchronicities that day whose significance was not clear to him at first. Only after reflecting back over the intervening years since 1995 did it become clear.

On Saturday morning, around 10:30 A.M., he was in a crowded local coffee shop when Lee, a Reiki practitioner, walked over to him. Raised Roman Catholic, Lee had once considered entering the priesthood. He was one of the kindest and most pure-of-heart men Stephen had ever met. Lee handed him a book entitled *Reiki and the Healing Buddha*. Lee just happened to appear and he just happened to have the book with him.

A few pages into the book, Stephen read a passage where a claim was made by a scholar of religion that he believed the evidence shows that Jesus was the Healing Buddha who lived circa 120 A.D. For one thing, the scholar found drawings of the Healing Buddha and his twelve assistants; they appear caucasian and not Asian. He also referenced the book *Jesus Lived in India* by Holger Kersten, another scholar of religion.

A few hours later, he saw his spiritually-minded friend Robert who was also raised Roman Catholic and, like Lee, he had also seriously considered becoming a priest when he was a young adult. As soon as he saw Stephen, Robert handed him a book, saying, "I felt guided to give this book to you." Robert had been working on a client's computer and happened to look up to see the book on the shelf above the computer. Robert began reading it and got the feeling he needed to borrow it for Stephen to read. The book was entitled *Jesus Lived in India*. Robert knew nothing of the book Stephen received from Lee that morning which referenced this book he was handing to Stephen.

The book had a major flaw. In order to explain the appearance of Jesus in India after his death on the cross, the author made the claim that Jesus did not die. He was somehow saved to carry on his ministry in the East. But Stephen knew Jesus could appear anywhere in His Resurrected or Glorified body as He did to the disciples in the forty days after the Resurrection. During that time, he ate with them, was touched by Thomas, and appeared to be in a real body to over five hundred people on three separate occasions. However, this was not the first time Stephen had come across the idea of Jesus being in India and Tibet.

Six years earlier, Stephen had come across the book *The Lost Years of Jesus* which discussed the years where nothing is noted in the Bible. These years extend from the time Jesus was teaching in the Temple at twelve until he shows up to be baptized by John at twenty nine or thirty. In this book, Stephen read recorded accounts about Jesus studying and teaching in India and Tibet during the eighteen year gap before he starts his ministry. After reading this book, Stephen remembered that right after the Reiki class in 1995, he heard about a book entitled *Jesus Was a Reiki Master*. He never read the book but he saw the blurb about the book in a catalog that claimed Jesus taught and studied in Tibet during the lost years.

Stephen wondered why he was being given this information. He really had no personal interest in whether Jesus had taught and studied in India and Tibet. So why was all of this being revealed to him? He prayed and asked God to reveal the purpose. First, it was to validate that Jesus being his Reiki Master Guide had some historical basis to it. It was not irreverent to refer to Him as such as some Christians might claim. Second, Stephen was also being assigned the role of revealing that Rudyard Kipling was wrong when he wrote in *The Ballad of East and West*, "Oh, East is East and West is West, and never the twain shall meet. . . ." Jesus was not to be found only in the history of the West but in the East. Nor was He restricted to only appearing to the white man.

Right after college, Stephen read a book (whose title he could not recall) in which a holy man fitting the description of Jesus appeared in Central America. To the Maya, He was Kukulcan and to the Aztecs, Quetzalcoatl. Jesus appearing to Stephen in the shadows of the Temple of the Sun in Tikal was not so strange after all.

Right after seeing Robert, Stephen met with Kathy, another one of his spiritually-minded friends. Kathy had the gift of prophecy. Stephen told her about the steps he had taken regarding Charley. And hours after their meeting, Kathy called to tell him about an experience her artist friend Jeanne had when she was meditating on Friday. Kathy had told Jeanne about Stephen's experience, and Jeanne replied, "That explains what I saw during my meditation." Jeanne was meditating peacefully when she had a strange vision. She told Kathy, "Suddenly, I saw a television set with all this white light carrying tons of information being downloaded into its screen."

It was determined that Jeanne's vision had occurred at the time Stephen was sending Reiki into the doppler radar image on the screen of his television set and commanding Charley to change direction.

"That's confirmation for Stephen," Kathy told Jeanne. The parallel was striking. So Stephen's vision of white light coming into his heart and out through his hands into the television set had registered on the inner planes of consciousness. Reverend Bill Johnson's quote mentioned earlier bears repeating, "The hands surrendered to God can release the power of Heaven into a situation. In the spirit world it is released like lightning."

* * *

THE REST OF THE 2004 HURRICANE SEASON WAS FAST AND furious. One storm after another appeared after Charley in the tight time frame of two months. August and September saw a lot of action. For the first time in the weather record books, four hurricanes hit the same state, and, to Stephen's dismay, the state was Florida. Stephen took on any and all hurricanes that threatened Sarasota and Tampa. His efforts were successful in protecting Florida's West Coast. (As an aside, when referring to hurricanes, Stephen prefers to use the personal pronouns of *he* or *she* instead of the impersonal "it" as the announcer had just done. After all, each storm was given a proper male or female name. In fact, each storm seemed to display a personality all his or her own.)

Frances followed Charley. She reached category four status. Although he was concerned, Stephen smiled because Frances was his mother's middle name. Sometimes his father Earl jokingly called her Gertrude Frances. Stephen began working on slowing Frances down and reducing the speed of her winds before she made landfall on Florida's Atlantic Coast. Stephen had some concern that she would hit Sarasota and Tampa by going through the back door of the Atlantic Coast instead of hitting them head on.

From September 2, 2004 to September 4, 2004, she weakened from a category four to a category two. Cupping his hands over a map he drew to represent Florida's Atlantic coastline, Stephen visualized a formidable energy barrier being erected right on the shore. He intended to keep Frances stalled until she lost more and more of her strength. Stephen turned on the Weather Channel, and at that very instant, he heard hurricane expert Steve Lyons say, "Frances is stalled as if she is up against some kind of a barrier." Later reports indicated that a "wind shear" had stopped her in her tracks. Later, in 2007, Stephen would hear the same feedback following his efforts to erect an energy barrier to block another hurricane. There was an interesting correlation between the intention to create an energy barrier and the sudden appearance of a powerful wind shear.

On September 5, 2004, Frances remained stationary for nearly twenty four hours before proceeding over Florida soil as a tropical depression and not a hurricane.

Hurricane Ivan appeared and Stephen was in Sarasota. He began using prayer and Reiki to steer Ivan away from Florida's West Coast and into the Gulf of Mexico. Ivan went toward Alabama. Stephen kept trying to reduce the wind speed of Ivan but he had to shift his focus to another threat.

On the heels of Frances and Ivan, Jeanne appeared. Then, while he was watching the Weather Channel on September 25, 2004, he saw Jeanne become a category three. Immediately, Stephen began working on weakening her wind speed and slowing down her progress as she headed toward Florida. She made landfall just a few miles from where Frances had. Once again, Sarasota and Tampa could be hit by a hurricane entering on the Atlantic Coast and cutting across the state.

Here he was now situated in Sarasota in the line of fire. However, his strategy was the same: imagine Jeanne shrunk down, cup his hands over her, and send the energy and intention to slow her wind speed. She did cut across the state, not as a hurricane but as a tropical storm. She passed over Sarasota and moved on to Tampa. For a few hours in the afternoon, the power went out where Stephen was staying. Jeanne's storm speed was very slow and caused considerable flooding from the heavy rains. Stephen saw a few branches down but there was no damage. He had been worried that the two tall palm trees near the house of his sweetheart's family might topple and rip the roof. During the hours the storm was passing through the state, he had cupped his hands over the house. It was similar to what he did when he was seated in any airplane beset by turbulence. Just as he did with airplanes, he imagined the house he was sitting in shrunk down and fitting under his cupped hands. The turbulence subsided just as quickly while he sat calmly with a firm faith as it did when he was on airplanes. The storm passed over in its weakened state without incident.

Even while in the storm, he watched it from the mountaintop perspective that Carl Jung had described. By being receptive to me and my inner prompting, he was seeing the material world from my spiritual perspective. Stephen was developing his ability to see through my spiritual eyes instead of seeing only through his physical eyes. What he was doing seemed simply silly from the point of view of his physical eyes. Now, quite literally, he knew what Saint Paul meant when he said, "We walk by faith, not by sight" (2 Corinthians 5:7). He was being called to *see* beyond the world as it is seen, heard, smelled, touched, and tasted by the five senses. His advanced and advancing glaucoma also had a spiritual benefit: he was forced to "walk by faith, not by sight." The next storm on the horizon posed quite a challenge to his faith.

* * *

"THIS IS THE MOST POWERFUL CATEGORY FIVE hurricane on record!" exclaimed the reporter on the Weather Channel. He seemed in awe of the statistics on Hurricane Wilma. She had formed on October 17, 2005, in the western part of the Caribbean, southwest of Jamaica. By October nineteenth, Wilma was a category five with winds of 185 miles per hour and an unparalleled core pressure of 882 MBAR. Spurred on by the information, Stephen intensified his efforts to protect his loved ones from Wilma's wrath. At the same time, he asked for God's guidance to shift Wilma's winds on a path to do the least amount of damage and no more harm to people in her path. There was something else Stephen had in his armamentarium to shore up his faith and the specificity of his prayer requests and visualizations.

In the springtime of 2005, Stephen had been reading *The Field*, a book which described the work of various scientists that verified the power of thought to influence physical reality. For all of the material world is essentially energy appearing in different material forms, including weather. In quantum physics, the underlying harmony of all forms is called the "zero-point field." Stephen was now reinforcing his Reiki and prayer interventions with a sound scientific perspective. He could strengthen his faith in the impossible being possible. The research on thought influencing matter in the quantum field was considerable and convincing.

A simple example was the saying, "The sun always shines on a

Princeton graduate." It was not just a metaphor. Many were said to believe it literally and figuratively. A review of weather reports on Princeton graduation days over a number of years revealed that even when neighboring towns had rain, Princeton did not. Sometimes reports revealed that the rain was delayed; it did come but only after graduation was over and everyone had left.

Needless to say, Stephen was filled with fear when he heard the newscasters indicate that Wilma was the most powerful hurricane to date. He shifted his *fear focus* to a *love focus* by zeroing in on what he would love to have happen instead of focusing on what he feared could happen. He would love to see Wilma steer clear of Florida's West Coast, fly out into the Atlantic, dissipate, and die out.

On Wednesday afternoon, while Wilma was moving through the Caribbean, he began his first intervention; he started using Reiki and prayer to contain and squeeze Wilma. He focused on containing her for half an hour. Hopefully, Wilma would slow down. At her current speed, she would proceed past the Yucatan where a low pressure system coming from California would catch her and hurl her directly into Florida's West Coast. Once again, the densely populated areas in and around Sarasota and Tampa were in danger.

He took a break to get back to his task for that day: reviewing the manuscript of *Words Become Flesh*. The instant his eyes lit on the word *container* in the book, he heard the reporter on the Weather Channel describe how the storm was *contained*. She was not expanding in her core: "Wilma is compact and its [her] high winds extend only fifteen miles." Here was his first feedback from God. Yes, he was acting as a container. The facts and words matched.

Feeling encouraged by this message, he then worked on Wilma for another half hour with the command: "Dissipate! Do no damage! Do no harm!" When he stopped, he turned on the Weather Channel and Wilma was weakening; the pressure at her core had changed by eighteen points and her wind speed had decreased by fifteen miles per hour.

Overnight, he worked on slowing down Wilma's storm speed by cupping his hands on the area of the map where she was traveling. Then, he delivered a command: "Father God, with Your permission, I AM an extension of Your Almighty I AM Presence in action now! And in the name of my Reiki Master Guide, Lord Jesus Christ, I command you to turn left (West)! Hang up on the Yucatan! Dissipate! Do no harm! And do the least amount of damage possible!"

In the morning, at the very moment he turned on the Weather Channel, Stephen heard the reporter announce that, instead of heading north as was expected, Wilma started moving west. He also heard that Wilma was "slowing down and proceeding more slowly" than was forecasted. He was delighted to hear the reporter announce, "The predicted path has changed from Florida to south of Florida." Wilma was moving left (west) to the Yucatan. This was to the left just as Stephen had commanded in the name of Jesus.

The focus of his afternoon intervention was to keep Wilma moving into the sparsely-populated jungles of the Yucatan. But before attempting to accomplish this task there was something else he had to do. He remembered his time studying the ways of the Mayan shamans. They stressed the importance of asking permission of the spiritual guardians, in effect guardian angels, of a place before entering it. For example, before entering an area of the jungle, the shamans taught him to address the guardian angels by asking in Spanish, "'Con su permiso?" The literal translation: "With your permission?" Stephen was impressed with how shamans exuded sincere spiritual humility and reverence for all of life. All of nature was imbued with the spiritual presence of God and his messengers. God was talking to all embodied souls all the time. From the wet jungle to the expansive sea and on to the airy mountaintops and from there to the sun, moon, and stars, God and His messengers were everywhere. Nature was their sacred cathedral.

Therefore, out of respect for his shaman mentors, he called to the four Lords of the Maya to request their permission for Wilma to move into the least populated areas of the jungle. Each Lord is associated with one of the four directions: Balam Quiché (East),

Balam Akab (West), Macutah (North), and Ik Balam (South). (Balam is the Mayan word for Lord.) With his cupped hands sweeping over the map, he kept reciting the command, "Cease and desist!" Suddenly, he had a vision of the jaguar, the sacred power animal the Maya associate with Ik Balam. The jaguar was gripping Wilma with his teeth and slowing her down. The jaguar was stalling the storm. Wilma was turning into life-giving rain. In accord with the vision, Stephen spent a half hour trying to make the storm stall and peter out. For half-hour stretches with brief breaks in between, he continuously kept repeating as tenaciously as a woodpecker chiseling a tree, "Hang up on the Yucatan! Hang up on the Yucatan! Hang up on the Yucatan!" He kept picturing a car whose engine keeps stalling as its wheels spin in the mud, making no headway.

By Thursday night, the Weather Channel's hurricane expert Steve Lyons announced, "For some reason, Wilma is *hanging up* on the Yucatan. The eye is now much wider. It went from three miles to thirty-five miles wide as the center winds lessened from 175 miles per hour to 145 miles per hour. Wilma has slowed down so much that Wilma is going to miss the low-pressure system coming from California." Hallelujah! Praise God! Stephen was grateful.

You may recall, this low-pressure system was going to intercept Wilma and carry her to Florida's West Coast. Lyons added, "Wilma is expected to spend thirty hours in the area of the Yucatan." Lyons then predicted, "When Wilma does turn it [she] will be a much weaker storm, limping along toward Florida."

On Friday, Stephen continued to focus on keeping her hung up on the Yucatan. Then, on Friday night, the Weather Channel's Jennifer Lopez (not the actress and singer) said, "We hope that Wilma will do no harm." She used the very phrase Stephen had been relentlessly repeating, "Do no harm!" Immediately in response to Lopez's report, Stephen cupped his hands over the area of the map where Wilma was stalled and commanded: "In the name of my Reiki Master Guide Lord Jesus Christ, I command you [Wilma] to dissipate, weaken, and die out!"

Stephen planned to concentrate on having Wilma weaken more

and more by barricading her in a field of energy and continuing to repeat the command, "Dissipate! Die out! And do no more damage!" When Wilma was finally beginning to leave the Yucatan, he started concentrating on using Reiki to direct Wilma to go under Florida and out to the Atlantic to dissipate and die out. To this end, he declared, "I command you [Wilma] to miss Florida, dissipate, and die out in the Atlantic where you can be reabsorbed by the quantum field!"

Sweeping his cupped hands, he focused on sending Wilma along an energy path beneath Florida, far from Sarasota and Tampa. While doing this for half hour blocks of time, he kept issuing the command, "Do the least amount of damage as possible!" His focused intention had been on dissipating the power, and slowing down the winds.

As of Saturday afternoon, Wilma had dipped to 110 miles per hour. Wilma went from a category four and then to a category three by Saturday morning. By Saturday afternoon, she became a category two. Stephen then heard Steve Lyons come on the Weather Channel and say, "Wilma is beginning to dissipate."

From daybreak until 11 A.M. Monday, he cupped his hands and kept making a sweeping gesture over the map beneath Florida and out into the Atlantic. He paired his hand movements with the command to Wilma: "Move as swiftly past Florida as an empty freight train carrying no cargo and out into the Atlantic! Do no harm! Do no more damage! And die out!"

The 11 A.M. report from Steve Lyons on October 22, 2005: "The worst of the storm moved in and out in two hours. Tornado watch has expired." The danger was over. Wilma had rushed across the bottom of Florida. The words matched Stephen's image of a swiftly-moving, empty freight train. Hallelujah! Relief. Gratitude. Stephen thanked God for the waning of Wilma. He was a little tired from all the sustained focusing. As always, the Reiki energy flowing through him was replenishing. The draining part was the focusing. From Wednesday until midday Monday, he found it mentally and emotionally taxing.

The hurricanes in 2004 and 2005 had not behaved as experts had anticipated. Experts' expectations of various hurricanes delivering a blow to the West Coast of Florida did not materialize. Stephen's prayers had been answered and his interventions had been successful. Then, from my higher and wider perspective, I seeded the thought for him to do something different for the 2006, 2007, and 2008 hurricane seasons. . . .

$$* * *$$

IT WAS EARLY MAY AND THE 2006 HURRICANE SEASON HAD not yet begun but would begin in less than a month. The 2005 season had been called "the deadliest one to date." It surpassed all records for what Weather reporters call "storm formation" in the Atlantic: twenty-eight storms, fifteen hurricanes, seven category three, four category five. Taking on every hurricane that posed a threat to his loved ones, and that involved nearly all fifteen of the mighty storms, had been extremely trying and time consuming to say the least. *Is there another approach?* he would wonder one day in May of 2006.

A novel thought came to him. *Why not a preemptive-prayer strike?!* Why should he wait for one hurricane after another to appear? Why couldn't he just pray and use Reiki well in advance?

He visualized the Atlantic Ocean from the coast of North Africa and the Canary Islands to Florida and the waters of the Caribbean. Then he prayed while placing his hands over a drawing of the above and creating an energy barrier in the form of a chute. The chute was intended to catch hurricanes in their transit across the Atlantic. Instead of making landfall, the storms were intended to be sent back up into the Atlantic as surely as children at play on a playground shoot down the slippery slope of a sliding board. Imagining the energy chute, he prayed, "Father God with Your permission, I intend that no hurricanes make landfall. Please send the almighty power of Your Holy Spirit through my hands so that *no* hurricanes come ashore but, instead, are sent back up into the Atlantic to dissipate and die out. I ask this in the name of Jesus. Amen."

For approximately half an hour, Stephen engaged in a meditative prayer while he held his hands over the makeshift map. Every so often, he would move his hands across the Atlantic as though he were digging a trench to guide the route for any and all hurricanes.

He held firmly to his faith and intention. This meant that he never wavered by taking any other precautions. He did not waver in his faith by anxiously checking the Weather Channel! He did no interventions, no more prayers or Reiki when he happened to hear news reports of any tropical storms. To do so, he believed, would undermine the power of his prayers. He did not doubt but believed what he said was going to happen would happen just as Jesus said it would (Mark 11:23-24). Faith *could* move mountains.

On November 30, 2005, Stephen turned on the Weather Channel for the local forecast of the day. It was the last day of the hurricane season. The first thing he happened to hear was a reporter announcing that the track of most of the storms did not make landfall and headed back into the Atlantic. A total of seventeen storms had been predicted in 2006 with nine of them to be hurricanes. The final outcome of 2006: total storms were ten with five of them becoming hurricanes. The really significant statistic was that *none* made landfall.

The results conformed to Stephen's intentions and prayers that there be a kind of energy barrier in the form of a chute to catch and send hurricanes and tropical storms that could become a hurricane back into the Atlantic to dissipate and die out. He immediately dropped to his knees to thank God.

A little over six months later, Stephen would think of how to modify the preemptive-prayer-strike approach he used in 2006 for the 2007 and 2008 hurricane seasons. He would consider keeping the energy barrier in the form of a chute and add something about eliminating the conditions that help create hurricanes. He zeroed in on the area of ocean by Africa and the Canary Islands: the so-called birthplace of tropical storms that form in the Atlantic.

To this end, he began his prayer by once again placing his hands on the same makeshift map from the year before. This time, he added to his prayer-command, "May any storms crossing the Atlantic bring only life-giving rain and no damaging winds!"

During the months of September and October, he heard from his sweetheart in Florida, "We sure are getting a lot more rain than we usually get this time of year." Stephen thanked God. This was confirmation that his prayers were answered. He had not told her that he had prayed for life-giving rain in place of damaging hurricanes.

In late September, Stephen just happened to check the Weather Channel for the local forecast. Of course, he knew there were no mere coincidences. He was meant to see that Hurricane Karen was in a position to threaten Florida. Karen was about to breach the energy barrier in the form of a chute that he set in place in May.

He sat down, closed his eyes, and began visualizing the doppler radar map he had just seen on the television. Then he placed his hands over the image of Karen and started sending Reiki to shore up the chute. He silently shouted, "In the name of Jesus, I command you, Karen, to dissipate! Do no harm and do no damage! Turn North and follow the chute into the Atlantic and die out!" He felt an energy surge through his body. It was similar to the one he felt with Charley. The electrifying sensations tingling in his back formed a steady flow but not as strong as happened with Charley.

Many months later, Stephen would do some follow-up research on the 2006, 2007h, and 2008 hurricane seasons. And when he did, he was astonished. Along with the fact that not even one hurricane made landfall, he saw the National Hurricane Center Map. There before his eyes, he could see how the tracks of all the hurricanes followed the outline of his energy barrier chute. It was just as he had intended; the storms appeared to follow the makeshift map he had made.

Then he read about Hurricane Karen. She was stopped in her tracks by a "relentless wind shear." It wore her down and sent her north into the Atlantic. Just as had happened with Frances when he erected an energy barrier, a wind shear manifested. He was fascinated by the contiguity and correlation between two events: cupped hands sending energy over a map and a substantial wind shear appearing over land in one case and over sea in another.

Next, he noticed how Hurricane Noel's course shifted. A month after Karen threatened Florida, Noel was poised to strike. Noel's path configured to the shape of the energy-barrier chute that

Stephen had put in place in the 2006 season and reaffirmed for the 2007 and 2008 seasons. From the National Hurricane Center Map for 2007, he noticed how Noel appeared to have been caught in the chute and flung North into the Atlantic. Mission accomplished.

In 2007, the results were as follows: fourteen storms were predicted with seven reaching hurricane status. The end result of 2007 was that there were fifteen storms with six becoming hurricanes. Only one named Umberto made landfall in the U.S., and he did not touch down in Florida but landed in the vicinity of Texas and Louisiana. The winds of two hurricanes that had the potential to hit Florida, Karen and Noel, shifted course and missed their mark.

The 2008 season was similar to 2007 in that, as Stephen intended, no hurricanes hit the Sunshine State, and he used prayer and Reiki to successfully redirect two storms projected to hit Sarasota and Tampa: Tropical Storm Fay and Hurricane Ike. Of the sixteen named storms, five became major hurricanes: Bertha, Gustav, Ike, Omar, and Paloma. The tracks of Bertha, Omar, and Paloma conformed to the energy barrier Stephen set in place. Gustav and Ike breached the barrier but posed no threat to Florida's West Coast. Gustav landed in Louisiana and Ike in Texas. Once again, mission accomplished.

* * *

LOOKING OUT THE WINDOW OF THE TRAIN, HE COULD NOT help noticing the space between stars in the night sky. He asked himself, *Was there anything else to glean from the miracles he had both witnessed and participated in?* Shifting winds had shifted his sense of himself and his notion of so-called reality. He shifted from a body-based identity and sense of self to a spirit-based identity and sense of self. He knew he was more than what his physical eyes could see and so was all of the visible world of material reality.

Underlying all that the physical eyes could see was an invisible energy. This *unseen* energy was the common denominator of the whole *seen* world of matter. He realized Reiki was defined as universal energy. This universal energy extended from his body to the bodies of all other living beings: people, animals, birds, fish, plants, trees, and so forth. His experiences with sending Reiki and his mystical moments of God the Father in the Temple of the Moon and of the Holy Spirit led him to conclude that this energy was love. He remembered some other words attributed to Jesus in Glenda Green's *Love Without End: Jesus Speaks.*

When you are fully certain in the wholeness of your being that you are love . . . you will say to the mountain, 'come!' and it will come and you will say to the wind, 'be still!' and the storm will cease.

* * *

YES, THE MIRACLE OF SHIFTING WINDS HAD OCCURRED naturally as an expression of love. Stephen's love for his sweetheart, her family, and his friends had *inspired* his efforts. He went back to what he had read in the beginning of *A Course in Miracles.*

1.) There is no order of difficulty in miracles. One is not harder or bigger than another. 2.) Miracles as such do not matter. The only thing that matters is their Source which is far beyond evaluation. 3.) Miracles occur as a natural expression of love. The real miracle is the love that inspires them. In this sense, everything that comes from love is a miracle.

Stephen found the last comment very interesting. Who or what is that love behind miracles? In *8 Steps to Love*, Stephen wrote this about love:

Love? To Freud, it was the only socially acceptable psychosis. To Plato, it was divine madness. But to Saint John love was nothing less than God, the ultimate power of the universe.

What had he learned about love and miracles? Now he realized that it was more accurate to say that love was the ultimate power operating "in" the universe but love itself was not "of" the universe. Miracles manifest in material reality when love and faith fill the space between Heaven and Earth and between what is and what an embodied soul would love to have happen. In his attempts to shift and calm the hurricanes threatening his loved ones, Stephen filled the space between what was happening (storms threatening to harm loved ones) and what he would love to have happen (storms subsiding) with the energy of love bolstered by faith. He held an unwavering love focus on the outcome he desired (his loved ones safe) instead of a fear focus on feared outcomes (images of death and destruction).

While the train rumbled along the last leg of tracks from Philadelphia to Wilmington, Stephen wondered what else he had learned from the miracles he had witnessed and participated in, especially the shifting of winds. Stephen then thought, *Jesus Himself proclaimed we would be able to do what he did and more when He said, "He that believeth on me, the works that I do, he shall do, and greater works than these because I go to the Father" (John 14:12).*

Reflecting on these words, he asked himself, *What about the preposition* on *instead of* in? Immediately an answer came. He thought of a metaphor often used for describing the advancement of knowledge in science. It is said that the current practitioners in any given field "stand on the shoulders" of those who came before. The better view afforded by such a position is like that of a child standing on his father's shoulders in a crowd watching a parade. The child can see farther than his father. In the field of psychology, Stephen visualized himself standing on the shoulders of the founding fathers of the field and its various branches: Freud and Jung as well as William James, Heinz Kohut, B. F. Skinner and many, many more.

Certainly, standing on the foundation of faith in Jesus and in God's love provided a power like no other. In the Bible, the Greek word for this power is *dunamis*; it is the origin of the English word dynamite. Embodied souls calling on Jesus, while standing on the firm foundation of faith in Him and His love, have a delegated *dunamis* (power or authority) which He grants to them. In the Greek this delegated *dunamis* is called *exousia*. However, unlike the many mentors Stephen had as a psychologist, Jesus, as part of the Trinity of God, is omniscient (all knowing), omnipotent (all powerful), and omnipresent (always present everywhere). Stephen had witnessed firsthand how Jesus can be called upon and miraculous things happen. This was an empirical fact. And observable facts are the kind of thing on which science is built. This fact was true for all believers, and Stephen was a believer. Stephen noted in *Words Become Flesh* that Jesus was the Word of Love that became flesh. And with words, God spoke the world into existence in Genesis: "Let there be light!" Actually, Stephen heard the more exact translation was, "Light, be!" God offered a model for commanding with words.

Stephen recalled the time he just finished writing about Jesus as *the* Word of Love. He had taken a break from writing and turned on the television. With his eyesight impaired by glaucoma, he found it easier to feel for the position of the numbers on the TV remote rather than struggle to see them. He thought he had pressed the numbers 10 for NBC Nightly News; instead he had pressed 18 which turned out to be TBN (Trinity Broadcasting Network). There he saw a man named Richard, a Native American with shoulder-length dark hair. Richard was talking about his path to becoming a follower of Christ Jesus.

Richard described how he had been a very angry activist. He had grown up resenting the Christian missionaries with their white man's culture. Richard had gotten into drugs and was wanted by the police. He fled to Hawaii. After arriving, he began walking from the airport. Two men picked him up and started to share their faith in Jesus. Richard listened but he still felt resentful of the missionaries he encountered on the reservation where he grew up. Later that day, he ingested some drugs.

A few hours into his drug trip, Richard felt like he was gong to die. He was terrified. Over the years, he had studied other sacred traditions and religions. He started chanting Hindu mantras to calm down. When that didn't work, he prayed to Buddha. And when that was unsuccessful, he prayed to Allah. Minutes passed. Nothing happened. Feeling desperate, he called on Jesus, saying, "Jesus, if You are real as these guys [referring to the two men who picked him up earlier] say, please forgive me and come into my heart!"

Instantly, Richard felt calm and peaceful. His mind became clear. The effects of the drugs, which would usually have lasted another ten or more hours, immediately subsided.

What an amazing testimony to the power of calling on Jesus from the depths of one's heart! Richard's story was confirmation of Jesus as the embodiment of God's Immense Love for each and every embodied soul. Empirical fact. Not fiction. Stephen remembered how he had instantly thought of the following verse: "For in Him [Christ Jesus] all the fullness of the Deity dwells in bodily form" (Colossians 2:9).

Following this experience, Richard was able to separate the truth of Jesus from the trappings of the white man's culture that had been forced on him. God revealed to him that the Gospel was a *seed* to be planted in the ground of the existing culture of any indigenous people. He began a ministry for Native Americans so they could worship God in harmony with their own traditions rather than be clones of the white man's ways. Instead of putting on coats and ties and going to church, they could wear their headdresses and ceremonial clothing to celebrate Jesus.

Visualizing Native Americans dancing and singing around a fire, Stephen recalled how God as the Father, Son, and Holy Spirit appeared to him amid ancient pyramids and during the sacred fire ceremonies. The head got hung up on form— the seen. The heart knew better. The unseen uses the seen. Jesus was his Lord and Savior *and* his Reiki Master Guide.

As always, Stephen was grateful for the message from God, the Divine Beloved, delivered by synchronicity. He had seen how synchronicity is always occurring in the space between Heaven and Earth. It's just that many do not notice God's little love letters.

* * *

STEPHEN PONDERED THE POWER OF LOVE UNDERLYING THE act of commanding a miracle in the name of Jesus. *For one thing*, Stephen thought, reflecting on the life of Jesus, *His name exemplifies love. Jesus the Christ is a model of being, doing, and having love for all embodied souls under all conditions and circumstances.* Yes. Stephen was beginning to feel more and more deeply how the name of Jesus the Christ is synonymous with the power of unconditional love: the no-matter-what-is-happening or no-matter-who-it-is kind of love. His name conjures up scenes of loving friend or foe and loving whether being loved or persecuted in return. What power!

From his knowledge of psychology, Stephen saw how this was truly powerful on many levels, not the least of which was to be free to feel joy and happiness despite the dictates of any given situation. In *8 Steps to Love*, he had written of this kind of power when he discussed the prisoner-of-war survivors. The ones who focused on whom and what they loved not only survived, they transcended the bleakness and desolation.

He then thought, *Didn't the life and sacrifice of Jesus to save the souls of humanity past, present, and future* embody *an immensely powerful and awesome act of love on the part of God the Father, the Creator and Source of all? Yes, indeed,* he concluded. *Absolutely.* He found his whole being ignited with the desire to be loving under all the circumstances of life as Jesus had done in his life on Earth.

To keep him on track, I, as his invisible guidance system, reminded him of the the passage in *A Course in Miracles,* "love [itself] is the true miracle." To further reinforce this insight, I led him back to the Bible. He found the story of the brothers in Acts 19:15 who were driving out demons using the phrase, "in the name of Jesus whom Paul preaches." The demon said, "I know of Paul and I know of Jesus, but who are you?" And the demon proceeded to pounce on the brothers. Using the name without a foundation in faith and love did not work. Then I led him to the following passage to strengthen the message on love.

> Not everyone who says to me, 'Lord! Lord!' will enter the kingdom of Heaven. But only he who does the will of my Father Who is in Heaven. Many will say to me on that day, 'Lord! Lord! Did we not prophesies in Your name? And in Your name drive out demons? And perform many miracles?' Then I will tell them plainly, 'I never knew you. Away from me you evildoers And therefore anyone who hears my words and puts them into practice is like a wise man who built his house upon a rock. The rain came down, the streams rose and the winds blew and beat against that house. Yet it did not fall because it had its founda-

tion on the rock. But everyone who hears these words of mine and does not put them into practice is like a foolish man who built his house on sand. The rain came down, the streams rose and the winds blew and beat against that house, and it fell with a great crash (Matthew 7:22-27).

What he needed to see was in this passage. With the almighty power of the love of the Holy Spirit working in and through him, Stephen had performed miracles. But that was not the most important thing. Practicing the commandment of love was the top priority. Once again, I brought him back to *A Course in Miracles*.

Miracles as such do not matter. The only thing that matters is their Source which is far beyond evaluation. Miracles occur as a natural expression of love. The real miracle is the love that inspires them. In this sense, everything that comes from love is a miracle.

Miracles, he now thought, feeling excited by the parallel between *A Course in Miracles,* and the Bible, *don't matter. And the Source,* he thought, *is God as Love! Or, you could say the Source is found in God's Great Love for each and every one of us. Miracles arise out of our love of God and His love for us. And the real miracle is love—the love that inspires miracles.*

* * *

LOVING UNDER ALL CONDITIONS IS THE REAL MIRACLE, especially the idea of all embodied souls being able to love their enemies. It is as radical a concept today as it was when Jesus first spoke of it two thousand years ago.

You have heard it said that you should love your neighbor and hate your enemy. But I say to you, 'Love your enemies, bless anyone who curses you, do good to anyone who hates you, and pray for those who carry you away by force and persecute you; that you may become sons of your Father Who is in Heaven; Who causes His sun to shine upon the good and the bad; and who pours down His rain upon the just and the unjust. For if you love only those who love you, what reward will you have: Do not even the tax collectors do the same thing? And if you salute only your brothers, what is it more that you do? Do not even the tax collectors do the same thing? Therefore, be perfect just as your Father in Heaven is perfect' (Matthew 5:44-48).

Later, in his final moments, Jesus demonstrated how to do this when he was in agony on the cross. Speaking to God the Father about those who had Him crucified, He said, "Father forgive them for they know not what they do" (Luke 23:24). Thinking about that scene, Stephen believed two things. First, he believed that the essence of what Jesus said could be summed up in what Stephen dubbed the mantra of compassion. It goes like this, "I know in my heart that you would do differently if you could do differently, but you can't (not yet anyway) so you don't."

Stephen believed that although not stated, Jesus not only forgave His enemies, he probably thanked them. In spite of His agony on the cross, He could thank them for helping Him fulfill and thereby reveal His divine destiny. No crucifixion. No resurrection. This points to the true miracle that takes place in the space between self and others and allows the blessings to flow between Heaven and Earth. The true accomplishment is the ability to not only love one's enemies but to thank them. Stephen sensed this when he developed the concept of "thanking stress." You can feel gratitude to an enemy because he or she helps you become a better person. He loved how his friend Dr. Shelly Stockwell put it, "Your tormentor is your greatest mentor."

In my own subtle way, I guided him to the discovery of the book *Radical Forgiveness*. Radical forgiveness involves an embodied soul having a sense of his or her spirit (sidereal self) working for his or her spiritual growth. He was pleased to find out that the core concepts of radical forgiveness were an extension of the principles presented in *A Course in Miracles*.

To Stephen, radical forgiveness could also be called *radical thankfulness*. Stephen first discovered how to love and thank his enemy in that college basketball game (discussed in chapter four) in which he entered the zone. His opponent, his enemy, helped him be the best basketball player he could be.

Storms strengthen us. Love thy enemies could be love thy storms,

Stephen thought. He was thinking of the inner storms of stress. Still, the hurricanes strengthened Stephen's faith. The outer storm, what psychologists call a stressor, acts as the stimulus that triggers the response of stress. All embodied souls experience the storms of life. The spiritual question is whether embodied souls experience the stress of these storms alone or with the supernatural help of God the Father, God the Son, and God the Holy Spirit. Stephen loved the way Saint Paul said it.

And we know that in all things, God works for the good of those who love Him, who are called according to His purpose" (Romans 8:28).

Stephen now saw how feeling love and gratitude toward one's enemies is an important element of spiritual maturity. His true calling was not calming outer hurricanes but teaching other embodied souls how to calm the inner storms, the cyclones of negative emotions. The goal of all his books could be summed up in what Mother Maria del Carmen said of his first book *8 Steps to Love*, "Reading this book helps us fulfill the commandment of love which Jesus gave us."

Facing the storms of stress with the help of Christ Jesus also meant following His example. All Stephen's study involved developing ways to live from love as Jesus did. This included the wisdom of other sacred spiritual traditions such as Buddhist meditation and psychology, Reiki, and the Kabbalah. He telescoped all he had learned in the space between polio and flow, surface and depth, and Heaven and Earth into the simple, practical steps and techniques found in his books.

* * *

BLINDED BY THE HEAVY RAIN OF RESENTMENT AND PANIC, blown about by the strong winds of fear and anger, the embodied soul is cut off from the blessings of God's love. Stephen smiled at the beautiful example of this in the Bible. Moses was cut off from entering the Promised Land because of an angry outburst. God told him to speak to a rock to bring forth water for the Israelites. Instead,

Moses struck the rock with his staff in anger. He was frustrated with the Israelites (Numbers 20:8-12). In this biblical account of the cost of acting out anger, Stephen saw an indirect confirmation of the steps—8 Steps to Love—he devised for managing stress. Embodied souls *can* make it to their personal Promised Land when they *express* rather than *aggress* their *stress* as Moses did.

To receive God's blessings and to manifest miracles, embodied souls need to learn how to be still and step out of the storms of stress. For as God said. "Be still and know that I AM God"(Psalm 46:10). And, in that peaceful stillness, embodied souls can view the storm of stress from the mountaintop of their spirit—sidereal self—instead of feeling victimized by negative emotions in the valley of victimhood.

Stephen realized that this is what happened in the womb when he was gripped by the fear of being swallowed up by the storm of the painful sensations of hunger and the fear of starvation. In that moment within the womb, he was absorbed by the focus of a body-based identity and sense of self, plagued and victimized by the body's appetites. But what saved him from being overwhelmed was his shift to a spirit-based identity and sense of self. Identifying with the body fills the space between Heaven and Earth with the storm clouds of stress which can block blessings and miracles. The spirit-based identity is a victor and the body-based identity, a victim. When Stephen witnessed the painful sensations of hunger from my transcendent perspective, he began calmly viewing the storm in the valley of his little-baby body.

Suddenly, Stephen realized in the depths of his being that shifting his body-based identity to the spirit-based identity had helped him to shift the winds of hurricanes. And now, he knew that the essence of the energy of the spirit (sidereal self) of all embodied souls is love. This shift in identity to the energy of love could help with shifting the winds of the inner and outer storms. Embodied souls need to clear away the storms of emotion clouding their vision of the love that they truly are and the miracles they are capable of manifesting.

Stephen then imagined that when beset by negative emotions,

the embodied soul is faced with a core choice: *Will "I" identify with the body, selfishly focusing on satisfying the desires of the body? Or, will "I" identify with my spirit (sidereal self), unselfishly rising above the appetites of the body and focusing on living from love?*

He then thought of the message God had given him in New York City when he entered what appeared to be a little, hole-in-the-wall donut shop. The owner was a jovial man from Trinidad. Stephen was amazed when he tasted the jelly donuts; they were filled with organic strawberry jelly from Italy. When the man found out Stephen had been in full-time practice as a psychologist, he became excited and asked him, "Why are people so angry?"

Stephen's first thought was because people identify with their body and not their spirit. Embodied souls identified with their body get angry when their needs are not met. Instead of saying that, Stephen gave a social and psychological explanation involving the breakdown of the family. When Stephen finished, the man said, "I think it is because we identify with our body, and with where we live. I'm from America. I'm from Europe. I'm better than you."

The man had said what Stephen first thought but censored. If there were only one of these delicious donuts left and two embodied souls wanted it, an embodied soul with a spirit-based identity would be willing to share or lovingly give away the tasty treat. In contrast, someone identified with the body and its appetites would not share and may even fight for the donut.

God had spoken through the donut man from Trinidad. Stephen smiled and thought, *Trini-dad and Trinity sound alike. God . . . the Triune Dad . . . does have a sense of humor.*

Unfortunately, many embodied souls are in bondage to the body and in slavery to a body-based sense of who they are instead of possessing the freedom of a love and spirit-based sense of themselves. Not until he was ready to relinquish a body-based identity did the Holy Spirit come to him.

* * *

STEPHEN RECALLED HOW HIS OWN BONDAGE TO THE BODY was

depicted in a dream. The dream occurred on the night before he was anointed by the Holy Spirit in Rockport. He was bound up in the cloth wrappings of an Egyptian mummy. However, his arms and legs were each wrapped separately which was unlike an actual Egyptian mummy with arms and legs bound to the body forming one unit. His wrists and ankles were shackled. Even after awakening, Stephen could still feel the heavy weight of the chains and thick iron bands on his wrists and ankles.

Using the technique of active imagination, he contemplated this image of being a slave to Rome. A picture popped into his mind. He saw himself gripping the handle of a long, wooden oar, and he also saw that he was chained to other men in the belly of a Roman ship. He and the other men were slaves whose rowing propelled the vessel. The shackles were rusty as though they had been on him for a long time. He had the feeling that, as an embodied soul, he had been in bondage for centuries. For a moment, he felt he was recalling a past life in Rome as a slave. But that was not what was important. What was significant was what it all symbolized. He wondered what the references to being a slave of Rome and bandaged in a manner resembling an Egyptian mummy was saying about the state of his spirituality.

Being a slave of Rome revealed his attitude to be like that of a Roman soldier before witnessing the Crucifixion and Resurrection of Christ Jesus and becoming a believer. His educated mind had strayed from his religious roots, and he was no longer experiencing the intimate relationship to Jesus that he had felt after his confirmation. Nonetheless, his heart had never abandoned his devotion to Jesus. Since childhood, his heart had always remained devoted to Jesus.

His deep love and devotion was reaffirmed later that day when he unexpectedly encountered Jesus in the meditation to meet his Reiki Master Guide. He recalled how his head was surprised but his heart did not skip a beat when he silently said to Jesus, "I've served you as a Roman soldier. . . ." Whether an actual past life memory or not, the significant thing was that a radical shift was taking place within him. He was moving from being enslaved by the Roman Empire to being a Roman soldier risking his life to follow Jesus. That night, his head would unite with his heart in the desire to serve Jesus as a healer and teacher. To serve Jesus was to live from love and to help others do the same. Jesus was the embodiment of God's love.

He then examined his associations to being bound in bandages like an Egyptian mummy. He thought of the spiritual attitude of ancient Egypt. In one of the volumes of the *Zohar*, he read how Egypt symbolized the attitude of being bound to the body and to a life of physical pleasures. As a mentality, Egypt represented being *wrapped* up in a body-centered lifestyle. In a nutshell, the dream depicted Stephen's spiritual bondage and his need to be liberated.

I led him to meet Mercedes in Salem. And that Friday night, I kept coming to him as a purple light pulsating in the middle of his forehead. I was leading him back to basics for the renewal of his mind and the harnessing of his mind for spiritual purposes. It was time to put his mind and all his extensive psychological knowledge in service to his heart and his sincere desire to live from love.

Now, a decade later, he saw how the dream and my coming to him led him to take the Reiki class later that day. It was during that class that he took his first step toward spiritual freedom. When he renewed his confirmation vow to serve Jesus in the meditation, he ripped off the wrappings and threw off the shackles of spiritual bondage.

Now with the benefit of hindsight, Stephen could see how his shackled mummy dream signalled the beginning of his spiritual awakening. This was his emergence from the bondage to a body-based identity and sense of self. His sense of self was now shifting to a spirit-based sense of self. The space between Heaven and Earth opened up so that the almighty healing energy of the Holy Spirit could flow in and through him to those lost in the dark night of pain and suffering. Miraculous healing and the miracle of shifting winds and calming storms followed. But of all this, what stood out was God's love that he experienced through the Holy Trinity. In that Reiki meditation, he had gone through the thick golden door of a golden-domed white temple and experienced the love of Jesus: God the Son. That night, he experienced the love of God the Holy

Spirit appearing as a white light in the shape of a dove. Then, three years later, he discovered the love of God the Father in Tikal.

At that moment, the psalmist's words came to him, "Although my mother and my father reject me, the Lord will take me in and adopt me as His very own child" (Psalm 27:10). Earl's criticism felt like a rejection. But through experiencing his Heavenly Father's love, Stephen was healed of that wound. By accepting God's love, he could love and accept himself as a son of God.

He gazed up at the stars; his heart was overflowing with thankfulness. The train was stopped at one of its many stops before reaching his destination. The final scenes from a movie he watched almost every Christmas as a child: the 1951 film version of *A Christmas Carol.* Why had he thought of this film? It seemed to best express what was happening inside. His heart was filled to overflowing with joy as Scrooge's heart had been on Christmas morning. Soon it would be Thanksgiving and then Christmas; he had so much to be thankful for, especially over these past ten years.

* * *

STEPHEN WAS STARTING TO SEE HIS WANING EYESIGHT AS A blessing and not a curse. He was uncertain whether he would regain his eyesight. Maybe. Maybe not. The doctors told him he would lose his sight if he did not get surgery immediately. And yet, even with surgery, the doctors concurred that it was just a matter of time before he would be totally blind. Lights out. Total darkness.

"I can't believe you are seeing at all, given the state of your optic nerves," said Dr. Ward, the eye doctor he saw for a second opinion about whether or not he should have traditional, under-the-knife surgery. Her tone was one of disbelief.

To Stephen, this was not a negative but a positive. This meant he was not seeing so much by way of the physical mechanism of the eyes but by God's grace. He knew in his heart that anything is possible when it comes to God the Creator of all including the marvelous mechanism of the eye.

Four years earlier, the eye doctor who was checking Stephen's prescription for glasses also did a comprehensive evaluation. He told Stephen that he had approximately ten percent of his optic fibers remaining in his left eye and fifteen percent in his right eye. On hearing this, Stephen imagined his optic nerves to look like the oak tree in the backyard of his former home in Connecticut did in late November. By then, only a few brown leaves were still hanging on the mostly bare branches. For a healthy optic nerve with all its fibers intact, he pictured a tree in late May with all its vibrantly green leaves in full bloom. Despite this bleak image of his optic nerves, he was doing what he could to preserve his diminishing eyesight.

Stephen was still legally blind following the surgery. It didn't help his eyesight improve but it did lower the deadly pressure that destroys the optic nerve. He was gradually losing his independence; he was no longer able to see well enough to drive. A very independent man all his life, he was now growing increasingly dependent on others.

With some assistance, he could still use public transportation. He would tell his friends that his new position in life is best expressed in the line delivered in the classic film *A Streetcar Named Desire*. Batting her eyelashes, the aging Southern Belle Blanche DuBois says, "I have always depended on the kindness of strangers." He now had to ask strangers for help. For example, looking up at the sign with a number on it, he was forced to ask, "Excuse me sir, I'm visually impaired (sometimes he would say the other label—legally blind), could you tell me if I am at the right gate for my departing flight to Philadelphia?" On another occasion, standing before the large board listing train arrivals and departures in New York's Pennsylvania Station, he had to ask for help. He approached a stranger, prefaced his question with reference to his impairment in order to justify his request for assistance. Then he asked, "Could you please tell me the time the next train to Trenton is leaving? And could you tell me what gate it is departing from? And, would you please point me in the direction of that gate?"

The loss of his central vision made it hard to do things like reading the mail or writing out checks to pay bills. And the special magnifying instruments could not overcome the lack of central vision.

By using his remaining peripheral vision, he could walk to the grocery store but he could not shop without assistance. Finding items took a lot of time and reading prices was not possible unless the display sign was huge.

Previous pleasures were now denied. He could no longer read and reading was one of his primary pleasures. He could still partially see movies by using his peripheral vision. Looking straight on, he would see a nearly blank screen; the actor's features were a blanched-out blur. Foreign films? Forget about it. They were out of the question unless his sweetheart or friends would whisper the words of the subtitles loud enough for him to hear without disturbing the other people in the theater.

In spite of all the obvious drawbacks, the lessening of his eyesight to the level of being legally blind was a blessing spiritually. He was truly walking by the lamp of faith and less by his physical sight. On the one hand, sometimes life was a chiascuro of light and shadow. On the other hand, life resembled a Monet painting; there was a light haze over all that he saw before him. The world had become his canvas and he was an impressionist painter. His impaired vision mirrored the mountaintop perspective; it was as if he were seeing everything from afar. The connectedness and oneness of the appearance world was being emphasized. When things are examined up close, the distinctions and differences stand out.

The lyrics from Billy Joel's song *River of Dreams*, "can only be seen with the eyes of the blind," described the spiritual value of his vision loss. Surely, there are spiritual truths that can be better seen through the spiritual eyes and not the physical eyes.

Looking up at the stars again, he thought of the photo taken by the Hubble Space Telescope entitled *The Eye of God* (the central image on the front cover of this book). It was a picture of a super nova exploding and it revealed a process of death and rebirth for stars. Now he could see for himself how, according to the observations of astronomers, the space between stars is where old stars die and new stars are born. In this space, a perpetual cycle of death and birth continually takes place. He found this a fascinating phenomenon filled with meaning. Out of physical destruction new stars are born. He wondered if this might mean that out of the death of physical sight, spiritual sight emerges.

He rubbed his chin, felt the stubble of his well-past five o'clock shadow, and continued his thoughts, *As we learn to see as God sees with total love and no fear, our vision becomes clear. When we can see the spiritual perfection hidden in the apparent physical imperfection as God does, we can bring about what we would love to have happen.* I was happy to see that he was beginning to *see* how God exists both beyond and within the dimension of time and space. He could now see that embodied souls become creators in the image of God when they develop a love focus instead of a fear focus. Then, in the space between what is and what they would love to see happen, embodied souls create desired outcomes instead of feared outcomes. Stephen would say it this way, "See it, believe it, and it becomes reality."

* * *

NOVEMBER'S FROST MOON WAS THERE TO GREET STEPHEN upon his return home just as she had been there to see him off that morning. The train was slowing down as it approached his final destination. Stephen stepped off the train and walked a few paces across the station platform. He opened the glass exit door, and began his descent down the stairway leading to the street below. Exiting the train station, he eyed the long line of yellow taxis stretched out before him; there was one solitary white cab at the head of the line. He climbed into it since taxi etiquette dictated taking the first one in line.

Like a comet streaking across the night sky, the glistening white vehicle sped along the dark stretch of three-lane highway. He looked up again at November's Frost Moon and smiled. A memorable scene from Steven Spielberg's film *E.T. The Extraterrestrial* flashed into his mind. E.T. was heading home seated on the back of the bike of the boy who had befriended him. The bike carrying the endearing little alien was flying high in the night sky; the bike and its two passengers were silhouetted across the face of a full moon.

Soon E.T. would be aboard the spacecraft that would take him home. The scene faded from Stephen's memory as the taxi pulled up in front of his home.

After paying the fare and exiting the taxi, he slowly made his way up the leaf-covered sidewalk leading to his front door. The rustling of brittle-brown autumn leaves made him think of the last line of a Pablo Neruda poem: "Dry autumn leaves revolved in your soul." Then he found himself recalling the words of Saint Paul, "So we fix our attention not on what is seen but on what is unseen. For what is seen is temporary and what is unseen is eternal" (2 Corinthians 4:17-18). Stephen knew that to do what Paul was saying, he must start seeing more through my spiritual eyes and not through the damaged goggles of his soul suit. Perhaps the damage done by glaucoma was a blessing that forced him to rely more on my eyes, the eyes of his spirit.

Glancing up at the stars, he smiled again. His thoughts were fixed on the mystery of the magical space where the starry heavens of inner and outer space converge . . . the dark, in a sense, invisible, space where stars and miracles are born. *Was that where the unseen place that embodied souls call home is to be found?* he wondered while turning the key and opening the front door to his home. Stephen was home in more ways than one. . . .

He considered how the moon does not have its own light but reflects the rays of the sun. He considered how the whole of creation reflects the light of God's love. He was home in the sense of being conscious that God is reflected in all that is. It was interesting that it was in the Temple of the Moon in Tikal that he had experienced the blinding light of God's love directly. For the Maya sensitized him to how God talks to embodied souls all the time through nature. Being home while still in the form of a body meant an embodied soul had a constant consciousness of God's loving presence. It meant knowing, as the Indian saint Yogananda put it, "Just as oil is in every part of the olive so love permeates all of creation." Stephen also remembered how he always loved what he heard world-class athlete and author Dan Millman say at a lecture in Philadelphia, "There's God and then there's not paying attention."

Spiritual maturity involved seeing God in and through the seen world of form with all its variety. He smiled, raised his arm, pointed his finger at November's Frost Moon, and repeated to himself the words of a Zen master. To the best of his recollection, it went something like this, *We must not confuse the finger pointing at the moon for the moon.* It had been over thirty years since he read the words.

Satan, the dragon, wanted us to confuse the finger for the moon and get caught up in the world of form. He was said to rule the material world. For Stephen, he was best described as the dragon of dependency: the mistaken belief that the peace of mind, well-being, and happiness of all embodied souls depend on something in the material world such as sex, drugs, and Rock 'n' Roll—the cry of his generation in the sixties. Looking to the things of the world is wired into the gray matter of the reptile brain in order to insure the survival of the physical body. The Bible tells of how Satan tried to tempt Jesus to turn stones into bread when Jesus was hungry. Satan also took Jesus to the top of a mountain and offered Him all the kingdoms and wealth of the material world. All Jesus had to do was worship him, Satan, the god of materialism. Instead, Jesus chose the unseen over the seen—the eternal over the temporary.

Stephen now saw how materialism—seeing matter as primary—was spiritually immature. His experience with distant healings and hurricanes had revealed to him that the unseen world of spirit (energy) was primary. But materialism can be quite compelling since the five senses of the soul suit constantly convey the primacy of matter to the embodied soul. In effect, scientific materialism worships matter and material explanations of phenomena. For example, disease is traced to chemicals and physical forms: malignant tissue, bacteria, etcetera. Such a view receives support because it is often successful in providing relief through drugs and surgery. The problem is that the sickness in the soul cut off from his or her spirit is ignored.

* * *

NOW, AT THIS VERY MOMENT, HE HAD AN IMPORTANT EPIPHANY that was the culmination of years of searching. For years, he paid attention to God in the form of his daily dialogue with the Divine: the synchronicities in his daily life. And for years, he delved into his dreams, and he diligently deciphered the meaning hidden in those seemingly nonsensical nocturnal images. Since college, he also explored other religions and esoteric writings. What was this epiphany? *It's all been about relationship, not religion!* All sacred traditions find their fulfillment in an intimate personal relationship with God.

He was well aware, however, that to some self-proclaimed "sophisticated" spiritual seekers, it seemed that it was more spiritually advanced to move beyond an anthropomorphic image of God as personal. Eliminating a theistic concept of God and substituting something impersonal such as the empty void of Buddhism may *seem* to be more scientifically, psychologically, and spiritually mature. Such a view was thought to help eliminate an egoistic and self-centered approach to life. Supposedly, it fostered humility.

Nevertheless, he had experienced how maintaining a spirit-based sense of self in relationship to God also helped eliminate ego and self-centeredness. God was love and the problem was maintaining a body-based sense of self instead of a spirit-based identity. The former was egoistic and driven by body-based hungers while the latter was governed by love for God, others, and self in that order.

Suddenly, he was seized by the thought of how the history of all religion was a record of how God had lovingly pursued intimacy with humankind all over the globe. The dance of different forms of religion sprang up in response to God's revelations in different social, historical, and cultural contexts.

Now looking at the stars from the large window in his bedroom, Stephen felt deeply grateful for the intimate and personal relationship he experienced with God. To borrow some words from T. S. Eliot, Stephen had never ceased from his explorations and the end of his exploring was to return to the place where he started and see it for the first time. The religious tradition he was raised within was right. The Creator of the universe and all the stars is a loving Father and not simply an impersonal force. Stephen realized he had incarnated in the time and place he did in order to be raised by Gerry and Earl and to attend the Episcopal Church: a compromise between being raised a Roman Catholic or Evangelical Protestant. He later learned that, indeed, from its inception, the Anglican movement had considered itself the *via media* (middle way).

Even though he was more spiritual than religious (over the years only attending church on rare occasions), he loved the forms—icons, rituals, sacraments, and overall aesthetic—of Roman Catholic, Episcopal, and Anglican churches. He especially loved visiting the old churches in England, France, Portugal, Mexico, and Greece. He had not yet been to Italy. But he knew that loving the forms of Christian worship was okay; it was not idolatry as long as he did not confuse his finger for the moon. When he took in the bread and the wine during the sacrament of Holy Communion, he felt blessed. For he often felt the tingling of electrifying energy up his spine that he had come to associate with the presence of Jesus and the Holy Spirit.

Stephen *knew* that God as a force or universal (Rei) energy (ki) permeating and animating all of life was love. This was not just an abstract notion; he had direct spiritual experiences of God, mystical moments, as he liked to call them, that revealed how God was love.

Since 1995, God revealed to him in subtle ways how it could be helpful to incorporate the wisdom from the traditions predating Christianity. For example, he found what Buddha taught about dealing with desire and working with the waywardness of the mind extremely helpful. These teachings were five hundred years before Jesus appeared.

In Tibetan Buddhism, Stephen loved the link of enlightenment with love and compassion. He loved the concept that those who have attained enlightenment often appear as suffering beings. They could appear as human or animal. The hurting homeless man or the stray cat crying outside could be one.

He would never forget the dog with the large and raw-looking open sore on his neck, lying in front of the church in Mexico City.

The poor dog looked half dead. People were rushing past the dog on their way into the large Church. He went into the church and prayed. The words of Jesus flashed into his mind, "That which you do to the least among us, you do unto me" (Matthew 25:24). He also recalled the story about the Buddhist monk Asanga. Seven years later, he wrote about this stirring story in *A Matter of Love*.

In the story, a mangy dog was suffering as it lay dying by the side of a busy road. Everyone was passing by the dog and ignoring it. Asanga stopped to comfort the dog and to give it some water. Just as the monk acted kindly toward the dog, it sprang up and transformed into the beautiful and radiant Lord of Love: Buddha Maitreya.

Asanga spent many years alone, meditating in the mountains. He concentrated his meditation on the Buddha Maitreya whose name meant "loving kindness." Asanga hoped to have a vision of Buddha Maitreya and he longed to receive teachings from him. But it was not until Asanga came down from the mountain and had his heart awakened by the suffering dog that the Lord of Love finally appeared to him. Likewise, the people rushing into the church to receive God's blessings were missing the true blessing lying by their feet. This lowly dog offered them the great spiritual opportunity to awaken their hearts to the heart of Jesus: the compassion of Christ.

Still filled with compassion for the poor creature, he exited the church and moved off to the side of the steady stream of people. Then he began praying and sending Reiki to the dog. The dog sprang up full of life as if raised from the dead and proceeded over to a shady tree to lie down. Stephen was deeply moved. His eyes filled with tears of thankfulness that his prayer and Reiki had helped the dog. A few days after the event, he smiled when I brought it to his attention that DOG is GOD spelled backwards. Now, eight years later, he thought of how Mother Teresa had said that each day in the streets of Calcutta, she touched Jesus Christ in all His "distressing disguises."

In Buddhism, bodhisattvas are the enlightened ones who do not have to return to Earth after they die. But they do anyway. Rather than stay in the bliss of Heaven or Nirvana as it is described in

Buddhism, they decide to come back out of a great love and compassion for those suffering on Earth. They want to help others become enlightened. In this sense, Stephen could see Jesus as the ultimate bodhisattva whose suffering opened the hearts of countless millions for two millennia.

He recalled his heart-opening experience when watching Mel Gibson's film, *The Passion of the Christ.* Witnessing, the barbaric behavior of the Romans was not simply a matter of being exposed to gratuitous violence. It served to awaken an even deeper love than he felt before. He felt his heart open up. With tears in his eyes, he found himself saying, "I'm so sorry you had to suffer like this. If I could have, I'd have taken your place to spare you all that pain."

* * *

A MONTH AFTER THIS TRAIN RIDE, STEPHEN WOULD HAVE A dream that would be followed by an incredible synchronicity. In the dream, he saw a young woman with light-brown hair standing on the platform of one of the floating docks in Bangkok, Thailand. Having visited Bangkok, he recognized it was part of the floating market where locals hawked their wares to tourists. The usual bustling crowd was gone.

She stood alone framed by a grove of leafy-green tree branches forming an arched canopy over her head. A solitary figure with downcast eyes, she stood there staring at the slowly rippling water. The sun was setting over the open expanse of water behind her. She was in deep contemplation. Stephen heard a man's voice say, "She studied Buddhism in Thailand but decided to return home to her Christian roots."

One early afternoon, two weeks later, the phone rang in his home. The call was from Canada. A woman named Vanessa was promoting a nutritional supplement. Her job was not to sell the product but to introduce it, ask health-related questions, and see if the person she called had any interest. Someone else handled the sales end.

As soon as he heard Vanessa's voice, he felt what he could only describe as a soul recognition. In the course of her presentation, she asked him if he took any supplements and if he did anything else to promote his health and well-being. He mentioned Reiki. She then said, "I've heard of Reiki and I wonder if it might help me. Ever since I was in Thailand studying Buddhism, I've had a hard time protecting my own energy and personal boundaries."

Instantly, he thought of his dream and felt a shiver go up his spine. *Was* she *the female in the dream?* he wondered and began by inquiring, "May I ask what color hair you have?" She said it was blonde and long. He told her about his dream and said, "For a moment, I thought the female in my dream might be you but she had light-brown hair."

Vanessa then told him, "That was me. My natural hair color is light brown. I had my natural hair color then and I cut my hair very short when I was staying in the Buddhist monastery. What you saw was when my hair was growing back. I remember that time in my life. It was just a few years ago. I was sad. I had gotten to a place in meditation where I was really able to transcend desire. And I lost interest in living. I asked one of the Buddhist monks at the monastery for help. He told me that there was a Buddhist sect in India where some of its members commit suicide once they have attained the degree of detachment from desire that I had just attained. I knew I wanted to live but life seemed totally devoid of meaning.

"That's when I knew it was time to go home and return to my Christian roots in the Anglican Church. In the States, you would call it Episcopal. I still value what I learned in practicing Buddhist meditation. I love having the ability to detach from desires as they arise in my awareness. But there is nothing like the peace I get when I awaken afraid in the middle of the night and call on Jesus."

God truly does work in mysterious ways to reach His lost sheep. Vanessa had prayed for God to provide someone who could help her understand what she had been through both psychologically and spiritually. And she asked for someone who could help her heal. Stephen was able to help her understand and he did distant Reiki to help her heal.

In turn, she helped him in his effort to integrate the wisdom of Buddhism with his return to his Christian religious roots. She showed him how the practice of Buddhist meditation could distort the teachings of the Buddha who had emphasized the middle way between the extremes of self-denial and overindulgence. Death was the danger when meditation was taken to the extreme. Buddhism lacked an awareness of a loving God who created embodied souls with desires that were to be controlled but not denied.

Vanessa's experience reminded him that embodied souls did not come to Earth to deny desires. Rather, souls incarnated to love and enjoy the things of the world without sticky fingers. *Otherwise,* Stephen reasoned, fondly recalling childhood memories of Walt Disney's portrayal of the stories of Uncle Remus, *the material world becomes the Tar Baby—the sticky trap set by Br'er Fox to ensnare Br'er Rabbit. Br'er Fox can be seen as the Evil One, the Tempter, who sets the trap for each and every embodied soul (Br'er Rabbit).* He then found himself singing that upbeat song sung by Uncle Remus, only he added his own spin in gratitude for how Vanessa's story deepened his faith in how much God loves each and every embodied soul: *Zippity do dah, zippity a! My oh my what a wonderful day! Plenty of sunshine—filled with God's love and blessings—coming our way! Zippity do dah, zippity a! . . .*

* * *

LOOKING AT THE MOON AND THINKING OF IT AS THE reflected light of the sun, Stephen considered the significance of the full moon of February. For it had been the February Moon that preceded his experience of the Trinity in Tikal on the first day of spring in 1998.

He recalled how he once heard that in times past, when people lived closer to nature and the rhythm of the seasons, the February Moon was an important marker in the yearly cycle. The last full moon of winter before spring, the February Moon casts its glow on the bleakness of the barren winter landscape. With food supplies running low, the February Moon had three names: the Wolf

Moon, the Snow Moon, and the Hunger Moon. They all captured the desolate feeling of those embodied souls in tribes and villages who were anxiously awaiting the spring.

Stephen imagined how all three names could be pictured in one image. Set against the round disk of the full moon, he could see the dark shadow of the hungry wolf perched atop a snow-covered peak; his mouth held high as he howls at the moon that frames his lean dark shape. At this moment, Stephen saw that the image expressed the primordial hunger and longing the embodied soul feels for God. Whether it is a time of feast or famine, deep down, all embodied souls know that the ever-changing forms of material reality cannot offer lasting happiness and fulfillment. He now realized all embodied souls are hungry wolves howling at the moon. It seemed significant that the wolf was howling at something whose light is not its own but is created by another heavenly body: the sun.

To Stephen, the wolf symbolized the body-based identity that keeps an embodied soul in bondage to the appetites of the body. Like the hungry wolf howling at the moon, the embodied soul identified with the body howls at the visible world which can never satisfy his or her hunger for lasting happiness. True freedom, Stephen now realized, does not come until the body-based sense of self dies and a spirit-based identity is born from this death.

With the death of a body-based identity and the birth of a spirit-based sense of self, embodied souls find themselves as dramatically transformed as the caterpillar is when it becomes a butterfly. With a spirit-based sense of self, embodied souls are able to love and enjoy freely all that life has to offer. To borrow the words of William Blake, it could be said that loving freely occurs when embodied souls, "kiss the joy as it flies." Loving life freely without clinging is like blowing a kiss to the butterfly as it flies rather than snatching it out of the air and destroying its "winged life." Similarly, when embodied souls love their loved ones freely, they help their loved ones soar on the wings of their joy toward the realization of their hopes and dreams.

Unlike the explosion signalling the death of stars, the inner death of the body-based identity is perhaps best depicted by the death of Jesus on the cross. Contemplating the cross, Stephen thought of something he had not considered before. The vertical and horizontal dimensions of human existence are expressed in the cross. The vertical dimension points to Heaven and represents the embodied soul's need to love God. In contrast, the horizontal dimension points across the plane of the Earth and represents the need for embodied souls to love others as well as themselves. These are the two commandments Jesus gave all embodied souls.

By following the two commandments of love, an embodied soul replaces a body-based identity and life with a spirit-based identity. Only then can all embodied souls realize that love is who they are. The energy of God's love is everywhere. It extends from the tiniest subatomic particle to the vastness of the universe with its countless galaxies as well as to the space between stars. . . .

* * *

DRIFTING OFF TO SLEEP, STEPHEN RECALLED THE WORDS OF a priest being interviewed in a documentary on the life of film director Martin Scorsese. The priest told the interviewer that he advised the famous film director, "Marty, you have too much Good Friday in your films. You need more Easter!"

Stephen smiled as he thought of how right the priest was in his assessment of Scorsese's films. All the films he had seen and would see sure had their share of bloodshed: *Mean Streets, Taxi Driver, Goodfellas, and Gangs of New York,* and *The Departed* for which Scorsese would finally win the Oscar for best director in 2007.

Good advice, Stephen thought, *everyone could benefit from less Good Friday and more Easter in their lives.* . . . Stephen then thought of the Easter aspect of the Good Friday of his fading eyesight. He was thankful for his spiritual eyes being opened. The words of the man blind from birth who was healed by Jesus (John 9:25) applied to him, "One thing I do know. I was blind but now I see."

Epilogue

The Space Between Breaths

EASTER 2008

IT WAS STILL DARK AS STEPHEN WAS AWAKENED BY THE symphony of the birds in the trees. The digital clock flashed 4:59 A.M. It was too early to get up. In an hour and a half, he would be attending the Easter Sunrise Service held on the beach of Siesta Key, overlooking the Gulf of Mexico. Last night, he saw the Cecil B. De Mille classic, *The Ten Commandments.* A favorite of his since childhood, he never tired of viewing it at Easter. He found himself focusing on the scene where God speaks His name to Moses (Charlton Heston). A booming voice from out of the Burning Bush, proclaims, "I AM THAT I AM."

Lying still in the predawn darkness, he thought, *We find peace when we pin our body-based sense of self with all its hungers and desires on the vertical and horizontal dimensions of the cross of full awareness. Basketball taught me that having a participant (horizontal) awareness and an observer (vertical) awareness can help us master the storms of stress in life.* To this end, he devised the following meditations.

Be Still & Cease Striving

Reflect on God's words, "Be still and know that I AM God" (Psalm 46:10). Consider how the original Hebrew word *raphah* translated as "still" literally means cease. The word added by translators is "striving." Hence its literal meaning is more the command, "Cease striving!" You could record yourself reading the following meditations and play them back to listen to them or create your own.

Begin by breathing in and silently saying, "Breathing in, I stop and still my mind. Breathing out, I stop and still my body." Focus on the

300

sensations of the air moving over your nasal membranes with each in-breath and out-breath. Bring your attention to the stillness in the barely noticeable pause after exhaling and before inhaling. Notice that as minutes pass, and you become more deeply relaxed, the space between exhale and inhale lengthens. Being still, you need less oxygen. Silently and slowly say, "The one and only stable aspect of my identity is the fact that I exist: I AM. All else is subject to change such as I feel sad, angry, or happy." Now silently say, "I . . ." drawing out the "I" sound while inhaling and focusing on feeling the sensations of the air passing over your nasal membranes. And then, as you exhale, silently and slowly say, "AM . . ." drawing out the "M" sound in accord with the sensations of air leaving your body. Notice how the air exiting your nose is barely noticeable since the air warming up in your body so that it matches the temperature of your nasal membranes. The air entering your nostrils is usually cooler than your body temperature so that it is more easily experienced. Now after each exhalation simply experience the still space between breaths instead of silently saying still.

Notice the expanding stillness begin to envelop you as you continue focusing on the still space between breaths. Keep repeating "I . . ." with each in-breath and "AM . . ." with each out-breath. Notice a deepening peace and serenity moving within, through, and around your body with each "I . . . AM. . . ." Continue for twenty minutes.

Still the Storm:
Accessing the Peace of Your Spirit

Now just let your breathing be slow and deep as you affirm the following. Breathe in and silently say, "I AM an extension of God," and breathing out silently say, "the Almighty I AM." Breathing in, silently say, "I AM in this world," and, breathing out, silently say, "but not of this world." I AM NOT my hungers and desires. I AM the expanded and formless awareness who is aware of the smaller awareness encased in my body. I AM the expanded, formless me who is aware of the contracted little me feeling the inner storms of hunger, desire, anger, and fear. I AM the one who experiences all that is occurring within the spaciousness of my awareness without trying to change any of it.

I AM still and from this still space between breaths, I watch and listen, see and hear, whatever thoughts, feelings, desires, and impulses arise into the spaciousness of my awareness. Reflect on how stress relief is found in the space between breaths and between desire and satisfaction, between impulse and action, between pain and the relief of pain. I AM the higher consciousness that can provide solace when stress strikes the smaller consciousness inhabiting my body. I AM the awareness at the apex of the triangle of awareness, looking down on the two points below: the stress and the desire for relief, between desire and satisfaction, between impulse and action, between pain and the relief of pain. I AM the expanded awareness who is aware of the space between these two states. I watch without reacting to the itch and the urge to scratch and remove the itch. I AM the expansive awareness of all that the embodied soul experiences through the human form. I AM the awareness who is experiencing hunger and the desire to eat to remove that hunger. I AM the pure and loving consciousness who is aware of what is and what the little-embodied-soul me would love to have happen. I AM the awareness who hovers in the stillness of the space between what the embodied soul does not want and what the embodied soul does want. I AM the larger awareness watching over the smaller awareness inhabiting my body. I watch as this smaller awareness is constantly assailed by the endless desires arising in my mind-body impelling me to action. I AM the loving awareness in the still space between breaths. . . . God is love, and, since I AM made in the image of God, I AM also love . . . Above all else, I AM love. . . .

* * *

AFTER MEDITATING, STEPHEN BEGAN HIS DAY AS HE HAD since his time in Tikal in 1998. He addressed God, "Father, thank You. . . ." He filled in the blank with one thing after another. His final entry: Father, thank You for revealing that with faith and love, we have power and authority over the inner and outer storms of life."

When Stephen arrived at the beach for the sunrise service, he gazed at the ocean and thought, *Peter walked on water until he looked away from Jesus and focused on the wind* (Matthew 14:28-30). *Peter sank when fear replaced faith and love. Wow! What a message! Fear sinks us. Faith elevates us. We can rise above life's stormy seas.*

About the Author

Dr. Stephen Royal Jackson has been a stress specialist in the field of psychology for more than two decades. He received his doctorate in clinical and child psychology from the University of Virginia.

Late in 1995, Dr. Jackson had a life-changing spiritual experience. Within a year, he decided it was time to leave the clinical practice of psychology to teach and write, and by the summer of 1998 he founded SET for Life Seminars, Inc.

Through his writing and seminars, Dr. Jackson is dedicated to helping people all over the world eliminate the needless suffering and senseless evil caused by ineffective ways of handling stress and conflict.

To this end, Dr. Jackson lectures and conducts seminars, and he has often appeared on national television and radio. Since 1995, he has been using a Christian—inspired and guided by the Holy Spirit—form of the deeply relaxing ancient healing art of Reiki. With the healing power of the Holy Spirit working through him, he has helped many people here and abroad find relief from stress and stress-related pain and disease.

Printed in the United States
133369LV00004B/65/P

9 780966 480962